USING EVIDENCE OF
STUDENT LEARNING TO IMPROVE
HIGHER EDUCATION

USING EVIDENCE OF STUDENT LEARNING TO IMPROVE HIGHER EDUCATION

George D. Kuh, Stanley O. Ikenberry,
Natasha A. Jankowski, Timothy Reese Cain,
Peter T. Ewell, Pat Hutchings, and Jillian Kinzie

National Institute for
Learning Outcomes
Assessment

JOSSEY-BASS
A Wiley Imprint
www.josseybass.com

Published by Jossey-Bass
A Wiley Brand
One Montgomery Street, Suite 1200, San Francisco, CA 94104-4594—www.wiley.com,
www.josseybass.com/highereducation

Jossey-Bass books and products are available through most bookstores. To contact
Jossey-Bass directly call our Customer Care Department within the U.S. at 800-956-7739,
outside the U.S. at 317-572-3986, or fax 317-572-4002.

Wiley publishes in a variety of print and electronic formats and by print-on-demand.
Some material included with standard print versions of this book may not be included in
e-books or in print-on-demand. If this book refers to media such as a CD or DVD that
is not included in the version you purchased, you may download this material at http://
booksupport.wiley.com. For more information about Wiley products, visit www.wiley.com.

Library of Congress Cataloging-in-Publication Data

Library of Congress Cataloging-in-Publication Data has been applied for and is on file
with the Library of Congress.

ISBN 9781118903391 (hardcover); ISBN 9781118903735 (ebk.);
ISBN 9781118903667 (ebk.)

Printed in the United States of America
FIRST EDITION
HB Printing   10 9 8 7 6 5 4 3 2

CONTENTS

PART THREE
What Now? Focusing Assessment on Learning

PREFACE

UNDERSTANDING WHAT STUDENTS know and are able to do as a result of their college education is no simple task, yet it is fundamental to student success and to the quality and effectiveness of American higher education. This volume grows out of a deep concern that the practical value of otherwise well-conceived efforts to assess student learning in American higher education is often diminished by deeply nested misconceptions. Many in the academy—especially those most directly responsible for the assessment of student learning—still view the assessment of student learning as an obligatory, externally imposed chore of compliance and accountability. Yes, to be fair, the capacity and commitment of colleges and universities to assess student learning outcomes have grown substantially, especially over the last decade. But the fruits of these investments— the tangible benefits to students and academic institutions—are embarrassingly modest.

What is required, we believe, is a fundamental reframing of the conversation around assessment and a clearer focus on the *use* of evidence of student learning in more productive and targeted ways. As we explain in this book, a complex, evolving combination of trends and forces makes evidence of student learning essential to improving student success and strengthening the vitality of colleges and universities. The quality of student learning at colleges and universities is inadequate—even declining, some say—and the meaning and coherence of a college degree are threatened as most undergraduates attend multiple institutions. New providers of higher education, transformative emergent technologies, anxiety over college costs, scarce and constrained resources, high levels of student debt, and the growing concerns of governing board members, employers, policymakers, accreditors, donors, and others have placed the gathering and use of evidence of student learning in a new light. Often missed in this cacophony of voices is the fact that many institutions have been responding to these challenges for years, but with too little to show for their efforts.

It is the *use* of evidence of student learning—its utility and impact on the lives of students and the prospects of campuses—that is the focus of this book. Documenting student learning and the conditions that promote high levels of student performance is a daunting task. Knowing how to harness evidence of student learning to improve teaching and learning and propel students to greater accomplishment is ultimately what matters.

This is the central challenge we take up in this book: identifying what colleges and universities must do to move the assessment of student learning from an act of compliance to the use of assessment results to guide changes that foster stronger student and institutional performance. Rather than accept the conventional view that going through the motions of assessment is a necessary burden, we argue that evidence of student learning is essential to strengthen the impact of courses, programs, and collegiate experiences; to ensure that students acquire the intended knowledge, proficiencies, and dispositions; to continuously improve teaching and learning; and to document the value of higher education to individuals and society. Thus conceived, gathering evidence of student learning is not for compliance with external demands but, rather, an institutional strategy, a core function of continuous improvement, and a means for faculty and staff to elevate student success and strengthen institutional health.

The Authors

The contributors to this book are especially well suited to take up its challenge. All are actively engaged with the work of the National Institute for Learning Outcomes Assessment (NILOA), which is colocated at the University of Illinois and Indiana University. Founded in 2008, NILOA is the leading national voice supporting efforts by colleges and universities to obtain, use, and share evidence of student learning to strengthen student attainment and improve undergraduate education. NILOA's monthly newsletter informs more than 6,500 college presidents, provosts, faculty, student affairs staff, institutional research directors, and assessment professionals about fresh thinking and new developments, resources including NILOA reports on special topics, case studies featuring best practices, and related topics. On average, more than 10,000 individuals each month visit the NILOA website (www.learningoutcomesassessment .org); most are from the United States, but academics from 120 countries and territories also draw on NILOA resources.

Since 2012, NILOA has tracked the use of Lumina Foundation's Degree Qualifications Profile (DQP) and related efforts to calibrate teaching and learning activities with desired outcomes, including developing a library of exemplary course assignments from different disciplines that

elicit essential learning outcomes. NILOA's Occasional Paper series—
with more than 20 releases at the time of this writing—has engaged the
nation's most prominent educational leaders and assessment scholars
and practitioners in a dialogue around contemporary issues. All of these
efforts are designed to increase the capacity of colleges and universities to
gather and use evidence of student learning to guide change in ways that
strengthen the quality and impact of American higher education.

Taken together, the contributors to this volume represent an exceptional blend of scholarly acumen and practical experience.

Tim Cain, a historian of higher education with a background in college
student development, brings to his inquiries related to faculty involvement in outcomes assessment both expertise on faculty and students and
experience codirecting a campus-wide undergraduate research initiative
at the University of Illinois.

Peter Ewell, at the National Center on Higher Education Management
Systems, inspired and chronicled many of the formative and contemporary events shaping assessment work since the mid-1980s by working
with hundreds of campuses and providing policy advice on assessment to
states and accreditors.

Pat Hutchings was among the pioneers at Alverno College in its early
years of outcomes assessment, served as the inaugural director of the
American Association for Higher Education Assessment Forum, and,
as a senior scholar at the Carnegie Foundation for the Advancement
of Teaching, worked with faculty who were studying their students'
learning.

Stan Ikenberry, president emeritus of the University of Illinois and
the American Council of Education and NILOA co-principal investigator, has a lifetime of experience in American higher education and
a deep understanding of why colleges and universities must harness
evidence of student learning to confront the challenges facing students
and institutions.

Natasha A. Jankowski manages the day-to-day work of NILOA and
is among the best-informed scholar-practitioners about issues related to
public reporting and use of assessment data to mobilize resources to realize the promises of data-informed efforts to promote student success and
institutional improvement.

Jillian Kinzie, through her work with hundreds of colleges and universities at the National Survey of Student Engagement (NSSE) Institute for
Effective Educational Practice and her experience with various accreditation organizations and review teams, brings deep insight into the applications of assessment results for institutional improvement.

George Kuh, also a NILOA co-principal investigator, with his leadership roles with national assessment programs such as NSSE, the Strategic National Arts Alumni Project (SNAAP), and the College Student Experiences Questionnaire (CSEQ) research program, coupled with a 35-year run as a university faculty member and academic administrator, brings another set of informed perspectives and expertise to the topics this book addresses.

Perhaps the most important qualification these authors share is a commitment to shift the functions and forms of assessment away from the conventional view that assessment is primarily an act of compliance to the realization that gathering and using evidence of student accomplishment are indispensable for addressing concerns about academic quality and informing institutional improvement.

The Organization of the Book

Stan Ikenberry and George Kuh open the book with their chapter "From Compliance to Ownership: Why and How Colleges and Universities Assess Student Learning." They present the contextualized rationale for why it is imperative for the focus of assessment to shift from an act of mere compliance to one of institutional ownership in which evidence of student learning is harnessed to make decisions and guide change. As signaled earlier, the guiding premise is that assessment of student learning is essential to student success and institutional performance. While this same work may also confirm the quality and benefit of higher education and may be useful to regional accreditors and policymakers, the value of evidence of student learning lies on campus, within the academy, where it can be harnessed to make wiser decisions and improve the learning experience of all students.

This volume is then divided into three main parts.

Part I: Making Assessment Work

In Chapter 2, "Evidence of Student Learning: What Counts and What Matters for Improvement," Pat Hutchings, Jillian Kinzie, and Kuh discuss what constitutes *actionable* evidence of student learning, as contrasted to other forms of data about the student experience, and consider the broad range of sources of relevant evidence, such as surveys, portfolios, classroom assignments, and external performances and their useful application for quality improvement.

In Chapter 3, "Fostering Greater Use of Assessment Results: Principles for Effective Practice," Kinzie, Hutchings, and Natasha Jankowski illustrate the broad range of effective uses of assessment evidence, drawing on case studies and focus groups conducted by NILOA and reports from institutional consortia and individual institutions to describe approaches that prompted meaningful use of assessment results and the principles that undergird these efforts.

Chapter 4, "Making Assessment Work Consequential: Organizing to Yield Results," examines different approaches to implementing assessment work as Kinzie and Jankowski illustrate how institutions with different missions use assessment committees, teaching and learning centers, faculty reward and governance structures, and institutional research and effectiveness offices to gather, use, and productively communicate evidence of student learning.

Part II: Who Cares? Key Stakeholders

In Chapter 5, "Faculty and Students: Assessment at the Intersection of Teaching and Learning," Tim Cain and Hutchings focus on what may be the most important but often the most frequently overlooked dimensions of assessment—faculty collaboration and student participation in the design and implementation of assessment approaches. They offer principles for how to make assessment more meaningful and useful for those who are central to student learning and institutional improvement.

In Chapter 6, "Leadership in Making Assessment Matter," Peter Ewell and Ikenberry explore the role of institutional leaders—specifically governing boards, presidents, provosts, deans, and department chairs—in managing and leading assessment efforts and in the practical use of evidence of student learning to inform institutional decision making and increase student learning and success.

In Chapter 7, "Accreditation as Opportunity: Serving Two Purposes with Assessment," Ewell and Jankowski address accreditors' need for evidence of student learning to assure quality and institutions' role in meaningful engagement with accreditation standards, with special emphasis on the ways institutions implement and respond to accreditation requirements and the role of learning outcomes frameworks such as the Degree Qualifications Profile (DQP).

In Chapter 8, "The Bigger Picture: Student Learning Outcomes Assessment and External Entities," Ikenberry, Kinzie, and Ewell examine state and federal policy related to assessing student learning as a means of quality improvement and consider the work of national organizations such as the American Association of State Colleges and Universities, the American Council on Education, the Association of American Colleges and Universities, the Association of Public and Land-Grant Universities, and the Council of Independent Colleges, among others.

Part III: What Now?

In Chapter 9, "Assessment and Initiative Fatigue: Keeping the Focus on Learning," Kuh and Hutchings discuss what campuses can do to ameliorate the potential debilitating effects when faculty and staff find themselves overwhelmed trying to implement multiple assessment projects and improvement initiatives along with their regular responsibilities.

In Chapter 10, "From Compliance Reporting to Effective Communication: Assessment and Transparency," Jankowski and Cain consider transparency not as a reporting or compliance exercise but as an effort to communicate to various internal and external audiences a variety of evidence on student learning. NILOA's transparency framework is highlighted as a means for thinking about the several dimensions of assessment that can be made more transparent, the interests of various audiences in such information, and the ways higher education can more effectively communicate evidence of student learning to both internal and external stakeholders.

In the closing chapter, the contributors to this volume ponder what the assessment movement has accomplished in providing useful evidence of student outcomes and the work left to be done.

This volume is very much a collaborative endeavor. From the beginning, all the contributors helped shape the book's purpose and structure. While certain authors took the lead on respective chapters, in every case, their good work benefitted from the comments and ideas of other contributors. And, in some instances, ideas that originally appeared in one chapter found their way to another when and where the material made for a stronger, more coherent, and persuasive presentation. The order of authorship reflects this collaborative nature. Kuh and Ikenberry, as NILOA co-principal investigators, and Jankowski, as associate director, are listed first. The other authors, all NILOA senior scholars, are listed in alphabetical order.

Audience

We intend for the book to spark a fresh and broad conversation on the future of higher education and the role of evidence of student learning in dealing with the contemporary challenges facing American higher education. Thus, the volume is especially relevant for those who lead, govern, and make America's colleges and universities among the best in the world—presidents and provosts, governing board members, and education policymakers. They are key players in positioning assessment work within the broader framework of higher education so that it informs institutional decision making and quality improvement efforts.

We expect the book to be particularly useful for faculty members and assessment professionals, institutional researchers, and those new to assessment, as it provides both practical and conceptual advice for thinking about and undertaking student learning outcomes assessment. For this reason, the contents are also instructive for graduate students aiming for a position in postsecondary education, along with administrators and staff members seeking to better understand how gathering and using student learning outcomes data—done well—can contribute to their effectiveness and to overall institutional performance.

ACKNOWLEDGMENTS

FROM ITS INCEPTION, NILOA has benefitted from sage counsel from national thought leaders who comprise NILOA's national advisory panel, listed in Appendix A. Their commitment to the core values of the academy and its obligations for societal betterment is inspiring and aspirational.

NILOA's work, along with numerous advances in the assessment field, would not be possible without the visionary leadership and generous support of philanthropic organizations. We are especially grateful to Lumina Foundation and Jamie Merisotis for the leadership grant that helped launch NILOA. The Carnegie Corporation of New York and the Teagle Foundation also provided resources at critical junctures, and we are most thankful for their interest and support.

The University of Illinois at Urbana-Champaign has been our principal home and a congenial host for NILOA and a superb staff, including graduate research assistants and senior scholars (Appendix B). We have been warmly welcomed and supported by this rich academic community. NILOA's impact and sustainability could not have been possible without the stimulating, engaged environment that makes it possible for us to thrive.

If there were an award for outstanding copyediting, it would surely belong to Sarah Martin from the Indiana University Center for Postsecondary Research. Her work and expertise have touched every page of this book, and the volume is much the better because of her. We also appreciate the good services provided by the Indiana University Center for Survey Research in conducting the three national NILOA surveys we refer to in this volume.

Finally, we tip our hats to countless colleagues across the country who responded to surveys, participated in focus groups, helped with case studies and reports, and otherwise shared their good work. It is through their efforts to assess student learning inside and outside the classroom that we have learned a great deal about the value of this important work and how it can be used to enhance student accomplishment and improve institutional performance. We are in their debt.

ABOUT THE AUTHORS

Timothy Reese Cain is associate professor at the University of Georgia's Institute of Higher Education and a senior scholar at the National Institute of Learning Outcomes Assessment. He writes and teaches about the history of higher education, college and university faculty, campus speech, and learning outcomes assessment. He has published in *Teachers College Record*, *Labor History*, and the *History of Education Quarterly*, among numerous other outlets, and his first book, *Establishing Academic Freedom: Politics, Principles, and the Development of Core Values*, was released in 2012. He earned his A.B. in history at Duke University, his M.A. in higher education and student affairs at The Ohio State University, and his Ph.D. in education at the University of Michigan. From 2005 to 2013, he was on the faculty at the University of Illinois, where he coordinated the higher education program and codirected the Ethnography of the University Initiative.

Peter T. Ewell is vice president at the National Center for Higher Education Management Systems (NCHEMS), a research and development center founded to improve the management effectiveness of colleges and universities. A member of the staff since 1981, his work focuses on assessing institutional effectiveness and the outcomes of college and involves both research and direct consulting with institutions and state systems on collecting and using assessment information in planning, evaluation, and budgeting. He has directed many projects on this topic, including initiatives funded by the W.K. Kellogg Foundation, Ford Foundation, Spencer Foundation, Lumina Foundation, Bill and Melinda Gates Foundation, and Pew Charitable Trusts. In addition, he has consulted with over 475 colleges and universities and more than 30 state or national governments internationally on topics including assessment, program review, enrollment management, and student retention. He has authored seven books and numerous articles on the topic of improving undergraduate instruction through the assessment of student outcomes. A graduate of Haverford College, he received his Ph.D. in political science from Yale University in 1976 and was on the faculty of the University of Chicago.

Stan Ikenberry is former president of the University of Illinois, serving from 1979 through 1995 and again in 2010. He presided over an era of major change at Illinois, including the founding of the University of Illinois at Chicago, the creation of the Beckman Institute and the National Center for Supercomputing Applications in Urbana-Champaign, the creation of a President's Award Program to enhance diversity and aid students, and a general strengthening of the university's academic programs and campus facilities. Following his departure from the Illinois presidency Ikenberry pursued a sabbatical at the Carnegie Foundation for Advancement of Teaching in Princeton and in 1996 became the tenth president, of the American Council on Education. He returned to the University of Illinois as professor in 2001, joining the graduate program in higher education on the Urbana campus. In 2008, along with his colleague George Kuh, he became co-principal investigator of the National Institute for Learning Outcomes Assessment. He earned a bachelor's degree from Shepherd College and his graduate degrees from Michigan State University. He is the recipient of 16 honorary degrees and is a fellow of the American Academy of Arts and Sciences.

Natasha A. Jankowski is associate director of the National Institute for Learning Outcomes Assessment and research assistant professor with the Department of Education Policy, Organization and Leadership at the University of Illinois Urbana-Champaign. She has presented at numerous national and international conferences as well as at many institutional events and assessment workshops. The author of multiple reports and case studies for NILOA, she has also elsewhere published on accountability and assessment. Her main research interests include assessment and evaluation, organizational evidence use, and evidence-based storytelling. She holds a Ph.D. in educational organization and leadership from the University of Illinois, an M.A. in higher education administration from Kent State University, and a B.A. in philosophy from Illinois State University.

Pat Hutchings is a senior scholar with the National Institute for Learning Outcomes Assessment and a scholar-in-residence with the Center for Teaching and Advising at Gonzaga University, in Spokane, Washington. From 1998 to 2009 she was a senior scholar and vice president at the Carnegie Foundation for the Advancement of Teaching, a position she moved to from the American Association for Higher Education where she was the inaugural director of the AAHE Assessment Forum and director of the Teaching Initiatives. Her work has focused on a variety of strategies for creating a campus culture of teaching and learning: student learning outcomes assessment, the peer collaboration and review of teaching, and the scholarship of teaching and learning. Her most recent book, coauthored with Mary Taylor Huber and Tony Ciccone, is *The Scholarship of Teaching and Learning Reconsidered: Institutional Integration and Impact*. She began her academic career as a faculty member and chair of the English department at Alverno College.

Jillian Kinzie is associate director of the NSSE Institute for Effective Educational Practice and the Indiana University Center for Postsecondary Research. She is also a senior scholar at the National Institute for Learning Outcomes Assessment. She worked as an administrator in academic and student affairs for many years at several institutions. When she was a visiting faculty member in the Higher Education and Student Affairs program at Indiana University, she received a Student Choice Award for outstanding teaching. Kinzie has coauthored a monograph on theories of teaching and learning and a Lumina Foundation monograph *Continuity and Change in College Choice: National Policy, Institutional Practices and Student Decision Making*. She has conducted research on women in undergraduate science, retention of underrepresented students and educational effectiveness and institutional change. She is coauthor of *Student Success in College: Creating Conditions That Matter* (Jossey-Bass, 2005); *One Size Does Not Fit All: Traditional and Innovative Models of Student Affairs Practice* (Routledge, 2006), and *Piecing Together the Student Success Puzzle: Research, Propositions, and Recommendations* (Jossey-Bass, 2007). Kinzie earned her Ph.D. in higher education with a minor in women's studies at Indiana University Bloomington.

George D. Kuh is adjunct research professor of education policy at the University of Illinois and Chancellor's Professor of Higher Education Emeritus at Indiana University Bloomington. He currently directs the National Institute of Learning Outcomes Assessment colocated at the University of Illinois and Indiana University. Founding director of the IU Center for Postsecondary Research and the widely used National Survey of Student Engagement (NSSE), he has written extensively about student engagement, assessment, institutional improvement, and college and university cultures. His recent publications include *Student Success in College: Creating Conditions That Matter* (2005, 2010), *High-Impact Practices* (2008), and Ensuring Quality & Taking High-Impact Practices to Scale (2013). Recipient of nine honorary degrees and numerous awards from professional associations, in 2014 he received the President's Medal for Excellence, the highest honor the president of Indiana University can bestow. In 2013, *The Chronicle of Higher Education* described George as a "towering figure" who "really launched the field of assessment of institutional quality." George earned the B.A. at Luther College, M.S. at the St. Cloud State University, and Ph.D. at the University of Iowa.

USING EVIDENCE OF STUDENT LEARNING TO IMPROVE HIGHER EDUCATION

FROM COMPLIANCE TO OWNERSHIP

WHY AND HOW COLLEGES AND UNIVERSITIES ASSESS STUDENT LEARNING

Stanley O. Ikenberry and George D. Kuh

Control leads to compliance; autonomy leads to engagement.

—Daniel H. Pink

EVERY ERA BRINGS CHALLENGES. Even so, by all accounts, this second decade of the twenty-first century has swept in a steady stream of disruptive developments that threaten some of the most basic assumptions on which the higher education enterprise rests—including how and by whom its core academic functions are delivered.

More than 18 million undergraduate students are currently enrolled at thousands of academic institutions—some quite large, others small, some public, others private, some for-profit, and still others virtual. Movement of students and faculty across these sectors has grown. On many campuses, a large portion of undergraduate teaching is provided by other-than-tenure-track faculty members: part-time adjunct faculty members and graduate teaching assistants. Soaring college costs, unacceptably low degree-completion rates, new technologies, and competitive new providers have become defining features of what some call higher education's "new normal." Further disruption comes from the uneasy sense that the quality of student learning may be falling well short of what the twenty-first century demands of our graduates, the economy, and our democracy. It is in this complex context that understanding student performance and optimizing success is not just important to maintain public confidence; it is even more necessary to guide and inform academic decisions and policies.

But with challenge comes opportunity. By every relevant measure, higher education adds value to individuals and to society (MacMahon, 2009). What today's students know and are able to do will shape their lives and determine their future prospects more than at any time in history. In addition to the numerous lifelong benefits college graduates enjoy, the performance of our colleges and universities has profound implications for the nation's economy, our quality of life, and America's place in the world. It is this *profound relevance and worth* of higher education that adds a palpable sense of urgency to the need to document how college affects students and to use this information effectively to enhance student attainment and institutional effectiveness.

The big question is this: How will colleges and universities in the United States both broaden access to higher learning and also enhance student accomplishment and success *for all students* while at the same time containing and reducing costs? This is higher education's signal challenge in this century. Any meaningful response requires accurate, reliable data about what students know and are able to do as a result of their collegiate experience. In the parlance of the academy, this systematic stock-taking—the gathering and use of evidence of student learning in decision making and in strengthening institutional performance and public accountability—is known as *student learning outcomes assessment.* Gathering evidence and understanding what students know and can do as a result of their college experience is not easy, but harnessing that evidence and using it to improve student success and institutional functioning is even more demanding. This second challenge is the subject of this volume.

Assessment should be *intentional* and *purposive,* relevant to deliberately posed questions important to both institutions and their stakeholders, and based on multiple data sources of information, according to the guidelines for evidence of the Western Association of Schools and Colleges (WASC, 2014). Evidence does not "speak for itself." Instead, it requires *interpretation, integration,* and *reflection* in the search for holistic understanding and implications for action. As did assessment pioneers at Alverno College many years ago, Larry Braskamp and Mark Engberg (2014) describe this work as "sitting beside" in an effort to assist and collaborate with members of the academy in ways that engender trust, involvement, and high quality performance.

Whatever the preferred formula or approach—and there are many—we are convinced that if campus leaders, faculty and staff, and assessment professionals change the way they think about and undertake their work, they can multiply the contributions of learning outcomes assessment to American higher education. The good news is that the *capacity* of the vast majority of American colleges and universities to assess student learning has expanded considerably during the past two decades, albeit largely in response to external pressures. Accreditors of academic institutions and programs have been the primary force leading to the material increase in assessment work, as these groups have consistently demanded more and better evidence of student learning to inform and exercise their quality assurance responsibilities (Kuh & Ikenberry, 2009; Kuh, Jankowski, Ikenberry, & Kinzie, 2014). Prior to the mid-1990s, accrediting groups tended to focus primarily on judgments about whether an institution's resources—credentials of the faculty, adequacy of facilities, coherence of the curriculum, number of library holdings, and fiscal soundness—were sufficient to deliver its academic programs. Over the past 15 years, however, both institutional and program accreditors have slowly shifted their focus and now expect colleges and universities to obtain and use evidence of student accomplishment (Gaston, 2014). In other words, the question has become "What have students learned, not just in a single course, but as a result of their overall college experience?" Still more recently, in addition to collecting evidence of student performance, accreditors are beginning to press institutions to direct more attention to the *consequential use* of assessment results for modifying campus policies and practices in ways that lead to improved learning outcomes.

The push from accrediting bodies for institutions to gather and use information about student learning has been reinforced by demands from policymakers at both the federal and state levels. As college costs continue to escalate and public investment in aid to students and institutions has grown, governmental entities have become more interested in how and to what extent students actually benefit, sometimes referred to as the "value added" of attending college. This, in turn, has brought even more attention to the processes and evidence accrediting groups use to make their decisions. Employers also have an obvious interest in knowing what students know and can do, prompting them to join the call for more transparent evidence of student accomplishment.

Taken together, this cacophony of calls for more attention to documenting student learning has not gone unheard by colleges and universities. Thought leaders in the field of assessment have developed tools and conceptual frameworks to guide assessment practice (Banta & Palomba, 2014; Suskie, 2009). In fact, the number of assessment approaches and related instruments jumped almost ten-fold between 2000 and 2009 (Borden & Kernel, 2013), both reflecting and driving increased assessment activity on campuses. Perhaps the best marker of the growth in the capacity and commitment of colleges and universities to assess student learning comes from two national surveys of provosts at accredited two- and four-year institutions conducted by the National Institute for Learning Outcomes Assessment (NILOA) (Kuh & Ikenberry, 2009; Kuh et al., 2014). The most recent of these studies found that 84% of all accredited colleges and universities now have stated learning goals for their undergraduate students, up from three-quarters just five years ago. Most institutions have organizational structures and policies in place to support learning outcomes assessment, including a faculty or professional staff member who coordinates institution-wide assessment and facilitates the assessment efforts of faculty in various academic units. While the majority of institutions use student surveys to collect information about the student experience, increasingly, classroom-based assessments such as portfolios and rubrics are employed. Taken together, this activity strongly suggests that many U.S. institutions of higher education are working to understand and document what students know and can do.

At the same time, all this effort to assess student learning, at best, seems to have had only a modest influence on academic decisions, policies, and practices. Make no mistake: the growth in assessment capacity is noteworthy and encouraging. But harnessing evidence of student learning, making it *consequential* in the improvement of student success and strengthened institutional performance is what matters to the long-term health and vitality of American higher education and the students and society we serve. Moreover, consequential use of evidence of student learning to solve problems and improve performance will also raise the public's confidence in its academic institutions and give accreditors empirical grounds on which to make high-stakes decisions.

What is needed to make student learning outcomes assessment more consequential? Answering that question first requires a deeper, more nuanced understanding of the motivations of different groups who conduct this work and their sometimes conflicting effects on faculty members—who are and must continue to be the primary arbiters of educational quality. That is the conundrum we take up in this volume.

A Culture of Compliance

To make evidence of student learning consequential, we must first address the *culture of compliance* that now tends to dominate the assessment of student learning outcomes at most colleges and universities. While external forces fueled the sharp growth of assessment activity in higher education over the past two decades, these same influences unintentionally nurtured the unfortunate side effect of casting student learning outcomes assessment as an act of compliance rather than a volitional faculty and institutional responsibility. As a result, a plethora of external pressures to collect and use student learning outcomes assessment data quickly filled the incentive vacuum, creating the dominant narrative for why and how institutions should set assessment priorities and design assessment programs. That is, instead of faculty members and institutional leaders declaring that improvement of student success and institutional performance was the guiding purpose for documenting student performance— and being encouraged and rewarded for doing so—the interests of others outside the institution with no direct role in the local process held sway. Thus, from the outset of the assessment movement circa 1985, complying with the expectations of those beyond the campus has tended to trump the internal academic needs of colleges and universities. Compounding the effects of what is sometimes called *initiative fatigue*, discussed in Chapter 9, a syndrome that commonly develops when campuses are swamped by the competing demands of multiple initiatives, assessment for compliance has meant second-guessing the interests and demands of external bodies with no clear vision of how the results can or will be used to help students and strengthen institutional performance.

So it is that by defaulting to the demands and expectations of others, the purposes and approaches of learning outcomes assessment morphed over time into a *compliance culture* that has effectively separated the work of assessment from those individuals and groups on campus who most need evidence of student learning and who are strategically positioned to apply assessment results productively. The assessment function—determining how well students are learning what institutions say they should know and be able to do—inadvertently became lodged at arm's length from its natural allies, partners, and end users—including the faculty, but others as well. Ironically, it is the faculty who are responsible for setting and upholding academic standards and who are in the best position to judge student accomplishment. Yet because the externally driven compliance culture has defined and framed assessment, the work of assessment is frequently off-putting, misguided, inadequately conceptualized, and poorly implemented.

Thus, rather than student learning outcomes assessment being embraced by the faculty and academic leadership as a useful tool focused on the core institutional functions of preparing students well for their lives after college and enabling continuous improvement in teaching and learning, on too many campuses this work remains separate from the academic mainstream, severely limiting its contribution to the very student learning and institutional performance it is designed to enhance. As a result, the *purposes and processes of assessment*—collecting and reporting data to external audiences—continue to take primacy over the institution's *consequential use* of the results of outcomes assessment.

Peter Ewell (2009) offers a cogent analysis of the implications of these conditions by describing two distinct, competing assessment paradigms, one that serves an accountability function and the other that addresses continuous quality improvement of both student learning and institutional effectiveness. In practice, the urgent necessity of accountability has tended to overwhelm the need and opportunity for improvement. It is these two worlds that must be joined.

Without question, providing data about student and institution performance to external entities for the purpose of accountability is both necessary and legitimate. Still, we believe that the two—the interest of faculty and staff to improve teaching and learning and the proper interest of external bodies for *accountability*—can be reconciled *if* college and university presidents, provosts, assessment professionals, and faculty members take ownership of assessment and align assessment work with campus needs and priorities in ways that focus on compelling questions and issues of student success and the myriad challenges to institutional effectiveness. Far more important than activity for mere accountability is the effective and productive use of student learning outcomes data by partners and end users inside the institution—faculty, staff, students, campus leaders, and governing board members. Failure to do so undermines the credibility and trust that is crucial in any system of accountability.

End users, as we apply the term in this chapter, are those who have occasion to use assessment results that frequently may be collected by a professional third party, perhaps an assessment or institutional research staff member, or by groups of faculty or student affairs staff. Thus, assessment work is performed as a service to those end users inside as well as outside the institution who, as a result of their roles and responsibilities, have a practical and functional need to know the answers to pressing questions about student learning and related topics.

The functional relationships between those formally charged with doing assessment and other faculty, staff, students, and campus leaders can also take the form of a partnership when those people work together to do some or all of the following: design the assessment priorities and strategy, collect and analyze the data, interpret the results, and take action based on the findings.

In this sense, individual faculty members are partners when they design and use in their classes assignments calibrated to address one or more of the institution's stated learning outcomes goals (along with specific course goals) and share the assessment findings with those charged with building an institutional profile of student attainment. Students are partners by putting forth their best effort on assignments and responding to information requests such as surveys about their experiences as well as helping faculty and staff interpret campus assessment results to determine how to improve the campus climate for engagement and learning (see Chapter 5). Later in this chapter, we talk more about why using partner and end-user relationships more effectively matters in making assessment work more consequential.

Realizing the Promise of Assessment

This volume is organized around the proposition that student learning outcomes assessment and the evidence it produces can be more consequential *if the work focuses squarely on the questions about student performance of institutions, partners, and end users.* These questions necessarily differ, depending on the partners' and end users' interests and needs. That is, faculty members want to know, among other things, whether students in their classes and programs are acquiring the knowledge, proficiencies, and dispositions valued by their disciplines. Campus leaders want to know whether graduates have attained the institutionally espoused outcomes that pertain to every student, such as those often associated with general education. Students want assurances they are well prepared for life after college, whether it is a job, graduate or professional school, or some other destination. Members of governing boards also need to know that the institution's academic quality assurance mechanisms are effectively functioning and that its commitment to continuous improvement is transparently active. Student learning outcomes indicators are a crucial source of that evidence.

In the process of serving the information needs of these various end users and as a result of engagement in that service, the multiple uses of evidence of student learning include calibrating and refining learning goals, revising courses and curricula, gauging the impact of technology, informing budget priorities, improving student retention and graduation rates, containing costs, and otherwise harnessing evidence of student learning to strengthen and improve American higher education and to brighten the prospects of graduates.

For evidence of student learning to be used these ways, the compliance culture that has captured the assessment function in higher education must change. On some campuses around the country, this is happening, but the pace is too slow and the progress too modest given the level of investment being made in assessment and the magnitude of the challenges now facing American colleges and universities. As George Kuh (2013a) argued elsewhere, changing—or *bending*—campus culture is more art than science. As with student-centered cultures, recalibrating the assumptions and norms that shape assessment work in colleges and universities will not just happen. Such conditions are built and sustained over time by institutional leaders, faculty and staff members, and governing boards. It is these same end-user groups who genuinely need evidence of student learning in order to improve academic outcomes. While consumers of evidence, many of these same people also are potential partners who can help interpret assessment results and envision the implications for change in policy and institutional practice. Even more relevant, these are the partners who must help bend the cultural properties in ways that elevate *improvement of student success* as an institutional priority and affirm the consequential value of learning outcomes data.

Bending the cultural properties that shape assessment of learning and the perceptions others have of that quest requires a shared purpose. A common, understandable language is needed to communicate to internal and external groups about the value of evidence of student learning and its potentially consequential impact. To be at least minimally effective, these efforts must extend across the campus, accepting that each academic community will bring its own perspective, assumptions, and norms and that these will affect how evidence-gathering and use are viewed.

To sum up to this point, as the need and value of higher education continue to grow, demands for public accountability will not diminish. Even so, gathering evidence of student learning in ways that address the genuine needs and questions of the many groups on and off the campus and using that evidence productively to improve performance will provide a stronger foundation from which to respond to the doubts of skeptical publics. To morph from a complacent culture of compliance to a sustainable, forward-looking enterprise, those engaged most directly in the assessment of student learning must lead by targeting their work on the everyday functional, structural, and cultural challenges of student learning and institutional performance facing their campus and virtually every other college and university in America.

Harvesting Results

At least three things must happen to make the assessment of student learning more meaningful and consequential. First, outcomes assessments must be more closely aligned with the major forces and challenges facing students and higher education institutions in the twenty-first century, including the specific *issues relevant to student learning* at individual campuses. Second, presidents, provosts, and assessment professionals must identify and *engage the key end users* or consumers of assessment results, working with them as full-fledged partners. For both end users and partners, the animating impulse is whether the results of outcomes assessment will be useful for performing their respective roles and responsibilities. Finally, for assessment results to be relevant and actionable, student learning outcomes assessment must have a clear focus—*an anticipated use*—that will shape the methodology and set the stage for the eventual consequential use of results. The anticipated use of assessment work should be made explicit at the outset of an assessment effort; it may or may not materialize after the fact.

Relevant Issues

As the prime societal institutions charged with discovering, preserving, and transmitting knowledge and its practical application, institutions of higher education need and must seek evidence of how well they are performing, especially with respect to their core function—teaching and learning. Every college or university confronts campus-specific questions that call for information about what students know and are able to do. For all these reasons, assessment priorities and practices will vary from campus to campus. At the same time, nearly every college and university in the country is at the mercy of five broad societal trends: changing student characteristics and needs; unrelenting technological advances that stretch institutional resources and revolutionize when, where, and how students learn; more intense competition for students; less forgiving economic circumstances that make efficient, effective management of the academic enterprise more challenging; and widespread skepticism about the quality of higher education.

The consequences of attending poorly to these forces are harsher today than at any previous time for both students and institutions. Priorities for the assessment of student learning must respond to these broader systemic challenges and at the same time align with very specific academic needs and priorities unique to the individual campus. What are the defining features of these broader forces?

CHANGING STUDENT CHARACTERISTICS AND NEEDS Students bring with them varying academic and personal qualities; they come from widely diverse family, educational, and community environments and have different preferred learning styles. Students are increasingly mobile, not only in terms of often traveling long distances to attend college, but also in terms of the number of institutions where they take courses or earn credits on the way to graduation. This increased diversity and mobility of college students adds an additional layer of complexity in assessing student proficiency. For example, if a student attends two or more postsecondary institutions on the way to a baccalaureate degree, as about two thirds of graduates now do, which institution is responsible for what portions of what a student has learned? Understanding the needs of learners, documenting student performance, and making adjustments in pedagogy that lead to improved learning outcomes—these constitute the core functions of assessment.

TECHNOLOGICAL ADVANCES The digital revolution is altering virtually every sector of society, including higher education. Many undergraduates today are digital natives, having grown up in a flat-screen world in constant contact with and instant access to information. Hundreds of institutions now offer online degree programs. More and more students enrolled in traditional residential programs also take one or more courses online. Massive open online courses (MOOCs) have entered the nation's vocabulary. On most campuses, technology is not likely to displace traditional pedagogy any time soon, yet hybrids of conventional and technology-driven learning systems are evolving quickly, and the education of increasing numbers of students is solely online. Understanding the implications of technology for what students know and are able to do may be essential, but we have only scratched that surface.

INTENSIFIED COMPETITION FOR STUDENTS The pool of applicants for college is changing and, in some states and regions, has diminished as growth in the numbers of high school graduates has leveled off or declined. *Student success* in the form of the completion agenda is important both for individual campuses and for the nation as a whole. The upshot is that it is essential for many campuses to implement an enrollment management strategy that attracts a strong pool of matriculates, sometimes reaching out to new populations, and to provide what is necessary to help more students persist and finish what they started. Increasing student persistence and graduation rates requires, among other things, an informed picture of how students are performing academically and what they are gaining from their experience. Assembling and using evidence of student learning to improve the prospects for student success—in the current context—is an essential competitive strategy.

ECONOMIC AND COMPETITIVE FORCES Much of the demand for a clearer understanding of the outcomes of student learning is driven by the changing economic and demographic forces that fueled expansion of higher education during the twentieth century but present a quite different reality in this century. All but a select handful of colleges and universities now cope with strained business models that functioned reasonably well in times past but now experience significant stress. Financial support for higher education from state governments has been in gradual decline for decades, and for most public colleges and universities state government is no longer seen as a reliable source of substantial support.

For private as well as public institutions, simply using tuition and fee increases to manage budget stress is no longer a viable option. Pushback from public opinion and the constraints of the academic marketplace itself make it harder for institutions to fill revenue gaps simply by raising tuition. Moody's Investors Service (Data retrieved 11/25/13 at https://m. moodys.com/mt/www.moodys.com/research/Moodys-New-Survey-Finds-Over-40-of-Universities-Face-Falling—PR_287436) reported that 28% of public institutions and 18% of private institutions expected *declines*, not increases, in net-tuition revenue—and this at a time when both sectors of schools are increasingly tuition dependent. Credit-rating agencies are more attentive and more likely to issue cautionary downgrades. And while income from gifts and grants from alumni and friends continues to grow, such gifts often are earmarked for purposes other than the core mission of the undergraduate education.

Controlling college costs while at the same time improving student success is no small order, yet as the financial strain felt by institutions grows and the debt load carried by students gets heavier, the pressure to contain and, where possible, to reduce college costs will escalate. Any successful effort at cost containment will require colleges and universities to do things differently—including altering approaches to teaching and learning. As this experimentation takes place, collecting and using evidence of student learning to inform decisions will be crucial for both students and institutions. This dynamic, uncertain economic environment has increased the urgency and elevated the stakes of institutional decisions and policies that affect student success and institutional performance.

SKEPTICISM ABOUT EDUCATIONAL QUALITY Public confidence in the quality and integrity of American higher education is indispensable. At the same time, confidence levels are waning in nearly all societal institutions—governmental, corporate, religious, and academic. In the end, enduring confidence in American higher education will be defined by our performance, by the quality of college graduates, and by the impact of the innovation, creativity, and service colleges and universities render society. If academic institutions are *collecting* and *using* evidence of student learning to inform decisions and guide change that can help students and institutions improve performance, the confidence of the American public is likely to follow.

The range of challenges that confront individual campuses is endless. The mission for those who are engaged in collecting and using evidence of student learning must be one of *cultivating institutional ownership* of student learning outcomes, *deploying assessment in ways that inform campus needs and priorities*, and *using the resulting information in consequential ways*.

Campus Partners and End Users

Consequential assessment work is a collaborative endeavor. Earlier, we identified two distinguishable roles for campus groups with an interest in assessment. Recall that partners in gathering evidence of student learning can be faculty, student affairs staff, students, and others who have much to contribute in designing the assessment strategy as well as in collecting and analyzing the data, interpreting the results, and taking action based on the findings. Members of these same groups—and others such as governing boards, senior campus administrators, and occasionally external bodies such as accreditors or governmental agencies—may also be end users of assessment in that they may find illuminating and useful the data collected by faculty members, librarians, student affairs staff, an assessment committee or task force, or the professionals in an assessment or institutional research office. Keep in mind that end users and partners—be they faculty members, students, board members, or administrators—are not self-generating; they must be systematically cultivated and their respective interests and contributions encouraged and renewed over time.

An effective assessment program requires both partners and end users who will (1) help shape or have a vested interest in the questions to be studied, (2) anticipate ways the assessment methodology or process will yield useful results, and (3) apply the evidence in ways that will improve students' prospects and institutional performance. Who are these likely partners and the potential end users of assessment evidence?

Accreditors and governments, no matter how reasonable and defensible their accountability demands, rarely become partners in the assessment work itself. Even as end users, such entities typically are not in a position to *use* assessment results to advance student success. For these external bodies, too often the end goal is making certain the institution is *in compliance*.

Virtually all of the potential partners and end users of assessment work are on campus. To be useful—to have a consequential impact on student learning and the health of academic institutions—they must be engaged. Assessment's attention must shift toward the campus and the academics who need and can use the evidence (Banta & Blaich, 2011).

FACULTY Faculty members are closest to the scene of the action and best understand the challenges related to student success. Assessment literature underscores the importance of faculty engagement (Hutchings, 2010), yet in NILOA's recent survey, when chief academic officers were asked what their institutions most needed to advance assessment work, their top two priorities related to faculty: more professional development opportunities for faculty; and more faculty members using and applying assessment results. For various reasons addressed in Chapter 5, faculty members too often neither are informed in advance about institutional assessment activities and (thus, not cultivated as potential end users) nor are recruited to be partners in the work. Despite the long-standing yearning that larger numbers of faculty members become more involved in assessment, many well-intentioned and hard-working academics are, through no fault of their own, excused and distanced from the action by a complacent compliance assessment culture that responds to one externally driven initiative after another.

If faculty members are engaged at the outset as partners in the assessment of student accomplishment, involved as the initiative is taking focus, consulted as questions and issues are being framed, and help shape and clarify the potential uses of evidence—if these principles are followed, prospects for collaboration and productive use of results can be greatly enhanced. The key is involving faculty members early, with the end in mind: the consequential use of data. Among the most promising approaches for engaging faculty is to engage them in reframing the conversation about documenting student learning as fundamental core teaching and inquiry responsibilities, with course assignments serving as the vehicle through student performance and instructional effectiveness are demonstrated and evaluated (Ewell, 2013a). More is said in later chapters about the importance of the assignments faculty design as a critical component of learning outcomes assessment.

STUDENTS Frequently overlooked as potential partners in an assessment program are the primary subjects of the inquiry—students. As Chapter 5 explains, there are pragmatic and salutary reasons to involve and consult with students who are at various stages of an assessment effort. Students can offer invaluable advice about how to garner student cooperation in assessment activities as well as selecting from the available assessment tools those that are most relevant to the nature of the learning experiences they have had, inside and outside the classroom. Students also can help interpret patterns of responses by different groups and may be best positioned to suggest the policy and programmatic implications of the results.

COMMITTEES AND SPECIAL TASK FORCES So far, we have referred to *faculty* in generic terms. To advance assessment work on campus, we need to think strategically about which members of the faculty and other campus educators—student affairs professionals, librarians, learning resource staff, academic advisors and writing program administrators, among others—are potential partners and possible end user-consumers of assessment evidence. The need for faculty engagement is not just representational—it is not simply the faculty voice that is desired. Faculty as well as staff engagement in assessment is about entering into a meaningful partnership to help define the key assessment questions, shape and refine the methodology, and clarify how assessment evidence can be most useful to improve student learning outcomes and completion.

Among the more obvious partners for assessment work are the many faculty and staff members who perform various institutional tasks that have student learning implications. They serve on campus committees on undergraduate education or general education, on ad hoc committees focused on student retention and graduation rates, or on faculty-staff study groups defining the learning goals of undergraduate education.

Other faculty members teach high enrollment gateway courses that—for better or worse—help define and shape the undergraduate experience and prospects for success of thousands of students. In professional and pre-professional programs such as engineering, business, education, medicine, and social work, still other faculty members are obvious partners when they take on a special responsibility for assessment of student learning for programs with specialized accreditation.

ACADEMIC LEADERS AS PARTNERS AND END USERS As just noted, provosts, deans, directors, program and department heads, and chairs are indispensable to an effective institutional assessment program, both as cheerleaders and through their day-to-day actions overseeing educational quality and institutional performance.

The chief academic officer by whatever title—provost, vice president for academic affairs, dean of the college—must be the prime strategic leader of academic quality assessment and its leading advocate. Provosts are the chief academic problem solvers and resource allocators. They must help shape the assessment agenda, articulate the questions about student and institutional performance that assessment can help answer, and influence priorities for the work to be done to understand what students are learning and how they are performing. The scope of these activities is broad, as student learning occurs at or is relevant for many different venues and levels: in individual classrooms, in professional and specialized academic programs, in graduate programs as well as those for undergraduate students, in connection with budget allocations, in understanding the link between student life and student academic success, in support of decisions to continue or terminate academic programs, in defining and shaping the curriculum, and in response to a host of ad hoc decisions that demand evidence of student learning outcomes.

Provosts operate at the intersections of each of these venues. Thus, they are in the best position to align assessment priorities with the campus strategic plan, and to oversee the consolidation and integration of the various strands of evidence collected by the multiple campus partners involved in assessment. Put another way, for those in the assessment community, the office of the provost is both the prime partner and the principal end user, crucial to shaping and championing the assessment agenda and essential to the productive use of findings.

As emphasized in Chapter 6, deans and department or program heads are crucial as well because they directly oversee and have frequent if not day-to-day contact with colleagues in the best position to generate the guiding assessment questions and to collect the data to answer these questions. And for assessment to be consequential, faculty and staff who have ongoing contact with students inside and outside the classroom, lab and studio are in the best position to use assessment evidence in significant ways. Moreover, in addition to the institution-level assessment approaches where standardized tests or student surveys may provide an estimate of performance based on a sample of students, other arguably more authentic measurement of student achievement takes place at the classroom or program level through the use of rubrics, portfolios, and demonstrations. To inform and drive campus improvement efforts, evidence of student learning must be harvested at multiple levels throughout the institution.

When those who lead assessment initiatives ignore or fail to capitalize on the various potential end user and partner relationships, others—especially faculty members—tend to adopt a role of passive resistance and often become a barrier rather than a pathway to consequential assessment work. Campus leaders, led by the provost, must champion and nurture faculty relationships in ways that acknowledge and speak to the interests of the various end user groups as well as engender authentic, long-term mutually beneficial partnerships.

PRESIDENTS Assessment of student learning has moved higher on the presidential agenda over the last decade. One such concrete and recent example is *Principles for Effective Assessment of Student Achievement* (2013), adopted by the presidents of major research universities in cooperation with the heads of the nation's regional accreditation bodies, which proclaims, ". . . all institutions should be expected to provide evidence of success in three domains" (p. 2), and lists the following: evidence of the student learning experience, evaluation of student academic performance, and articulation of postgraduation student outcomes (p. 2).

Almost certainly, the Association of American Universities and other college and university presidents will differ on exactly *what* constitutes evidence of student learning, precisely *how* student performance should be assessed, and specifically *which* postgraduation outcomes are most relevant to academic quality. Yet the emerging broad presidential consensus around the need for evidence of student learning outcomes in and after college represents an important milestone.

Symbolic and concrete milestones are important, but most faculty and staff are either unaware of or not persuaded by national movements—for some reasons explained in Chapter 5. Even so, it is both an article of faith as well as an empirical finding that presidents have more than a little influence in shaping campus culture and setting the institution's strategic priorities. Whether at a research university or a community college, striking the right tone at the top and working in partnership with the provost and with the support of the governing board, a president can do much to focus faculty and staff on the core function of the undergraduate experience: student learning. In so doing, through words and deeds the president can help infuse this preoccupation into the institutional culture.

GOVERNING BOARDS As guardians and fiduciaries of an institution of higher learning, governing boards are responsible for the oversight of the institution's academic quality as well as its financial soundness. On the financial side, the governing board provides for an independent financial audit, assures strong internal financial controls, adheres to generally accepted financial accounting policies and procedures, and oversees the financial performance (outcomes) of endowments and investments. A comparable level of oversight is essential to the quality and integrity of the institution's academic program. For all practical purposes, the governing board is an end user—albeit a very influential one—that needs assessment evidence to inform decision making and policy development. Frontline responsibility for questions on academic quality is typically delegated to a board committee on academic affairs to consider the following assessment evidence. To what degree do graduates demonstrate achievement of the institutional learning goals? That is, have they learned and can they do what the institution promised? What systems are in place in programs, departments, colleges, and institution wide to address these questions? What happens to the results? Is institutional performance and efficiency improving as a result?

Still, on many campuses, board engagement with academic issues, including weighing evidence of student learning, tends not to be a part of the board's culture. This, too, is changing as the Association of Governing Boards (2010) and other professional associations have placed more emphasis on boards being actively engaged in oversight of educational quality. However, specifying the board's role for assuring academic quality does not substitute for the authority and responsibility of the faculty for determining and upholding educational standards. Gathering and using evidence of student learning is a complex undertaking, and faculty and academic leaders are the daily arbiters of academic quality. At the same time, the governing board should expect that instances and examples of productive use of student learning outcomes assessment be presented in a way sufficiently understandable and coherent to support the board's confidence that the institution's internal academic quality controls are operating effectively (Chaffee, 2014; Ewell, 2013b, 2014).

Begin with the End in Mind: Anticipating Use

Too often, assessment activity fixates on executing an assessment process or approach to document student attainment rather than focusing on shedding light on a vexing issue and using evidence to address student and institutional needs and questions. Those charged with coordinating assessment frequently struggle to second-guess what might satisfy an accreditor or placate a state legislature or other government entity. Rather than taking account of genuine academic concerns and deploying assessment to inform change in pedagogy, the activity is preoccupied with "doing" assessment rather than using assessment results. The specific need for evidence of student learning—the central question or questions—and the particular uses the results will inform—these basics must be defined up front, at the beginning of the assessment process, not after the fact. St. Olaf's Jo Beld has advocated backward design assessment in ways that anticipate use of evidence—for purposes such as advising, curriculum revision, pedagogical changes, resource allocation, faculty development, and program review (American Association for Higher Education Assessment Forum, 1992; Beld, 2014; Blaich & Wise, 2011).

Whether through backward design or in forward-looking anticipation, consequential assessment begins with the articulation of an important question, such as the following. How does the prior academic preparation of incoming first-year students influence dropout rates at our institution and what are the implications? What assignments are used by faculty in capstone courses, and what can be learned from them in terms of student performance and pedagogical effectiveness? Does the evidence of student learning outcomes align with and confirm our institution's stated learning goals? Are there disparities in academic performance among students from various backgrounds? Are our students able to transfer knowledge learned in one course to another in the same discipline or allied discipline? How does student–faculty interaction influence our students' success and learning outcomes?

Assessment work preoccupied with collecting data rather than using evidence typically falls short of the mark. It is the articulation of an important question and an explicit understanding of the need for evidence that must drive the assessment process and empower the productive use of evidence.

The Voluntary System of Accountability (VSA), sparked by the last reauthorization of the Higher Education Act, suggests one instance in which the ultimate impact might have been greater had the focus and intended use been clearer. Growing out of the national conversation on accountability instigated by the Spellings Commission (Commission on the Future of Higher Education, Secretary of Education, U.S. Department of Education, 2006) and related Congressional hearings, public universities and colleges came forward with a simple plan: an approach to providing information about student performance in which participating institutions would voluntarily administer a standardized test to a random sample of their first-year and senior students, calculate a value-added index, and make the results public.

As it turned out, the VSA was a timely, prominent public policy response to a hot political issue—but it was less useful to institutions and those they serve. That is, while the VSA proved effective in breaking an otherwise intractable political logjam and attracted the attention of unprecedented numbers of university presidents and provosts to the challenges of assessment of student learning, it was less effective than needed for improving student success and strengthening academic quality. Hundreds of campuses administered the standardized tests and posted the results, but precious few found the test scores meaningful for decision making, problem solving, or curricular reform. Moreover, very few members of the public for whose benefit the VSA was ostensibly created actually visited the websites that contained this information. Simply put, *process* prevailed but *use* was minimal. Administering a standardized test and posting the results—for institutional *compliance* with the requirements—became ends in themselves. Other than policymakers, identifiable end users were lacking. Perhaps with a clearer sense of the target audiences and a sharper vision of how the results could be applied and used, the VSA could have had a more powerful and lasting impact.

A similar pattern often prevails in accreditation. On hundreds of campuses, a flurry of assessment activity takes place 12 to 18 months in advance of an accreditation site visit. A review team is appointed, a variety of assessment efforts launched, a report prepared, the campus visited, and, at the end of the process, accreditation likely affirmed, and the campus urged to do better—with impact on student success and institutional improvement modest at best.

Demands for institutional accountability and compliance with the dictates of external forces are unlikely to diminish. The challenge for higher education institutions and especially for those most directly engaged in the assessment of student learning is to anticipate and align external demands with authentic campus needs. As a response to expectations of external authorities, compliance is a practical necessity. Absent a clear focus and vision for the use of assessment results, as a tool for improving learning outcomes, compliance is a waste.

What This Book Promises

As may well be evident by now, this is not a how-to book on the assessment of student learning, as valuable and important as those volumes may be. *Our preoccupation is with making assessment consequential.* That is, for us, the gnawing question is this: What can institutions and others with an interest in quality assurance in American higher education do to make assessment more useful and productive so that the results of assessment efforts are put to better use? To address that challenge, the following chapters search for answers to nine key questions.

What Counts as Evidence?

Colleges and universities are collecting a broader range of information about student learning, and more of it, than even a few years ago. Evidence drawn from the regular work of teaching and learning, like portfolios and classroom assignments, is on the rise. Rubrics are increasingly used to assess student learning and guide changes in pedagogy. Surveys provide rich information about the behaviors of students and the perceptions of alumni and employers whose feedback can help to guide improvement. And learning analytics promise greater insight into conditions that foster (or impede) student success. The practical challenge is to translate this growing body of information into evidence that answers pressing questions about student and institutional performance in ways that will inform pedagogical changes and policy going forward. This means paying careful attention to what counts as evidence for different audiences and thinking not only about the technical properties of data but also about their potential to catalyze improvement.

What Are Relevant Examples of Productive Use of Evidence of Student Learning?

Many campuses are using evidence of student learning productively to set institutional priorities, to guide decision making, to clarify learning goals, to increase student persistence, to reallocate resources, to enrich and accelerate learning via technology, and in a host of other ways. What has worked for these campuses and what has been the impact? Much can be learned from the successes and frustrations of the early adopters, but the hard truth is that most campuses have too little to show and share in terms of productive *use* of evidence of student learning in ways that transform student success and institutional performance.

How Can Assessment Work Be Better Organized and Led?

The rich diversity of American higher education calls for a comparable variety of approaches to understand what students know and are able to do. Approaches necessary and suitable for large, complex universities with multiple missions may not fit smaller institutions with more focused or specialized educational programs. Moreover, most campuses are replete with the proverbial academic silos, which inhibit sharing information about student performance as well as promising practices. How can evidence of student learning be shared and used more broadly and with greater impact, and what does the sum of all parts tell us about the whole?

What Can Institutions Do to Involve in the Assessment Process Those Whose Contributions Are Most Central to Improving Student Learning?

Members of the faculty are closest to and most knowledgeable about what students know and are able to do as a result of their college experience, but they are often the most skeptical of attempts to assess student learning on a broader scale. Often not consulted in advance or viewed as partners, faculty members may see efforts to gauge student learning as threatening, unneeded, useless, intrusive, or irrelevant. Moreover, institutional cultures and reward structures might press against, rather than encourage, their active engagement with assessment. Yet many campuses are finding ways to involve faculty, and their engagement is crucial if assessment is going to be consequential. So, too, is the engagement of their partners in the teaching–learning process: the students whom assessment is supposed to benefit. Although too often left out of the assessment conversation, when meaningfully included, students can promote their understanding of their own educational experiences and outcomes, inform institutional practices, and help further engage faculty in assessment deeply embedded in the teaching and learning process.

How Can Campus Leaders at All Levels Create and Sustain a Culture of Evidence That Emphasizes Improvement?

The student learning assessment movement in higher education was prompted in large part by government agencies and accreditors wanting colleges and universities to be more accountable for their actions. While much progress has been made and assessment capacity has increased, too many institutions remain most focused on complying with the demands and expectations of others. This culture of compliance has clouded the most important, actionable purpose for collecting evidence of student accomplishment—improving teaching and learning. To shift the culture to one that harnesses evidence in ways that enhance student achievement, committed leadership is needed from presidents, governing boards, provosts, and deans, in partnership with an engaged faculty.

With Its Role in Prompting Assessment Well Established, What Can Accreditors Do to Become Even More Helpful to Promoting a Culture of Evidence for Improvement in Higher Education?

Accreditation of academic institutions has become the federal government's engine for change in higher education. Despite a cacophony of criticism of accreditation in recent years, we believe history will show it served well the postsecondary enterprise and society. As discussed earlier, NILOA's two national surveys of chief academic officers confirm that accreditation is seen by institutions as the prime force demanding more attention to the assessment of student learning. The best strategy for institutions and for those who wish to hold them accountable is a strong system of academic quality assurance that relies on relevant, reliable data accurately representing student and institutional needs and informing meaningful changes in policies and practices to promote student learning and institutional effectiveness.

What Has Been and Will Likely Be the Influence of State and Federal Policy and Higher Education Affinity Groups on Student Learning Outcomes Assessment?

Government entities—both federal and state—have played a major role in the growth of assessment by seeking more information, greater accountability, and better evidence of student learning. Thought leaders, higher education associations, and allied affinity groups have responded with efforts to frame and support the assessment agenda for the vast majority of U.S. colleges and universities. Despite the ebb and flow in the priorities of government and the work of associations, these entities have largely created and sustained demands for evidence of student learning. This was especially so in the early years of assessment. State mandates got assessment established in many states, and federal recognition of accreditation has kept it focused on student academic achievement. Moreover, these same forces largely generated the culture of compliance we know today. The key question becomes, "Where will these external forces take assessment from here?"

What Can Be Done to Ameliorate the Debilitating Effects of Initiative Fatigue That Often Come with Assessment Work and Related Improvement Efforts?

Initiative fatigue is one of the most troubling, and troublesome, side effects of the culture of compliance. As institutions take cues from government, accreditors, and their peer institutions on how to document and improve student and institutional performance, initiatives tend to pile up, multiply, duplicate—and become transitory. Not uncommonly, academic and student affairs faculty feel overwhelmed by the sense of "one more thing" and disenfranchised by someone else's notion of what constitutes improvement and accountability. The result is often pervasive frustration and a fragmented, burdensome, and less effective institutional investment in assessment.

How Can Institutions Best Respond to the Clamor for More Transparency About Student and Institutional Performance?

To be transparent—including sharing evidence of student learning—is not simply to make information available, nor necessarily public. Rather, transparency is meaningfully communicating actionable information to those who can *use* it, most of whom, in the case of learning outcomes assessment, are *internal partners and end users*: faculty, students, campus committees, provosts, deans, department chairs, budget officers, president, and members of governing boards. Other relevant, interested parties are external stakeholders: prospective students, parents and family members, governmental agencies, media, and the general public. The needs and interests of these groups differ, and they seek and consume information differently. What is needed is not so much for institutions to report more as for the information they do share to be meaningful and actionable to the targeted audiences.

On the pages that follow, we confront these and many other pertinent issues that bear on this central challenge: What must colleges and universities do to more effectively gather and use evidence of student learning in ways that will enhance student and institutional performance?

PART ONE

WHAT WORKS?
FINDING AND USING
EVIDENCE

2

EVIDENCE OF STUDENT LEARNING

WHAT COUNTS AND WHAT MATTERS FOR IMPROVEMENT

Pat Hutchings, Jillian Kinzie, and George D. Kuh

In God we trust; all others bring data.

—W. Edwards Deming

DOCUMENTING STUDENT LEARNING REQUIRES evidence. In its various forms—evaluations of performance on assignments, scores on exams, survey results, readings of portfolios, analyses of course-taking patterns, persistence, and graduation—evidence about students' educational experiences can tell a compelling story. Evidence calls attention to an institution's strengths and weaknesses, points to where changes might be made, and reveals whether those changes have had the intended effects. Simply put, evidence is essential to improving student learning and responding to accountability expectations.

Today, colleges and universities are collecting a broader range of information about student learning, and more of it, than even a few years ago.

Whereas in 2009 institutions reported gathering an average of three types of assessment information, by 2013 that number had risen to five (Kuh, Jankowski, Ikenberry, & Kinzie, 2014). Reports from provosts suggest that campuses have "shifted from being able to provide plans to assess student learning to instead being able to document and provide evidence of student learning" (Cain & Jankowski, 2013, p. 4).

Perhaps this is not surprising. The growing commitment to data about student learning in higher education is part of a larger social trend. Think of evidence-based medicine, the use of "people analytics" to make management and staffing decisions in business and industry (Peck, 2013), and the frequency, ease, and speed with which we access a world of information—simply using our phones, no less. In higher education, too, calls for evidence-based teaching are now widespread, data-informed practice in student affairs is gaining ground, and grant proposals require rigorous evaluation of outcomes. Big data has found a place at colleges and universities, with educational data mining and learning analytics now popular topics at higher education conferences and with campuses using these tools to explore the variables that contribute to or impede student success (Hrabowski, Suess, & Fritz, 2011; Mattingly, Rice, & Berge, 2012). Indeed, an abiding commitment to evidence from systematic inquiry is a defining value of academic life.

Unfortunately, evidence does not automatically translate into change. Human beings are amazingly able to ignore the data, even when it points overwhelmingly to the value of certain approaches over others. For instance, only one in seven cardiac patients modifies their behavior when told their life depends on it (Kegan & Lahey, 2009, p. 1). In student learning outcomes assessment (where the stakes, although serious, are fortunately lower), the same pattern persists. Faculty members typically seek out and value the highest quality, most compelling evidence to guide their disciplinary scholarship and practice, but that disposition is exercised far less when it comes to shaping practice in the classroom. Indeed, tales abound of fat black binders full of assessment findings stashed on shelves where no one sees them or seeks them out.

Moreover, what counts as evidence is sometimes contested, with the value and utility of data depending on where one stands—literally and metaphorically. What one person sees as persuasive, another sees as anecdotal. The chemistry department wants numbers and the English department eschews them (see Becher, 1987); student affairs professionals look to sources and types of evidence different from what interests their colleagues in institutional research. According to the Western Association of Schools and Colleges (WASC, 2014), *evidence* constitutes the substance of what is advanced to support a claim that something is true and differs from *information* in that it is more intentional and purposive, more a matter of reflection and deliberation. In other words, while information exists in a vacuum, evidence responds to a community's questions and is made meaningful through analysis and interpretation relevant to that community. In this sense, colleges and universities may be said to be information rich but evidence poor—and even poorer in *using* information to make changes to enhance performance (Seymour, 1995).

The good news is that provosts report the *use* of assessment results is on the rise at institutions (Kuh et al., 2014, p. 15), and over the years there have been notable examples of how evidence can catalyze significant change. Long-time assessment activists know the story of Northeast Missouri State University (now Truman State) discovering that students' mathematics proficiency actually declined as they moved through the curriculum—evidence that triggered a curricular change reversing that trend. Another example is the University of Texas at El Paso (UTEP), which implemented a learning community model as part of a grant to support Hispanic engineering students; this innovation worked so well to foster student persistence that the approach is now used with all entering students. But such examples are few and far between. In a review of campus assessment efforts, Trudy Banta and Charles Blaich (2011) noted that only 6% of such efforts "contained evidence that student learning had improved, no matter what measure had been used" (p. 22).

In the pages that follow, we examine the complex characteristics and role of evidence in assessment—its critical importance but also its complications and challenges—by exploring answers to the following questions:

1. What are the different sources and properties of assessment evidence now in use and what can be said about their respective strengths and limitations for stimulating improvement?

2. What are the obstacles to the effective use of evidence?

3. What counts as evidence for different audiences and purposes?

Sources and Properties of Assessment Evidence

In the early days of the assessment movement, the systematic collection of data about student performance was framed as an alternative to course grades assigned by individual faculty, which were viewed with suspicion by policymakers driving the movement (Ewell, 2009). As a consequence, assessment typically meant administering an off-the-shelf tool of one sort or another, often in the absence of a guiding institutional statement of desired learning outcomes. Today, a much broader array of approaches is in play, yielding more and more varied *kinds* of evidence (Figure 2.1). As noted earlier, the average number of different approaches used by campuses is now five, up from three in 2009.

The methodological pluralism reflected here is promising both for assessment practice and for institutional improvement efforts because a more expansive range of approaches and types of information make it more likely that a campus will uncover consequential evidence about the experience of its students—evidence that answers real questions for faculty and student affairs professionals. Variety is useful, as well, because what counts as evidence is often determined by the context of use and the audience at hand; multiple approaches raise the chances that different audiences (for instance, different disciplines) will find something that speaks to them. Further, the most compelling evidence is integrative, drawing as needed on both direct and indirect evidence of learning and bringing together quantitative and qualitative information—to both count and recount, as former Carnegie Foundation president Lee Shulman (2007) once advised campus leaders to do in their "quest for accountability."

At the same time, the array of evidentiary choices can be daunting. The temptation to do one of each (a portfolio, a student survey, an employer

---

Figure 2.1: Percentage of Institutions Employing Different Assessment Approaches at the Institution Level to Represent Undergraduate Learning in 2009 and 2013.

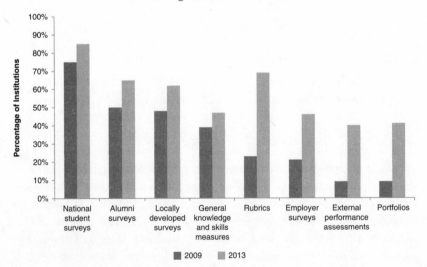

survey, a capstone project, a general educational skills test, and so on), and to gather information just because it is possible to do so can lead to a fragmented approach that does not serve improvement well.

What, then, do the various sources and types of evidence offer? What are their respective properties? And what are the benefits and limitations of the evidence they produce when it comes to stimulating change and improvement in student learning?

Surveys

Surveys have been the most popular campus assessment tool for some time now, and they continue to rise in use, whether focused on students, alums, or employers (Kuh et al., 2014).

National student surveys are the single most popular source of assessment evidence today, although their use is growing more slowly than that of some other approaches. They include the National Survey of Student Engagement (NSSE), administered by more than 1,500 colleges and universities in the United States and Canada, and the companion Community College Survey of Student Engagement (CCSSE), used by nearly 900 campuses. In the mix as well are both older and newer instruments, including the long-standing Cooperative Institutional Research Project (CIRP) Freshman Survey and the more recently developed survey of Student Experience in the Research University (SERU).

Surveys like these are an efficient way to get a wide range of information about the student experience. They do not provide evidence of learning itself but of the institutional processes and student behaviors and attitudes that impact student learning and success (Pascarella, Seifert, & Blaich, 2010)—that is, indirect evidence of learning. They also have the advantage of providing comparative information, allowing campuses to see themselves relative to similar institutions—although the more important, actionable differences are likely to be internal, within institutions' programs, than between institutions (Kuh, 2003).

Moreover, survey results can attract attention (sometimes also irritation and denial when results are disappointing) and thus motivate people to take action. When a campus learns that its students are studying on average only seven hours a week or that students at peer institutions are having more culminating capstone experiences (Hutchings, 2014b), alarms go off. Many open-ended responses in the NILOA survey of provosts mentioned valuable insights gained from surveys of students' educational experiences. One respondent, for example, described how survey results pointed to a lack of curricular integration and connection to real-world practice, which helped launch an initiative beginning with a first-year experience, sequenced interdisciplinary courses, a travel experience, and a culminating project to help students connect academic theory with practice in a global context. In short, survey results can quickly identify aspects of undergraduate education that are out of alignment with effective practice or institutional learning goals and provide the impetus for more extensive examination and evidence gathering. But surveys also produce a huge amount of information and require careful interpretation in order to connect findings to local questions, problems, and opportunities—to turn information into evidence, if you will.

In this regard, *locally designed surveys*—whether focused on students, alums, employers or other groups—can have an advantage. Although creating a good survey can be daunting, and poorly designed questionnaires can produce poor quality data, the task of formulating questions is an opportunity to bring members of the campus community together to decide what issues they most care about and what information would be most actionable. Consider, for example, the Essential Learning Outcomes Assessment, a 20-minute institution-level questionnaire developed by a team of faculty and student affairs staff at St. Olaf College. The instrument is used in the first-year orientation week, in which, according to one faculty member, it helps to "build the expectation for first-year students that providing assessment information—demonstrating what you know and how you are developing as a student—is just part of what being a St. Olaf student is about" (Jankowski, 2012a, p. 1).

Administering the survey as part of orientation also addresses what is clearly the biggest challenge in surveys of all types, whether national or locally designed, aimed at current students or at other populations: response rates can be distressingly low. Survey burnout among students was identified as a worry of provosts and many added that this has in turn depressed assessment momentum. Many campuses today administer multiple surveys in a given academic year—and often only the students who are asked to fill them out know how many surveys are actually in the in the field at a time—with predictable survey fatigue dampening response rates to unreliable percentages and reducing the capacity to meaningfully disaggregate by major field or student subpopulations. Even where response rates are technically high enough to warrant confidence in the findings, the results may be met with skepticism and mistrust—attitudes that undermine the goals of assessment and the likelihood that the results will qualify as evidence.

General Knowledge and Skills Tests

The majority of campuses (now about 84%) have developed institution-level outcomes expected of all students (Kuh et al., 2014, p. 8). Typically, these focus on general intellectual skills such as critical thinking, communication (especially writing), problem solving, and quantitative literacy. Over the years, many campuses have adopted nationally normed instruments as a way to collect evidence about students' progress toward these goals. These include, for instance, the Collegiate Learning Assessment, the ETS Proficiency Profile, and ACT's Collegiate Assessment of Academic Proficiency.

These kinds of tests have two noteworthy advantages. The first is convenience; they are off the shelf and ready to use for campuses willing to pay the price (which can be nontrivial). Second, they have established psychometric properties to ensure reliability and validity (*Rising to the Challenge,* 2010). In fact, the assessment movement has stimulated some creative advances in the design of these instruments. Rather than simple multiple-choice formats that require only the basic recall of information, performance tasks are increasingly the order of the day. For instance, the Collegiate Learning Assessment (CLA) poses complex case studies that students must analyze and write about.

These tests can be useful if they measure learning outcomes that the institution actually values and if the results are shared in a way that engages appropriate campus groups. For example, initially disappointing critical thinking results on the CLA prompted the provost at The Richard Stockton College of New Jersey to discuss results with the faculty through the Institute for Faculty Development and an all-faculty forum. This, in turn, catalyzed greater investment in critical thinking, including the establishment of a campus Critical Thinking Institute, the adoption of additional measures of critical thinking to triangulate with the CLA, and faculty-designed classroom-level performance tasks to familiarize students with complex performance tasks (see http://www.collegeportraits .org/NJ/RSCNJ/learning_outcomes).

The downside to such instruments is that they are often hard to align with local learning goals and claims about instructional practice, a problem exacerbated by a lack of buy-in on the part of faculty, who may see them as invasive or top-down and a further erosion of their own responsibility for academic quality. Several provosts responding to the NILOA survey commented that they worried about using external instruments and needed (as one said) assistance getting "results out in front of faculty in a meaningful way." Additionally, the results from these instruments generally represent generic, cross-cutting outcomes. Important as these may be, they can appear disconnected from the outcomes valued by specific disciplines (Heiland & Rosenthal, 2011), reinforcing the idea of assessment as an add-on, compliance activity. Not coincidentally, some of the test providers are creating products that more directly link with the work of faculty. The Critical Thinking Assessment Test, for instance, is externally developed but designed to be scored by local faculty, whose training in the process turns out to have professional development benefits (Skinner & Prager, 2013; Stein & Haynes, 2011). Similarly, the Collegiate Learning Assessment now offers a CLA in the Classroom experience in which faculty learn to develop performance tasks they can use in their own classrooms—essentially an exercise in assignment design.

While externally developed instruments, like all other sources of assessment evidence, are on the rise nationally (Kuh et al., 2014), this is not true across all sectors. A 2013 survey from the Association of American Universities shows that top-tier research universities are moving away from these tests (p. 2). The bottom line is that externally developed tests of general knowledge and skills often fall short when it comes to producing actionable evidence that can guide improvement efforts. To be useful, they require an extra measure of effort and creativity from the campus.

Classroom Assignments

The work assigned by faculty has always been the most meaningful and natural source of evidence for documenting student learning. But because the assessment movement was initially framed as a corrective to faculty subjectivity and policymakers' concerns about grade inflation, classroom work has had a difficult time establishing itself as a recognized source of evidence for student learning outcomes assessment. Some assessment scholars and practitioners have viewed the separation as a "safeguard to ensure objective measurement" (Richman & Ariovich, 2013, p. 4). Others have seen it as a way to protect faculty from unwelcome oversight in their classrooms. While both of these concerns are understandable, an emerging movement for authentic assessment—performances on complex, real-world tasks—has gone in the other direction, fueling an interest in evidence that comes from the classroom. Thus, as shown in Figure 2.1, the use of locally designed classroom assignments and assessments, including culminating projects or capstones, has risen dramatically in the last few years. Commenting on this shift at one campus, a provost noted that the most hopeful aspect of assessment was "the realization that classroom based learning assessment is both legitimate and valuable."

This trend is not without its challenges. Assignment design is not a part of the training most faculty receive, and classroom activities, projects, and exams are not always constructed to reliably elicit the desired learning from students. But where programs and campuses have developed clear, explicit outcomes—and assignments are aligned with those outcomes—assessment can be integrated into the ongoing work of faculty and students in ways that raise the likelihood of improvement by starting and staying closer to the action. This is the vision of assessment as "our students' best work" championed by the Association of American Colleges and Universities (AAC&U Board of Directors, 2008) in its framework for accountability, and it is also a defining feature of the Degree Qualifications Profile (DQP) introduced by Lumina Foundation in 2011, which "keeps faculty judgment at the center of assessment" by putting the focus on carefully designed (and aligned) assignments (Ewell, 2013a, p. 3).

The trend toward greater course-level assessment and assignments, illustrated in Figure 2.1 (which focuses on institution-level uses), has also been documented at the program level. The NILOA survey of program heads in the two- and four-year sectors revealed that academic programs used portfolios, measures of content knowledge, rubrics, and performance assessments more frequently than national surveys and general tests (Ewell, Paulson, & Kinzie, 2011). Two-thirds (68%) of academic programs reported using capstone assessments or rubrics, and more than half (58%) reported using performance assessments or final projects to measure learning. Some disciplines, moreover, appeared to employ "signature assignment" approaches. For example, 75% of education programs reported that all or most of their students completed portfolios, with the next most frequent being health sciences, at 41%. The greater use of assignments and course-based assessment in academic programs—and in particular in disciplines with a strong emphasis on practical, field-based experience—is perhaps not surprising. In fact, end-of-program courses or experiences that provide authentic, real-world application of learned concepts and skills are typically found in off-campus experiences such as student teaching, clinical nursing, internships, and cooperative education placements within professional disciplines. Student work produced in such settings may be evaluated by teams of faculty or field-based experts and then used in program accreditation or to inform program improvement.

The most persuasive brief for this kind of evidence is that its usefulness is built in; it is assessment not as aspiration but as an expectation and requirement, generating evidence that is used directly in ensuring each student's worthiness to be awarded a degree. And the results are clearly not at risk of being stashed and forgotten on a shelf; in such assessments, faculty members look carefully at their students' learning and care deeply about what they see. The challenge, on the other hand, is translating this fine-grained information at the level of the individual student into evidence that speaks meaningfully to audiences at other levels. Technology is now making this possible in new ways. Prince George's Community College's All in One system, for example, allows the campus to map student learning vertically starting with individual student performance and moving up to the course, program, and institution level (Richman & Ariovich, 2013). Some older, tried-and-true approaches are still in use as well. One of these—bringing faculty members together to read samples of work from the larger universe and draw more general conclusions—has a long and successful track record in the evaluation of writing. Another approach, portfolios, brings disparate classroom work together—and is our next category of evidence.

Portfolios

Like classroom-based assessments, the use of student portfolios for assessment has risen significantly. In their 2009 paper, Trudy Banta, Merilee Griffin, Teresa Flateby, and Susan Kahn identified portfolios as a "promising alternative" approach to student learning outcomes assessment. But by 2013, portfolios had become essentially "mainstream," with more than 40% of campuses using this approach (Figure 2.1) for institution-level assessment. If program-level use is included, that percentage clearly is much higher.

The evidence captured in portfolios has several significant advantages. As with classroom-based assessments, portfolios are a form of authentic assessment that draws on the work students do in regular course activities and assignments. It is no accident that these two developments—portfolios and classroom-based assessment—are trending in the same direction. As such, they reconnect assessment to the ongoing work of teaching and learning and to the work of faculty, raising the prospects for productive use. Additionally, because they represent work over time (not just a snapshot), they can capture more complex and evolving forms of learning (Banta et al., 2009) and experiences in the cocurriculum. Moreover, because most portfolios now call not only for artifacts but for student reflection, they are a vehicle for students to step back from their work, think about its meaning and trajectory, and how it comes together across contexts and over the college experience. "I have had many amazing experiences [as an undergraduate]," one senior student at the University of Michigan wrote in a portfolio, "but I didn't really know what they meant or how they all fit together. Now, I see patterns and themes. . . . There has been some direction to it all along" (Miller & Morgaine, 2009, p. 9). In this way, portfolios create "opportunities to move beyond assessment OF learning and move toward assessment FOR learning" (Eynon, Gambino, & Török, 2014, p. 107, emphasis in original).

Yet portfolios pose a variety of challenges. The evidence they provide is rich and authentic but it is also dense and potentially daunting. Without a system for making sense of that evidence, portfolios may be good for students but not very useful for making judgments about program quality. Additionally, they require a substantial dose of patience to design, implement, administer, codify, and interpret for the purposes of student outcomes assessment (Banta et al., 2009).

Today, thanks to the energy and commitment of a group of long-time champions of the method, much is known about how to use portfolios effectively. As reported by leaders of Connect to Learning, a 24-campus national ePortfolio project, the approach has been found to have three major benefits: (1) advancing student success; (2) making student learning visible (by supporting reflection, social pedagogy, and deep learning), and (3) catalyzing learning-centered institutional change (Eynon et al., 2014, p. 95). For these reasons, portfolios have become a major feature on the assessment landscape and a prominent source of evidence for improvement.

Rubrics

According to provosts, the use of rubrics has risen significantly, from 23% in 2009 to almost 70% in 2013 (Figure 2.1). Strictly speaking, a rubric is not evidence but rather a framework for interpreting information—for turning information or data into evidence. In that sense, a rubric articulates criteria for successive levels of performance.

The increase in the use of rubrics to analyze and collect evidence reflects the widespread acceptance of AAC&U's VALUE (Valid Assessment of Learning in Undergraduate Education) Rubrics, developed by teams of faculty from across the country for a wide range of outcomes (from writing to integrative learning, quantitative literacy to teamwork) (Figure 2.2). As AAC&U advises, these rubrics must be adapted to local circumstances, and many campuses have done so, in some cases creating their own.

For faculty, rubrics are a way of raising awareness of (and increasing explicitness about) the different levels of performance students may move

Figure 2.2: VALUE Rubric from the Association of American Colleges and Universities.

INQUIRY AND ANALYSIS VALUE RUBRIC

for more information, please contact value@aacu.org

Definition

Inquiry is a systematic process of exploring issues, objects or works through the collection and analysis of evidence that results in informed conclusions or judgments. Analysis is the process of breaking complex topics or issues into parts to gain a better understanding of them.

Evaluators are encouraged to assign a zero to any work sample or collection of work that does not meet benchmark (cell one) level performance.

	Capstone 4	Milestones 3	Milestones 2	Benchmark 1
Topic selection	Identifies a creative, focused, and manageable topic that addresses potentially significant yet previously less-explored aspects of the topic.	Identifies a focused and manageable/doable topic that appropriately addresses relevant aspects of the topic.	Identifies a topic that while manageable/doable, is too narrowly focused and leaves out relevant aspects of the topic.	Identifies a topic that is far too general and wide-ranging as to be manageable and doable.
Existing Knowledge, Research, and/or Views	Synthesizes in-depth information from relevant sources representing various points of view/approaches.	Presents in-depth information from relevant sources representing various points of view/approaches.	Presents information from relevant sources representing limited points of view/approaches.	Presents information from irrelevant sources representing limited points of view/approaches.
Design Process	All elements of the methodology or theoretical framework are skillfully developed. Appropriate methodology or theoretical frameworks may be synthesized from across disciplines or from relevant subdisciplines.	Critical elements of the methodology or theoretical framework are appropriately developed, however, more subtle elements are ignored or unaccounted for.	Critical elements of the methodology or theoretical framework are missing, incorrectly developed, or unfocused.	Inquiry design demonstrates a misunderstanding of the methodology or theoretical framework.
Analysis	Organizes and synthesizes evidence to reveal insightful patterns, differences, or similarities related to focus.	Organizes evidence to reveal important patterns, differences, or similarities related to focus.	Organizes evidence, but the organization is not effective in revealing important patterns, differences, or similarities.	Lists evidence, but it is not organized and/or is unrelated to focus.
Conclusions	States a conclusion that is a logical extrapolation from the inquiry findings.	States a conclusion focused solely on the inquiry findings. The conclusion arises specifically from and responds specifically to the inquiry findings.	States a general conclusion that, because it is so general, also applies beyond the scope of the inquiry findings.	States an ambiguous, illogical, or unsupportable conclusion from inquiry findings.
Limitations and Implications	Insightfully discusses in detail relevant and supported limitations and implications.	Discusses relevant and supported limitations and implications.	Presents relevant and supported limitations and implications.	Presents limitations and implications, but they are possibly irrelevant and unsupported.

Reprinted with permission from *Assessing Outcomes and Improving Achievement: Tips and Tools for Using Rubrics*, edited by Terrel Rhodes. Copyright 2010 by the Association of American Colleges and Universities.

through from beginning to more advanced proficiency. When shared with students, they have the additional advantage of providing a clear statement about expectations—although the amount of jargon in rubrics can sometimes lessen their utility for students (an argument for involving students in the development of rubrics). By providing a shared lens for making judgments, rubrics encourage the use of authentic student work for assessment such as portfolios, assignments that require the application of knowledge, and field-based work, illustrating a significant step in the shift from compliance to improvement.

Learning Analytics

A new source of information about student learning, made possible by growing computational power, is learning analytics—the so-called big data movement brought to bear on questions about the variables that contribute to or impede student progress and success. A number of institutions including Stanford University, the University of British Columbia and the University of Saskatchewan in Canada, the University of Queensland in Australia, and the Open University in the UK have joined together as the Society for Learning Analytics to "explore the intersection of learning analytics, and open learning, open technologies, and open research" (http://www.solaresearch.org/mission.ola/).

Not everyone would classify learning analytics as a form of student outcomes assessment. After all, it is concerned with large-scale patterns of course taking, student demographics, and other variables that can seem distinctly distant from the substance of learning. Yet, addressing the educational technology community, John Campbell, Peter DeBlois, and Diana Oblinger (2007) argue that "IT leaders may soon become critical partners with academic and student affairs [in answering the call] for accountability through *academic analytics*, which is emerging as a new tool for a new era" (p. 41). A growing number of campuses are now seeking to deploy this analytic capacity to improve student learning and success.

At the University of California–Davis, as part of the institution's work with the Bay View Alliance, an international network of research universities seeking to expand the use of evidence-based pedagogies, a pilot project is under way to engage faculty with learning analytics tools and data. Preliminary results suggest that this can lead to quick and positive shifts in the course planning process and the adoption of evidence-based teaching approaches (http://bayviewalliance.org/).

The University of Maryland–Baltimore County has also embraced learning analytics, using its tools to uncover obstacles to student success and evaluate attempts at intervention. What has been central to success has been "the insistence that all groups on campus take ownership of the challenge involving student performance and persistence" (Hrabowski et al., 2011, p. 26). In other words (as at UC–Davis), more sophisticated information is only part of the picture. As always with successful assessment, the academic community must be on board, engaged, part of the discussion, planning, and action—actively working to turn sometimes massive amounts of information into meaningful evidence for improvement.

Consequential Validity

Surveys, external instruments and exams, classroom assignments and assessments, portfolios, rubrics, and learning analytics constitute only a partial list of the potential sources of assessment evidence. They reflect some of the methods that are prominent today, and one—learning analytics—that appears to be gaining ground, especially in large research university settings. Twenty or even ten years ago, the list would have looked different, with more attention to standardized tests, less to classroom assignments, and little mention of rubrics. But what has been true throughout the several decades of the assessment movement is that much of the attention of assessment professionals has been focused on the psychometric properties of validity (asking whether the tool measures what it purports to measure) and reliability (whether the tool provides a consistent measure). There have been long-standing debates about whether it is possible to calculate value added and much discussion about sampling problems, student motivation, and response rates (see, for example, Banta & Pike, 2007; Hanson, 1988; McCormick & McClenney, 2012). All of these conversations are important. What has received far less attention is a different principle, central to this volume's focus on the use of assessment to catalyze productive change: the degree to which evidence stimulates improvement and, therefore, becomes consequential.

Of course, this concern does not and cannot exist in a vacuum. If evidence does not meet certain traditional standards of reliability, for instance, faculty—especially those with expertise in measurement—are unlikely to pay attention to or use it. But once measures of data quality and representativeness have been assured, and assessment results are found to generally comport with other assessment data or resonate with campus interests, then the next step is to use the results in the particular context. At that point, the utility of evidence for its intended purpose—consequential validity—becomes an important additional aspect of validity (Messick, 1989).

Consequential validity posits that assessment must be valid for the purposes for which it is used, consistent with relevant professional standards, and—this is the key point here—that the *impacts or consequences of its use* should be factors in determining validity. This focus on consequences underscores the fact—known all too well by anyone who has worked for long in assessment—that the relationship between evidence and action is not always neat, rational, or linear. Moreover, the fact that evidence meets the highest possible psychometric standards may have no bearing on its effectiveness in prompting action on campus. And vice versa: A locally designed student survey, for example, may not have the psychometric properties of a tool such as NSSE, but the process of designing it may start productive, generative conversations among faculty, and such conversations are often harbingers of meaningful change. Consequential validity thus brings an important new lens to questions about evidence by putting a premium on the productive use of information critical to student learning outcomes assessment that is more than compliance.

Obstacles to the Effective Use of Evidence

As noted earlier and throughout this volume, colleges and universities have made great progress in gathering information about student learning. Most higher education institutions today have an assessment office or assessment director. In addition, most are investing more in their analytical and research capacities and expanding their institutional research offices (Volkwein, 2011). Also, as we have seen, colleges and universities are generating more data through more varied approaches than in the past. But for all kinds of reasons, even where these efforts are well intended, using the results in an evidentiary manner is far from easy.

Assessment results can be ambiguous or inconclusive, making it difficult to take action. They can be disheartening or dispiriting, or can fly in the face of long-established habits and practices highly resistant to change. Results can be disconnected from local circumstances—too far from home, one might say—and hard to connect to immediate questions and needs. They can be poor quality, or viewed with skepticism in important quarters, and can engender mistrust. Collecting information about student learning and collegiate experiences, it turns out, is perhaps the easiest step in the assessment process. The hard part follows: "The real challenge begins once faculty, staff, administrators, and students at institutions try to use the evidence to improve student learning" (Kuh, 2011, p. 3).

Among the obstacles that make the use of evidence challenging, three warrant mention here. First, *evidence isn't accessed by those who could or might use it.* Data on the shelf—the report that is carefully put together and then sits in a binder, gathering dust in the office of assessment or institutional research—is an all-too-common problem, say Charles Blaich and Kathleen Wise (2011). Campuses gather information, sometimes circulate the results to a small number of people, and then store the reports in perpetuity where no one need bother with them.

This dynamic is the likely result of a circumstance noted in Chapter 1: when the information doesn't meaningfully address a question that someone (or some group) cares about or when the connection between questions and answers has not been sufficiently articulated. Put differently, these are data looking for a problem. Issues of attitude and framing may be part of this dynamic as well, illustrated in the comment of a campus accreditation committee member who, when asked how the campus would use its extensive exhibit of assessment results to improve student learning, said, "Oh, we just collected the data for SACS [Southern Association for Colleges and Schools]." When assessment is framed as a compliance activity—or only that—results are likely to be inert and to remain unengaged by those who might use them.

Second, *evidence of unacceptable performance is known and even acknowledged by those in a position to take action, but they do not.* Here, the issues are likely to be about motivation to do that very difficult thing: change behavior. (Recall the recalcitrant heart patients.) Writing about a science education initiative at the University of British Columbia (UBC), physics Nobel laureate Carl Wieman and his colleagues reported, "While research and data on student learning are important and useful, they were seldom compelling enough by themselves to change faculty members' pedagogy, particularly when that change conflicted with their beliefs about teaching and learning" (Wieman, Perkins, & Gilbert, 2010, p. 9).

Part of this dynamic is the familiar not-invented-here syndrome that plagues higher education. Especially when it comes to teaching, faculty value what they themselves invent, design, and experience—and look upon evidence generated elsewhere as not quite to the point. It is true that the evidence UBC faculty generated themselves on their own students and classrooms had greater power and was more likely to lead to change (Wieman et al., 2010). In fact, part of the power of assessment is that evidence from one's own setting, reflecting local contexts and conditions and answering local questions, is more likely to lead to change than research done elsewhere by others (even expert others). But even then, evidence comes up against preconceptions, habits, and powerful incentives to continue doing the same thing one has always done.

And third, *evidence is used but does not lead to real improvement.* Some institutions face challenges that are seemingly intractable, such as increasing the success rates of students required to complete a developmental mathematics course before they can take the required general education math class. Many Achieving the Dream colleges are working on this major challenge, with mixed outcomes (see http://www.achieving thedream.org/topics/use_evidence), and a major initiative of the Carnegie Foundation for the Advancement of Teaching now has significant progress to report (Clyburn, 2013). But individual campuses working on these problems alone, without major funding, are up against heavy odds indeed. Another all-but-intractable challenge is providing a high quality educational experience to students who want to take a full load of coursework to qualify for financial aid but who also must work 25 or more hours a week to make ends meet and, perhaps, support their family members (children, parents). Students who must manage such demanding circumstances are less likely to participate in high-impact activities (Kuh, 2008) or take advantage of other educationally enriching opportunities. Yet, while evidence suggests students would benefit from these high-impact practices, institutions may not be willing or able to address the stipulations for financial aid, or to think more creatively about how experiential activities could be scheduled to encourage the students' participation.

Information's Social Life

As these three types of challenges suggest, the relationship between evidence and action is complicated—and fragile. The problem lies partly in the character and quality of the evidence itself, but it can also be seen as a problem with what John Seely Brown and Paul Duguid (2000) call "the social life of information." That is, the power of evidence to stimulate productive use may depend on the human context in which it exists. Indeed, in a study of how new approaches to teaching travel (or don't), Mary Taylor Huber (2009) notes, "There has been a tendency to look for answers to these questions in matters of theory and method"—for instance, whether the evidence about the effectiveness of a particular teaching approach or curriculum is valid or generalizable. However, she cautions, "the very possibility of pedagogical travel is better understood as a function of the work's social life," and, particularly, the kinds of networks and communities in which the evidence is gathered, talked about, and traded (p. 1).

Huber's focus is the scholarship of teaching and learning, but her point is relevant to assessment as well. The Wabash National Study, a multicampus assessment project focused on the outcomes of liberal education, began with an assumption: "once faculty and staff had 'good' data from a high-quality research project, they would use it to improve student learning" (Blaich & Wise, 2011, p. 8). That assumption, its leaders say, turned out to be wrong. As they now argue, campuses tend to put too much of their energy into getting huge amounts of "perfect" data, and not enough time getting people organized, interested, and engaged all the way through the process (2011). As we argue in Chapter 5, some of those people should be students, who can be an important part of the force for improvement.

What Counts as Evidence

Acknowledging the importance of the social life of evidence brings us to questions about the range of audiences for assessment. Indeed, many of assessment's perennial and most pressing challenges stem from the need to provide meaningful, comprehensible evidence to very different stakeholders with very different needs and interests. Subsequent chapters will examine these groups in more depth. Here, we focus more briefly on the nature of evidence most likely to be compelling to each.

Policymakers

By *policymakers* we mean those outside of academe in positions to influence what institutions value and do. These include members of state or system governing and coordinating boards, state and federal legislators, and federal regulators including the U.S. Department of Education.

Generally, when policymakers ask for evidence, their need is for information they can understand quickly and clearly—numbers, broad trends, dashboard-like metrics. The demand for assessment evidence from state agencies—including state higher education offices, systems and coordinating boards and state legislatures—represents a mix of requirements for common testing, the identification of performance indicators, or policies forcing public institutions to conduct their own assessments and report results. Some state higher education systems, for example, require public institutions to collect evidence using specific instruments and tests and to identify indicators for performance funding, while other states simply have a requirement that students are surveyed regularly. State and federal policies and practices in assessing student outcomes are discussed more thoroughly in Chapter 8. However, for better or for worse (perhaps a little of both), policymakers are not necessarily interested in the nuances of how history majors perform in a culminating capstone experience. They want to know what percentage of students are graduating, how much it costs to educate them, whether they are finding employment, and whether—more generally—institutions are delivering on their promises to students.

The challenge is to respond to these questions in ways that are both straightforward and simple but also true to complex institutional realities—and this is a work in progress. Many academics are unhappy with the reliance on overly simple and often reductive measures like graduation rates and employment status, and probably many inside and outside of higher education would like to find simple ways to measure actual contributions to learning. At a symposium convened by the Association for the Study of Higher Education's Council on Public Policy in Higher Education, former U.S. Deputy Under Secretary of Education Robert Shireman quipped that the best-case scenario would be a sort of "Thinkbit" for students, modeled on the Fitbit device that tracks physical activity. "But the Thinkbit would tell you, 'Is there real learning going on?'" (quoted in Golden, 2013, para. 8).

We are not, as they say, there yet, but the assessment movement has made some progress in moving the policymaking appetite for evidence in useful directions, and this is an important role for higher education institutions and organizations. Whereas test scores were the default choice early on (this, at least, is what some vocal policymakers *thought* they wanted, borrowing from their experience with K–12), there is more openness to a range of evidence today. The Voluntary System of Accountability—higher education's response to the Spellings Commission, described in Chapter 1—invites a variety of types of evidence, from information about costs, to NSSE results, and (a more recent addition) evidence from classroom assignments and portfolios scored by faculty using AAC&U VALUE Rubrics (see https://cp-files.s3.amazonaws.com/32/AACU_VALUE_Rubrics_Administration_Guidelines_20121210.pdf). The next challenge is to bring more viewers to this information (Jankowski, et al., 2012).

Accreditors

The U.S. system of accreditation—particularly accreditation through the seven regional accrediting agencies—is an interesting hybrid. It is external in that it involves significant, regular review by experts from outside the institution, but those experts are also peers—fellow academics, often from similar institutions and with a feel for the realities facing the institution under review. As such, accreditors stand in a kind of middle position when it comes to what counts as evidence. They are in a position to understand and value more detailed and nuanced information than external policymakers, but they are necessarily focused on the big picture—on systems, processes, and structures more than on the particulars of each and every program (Gaston, 2014). Increasingly, they are focused not only on whether the institution is gathering evidence but also on whether it is "becoming more systematic and intentional about gathering data about the *right things*—performance and effectiveness—and on *using* the resulting information to continuously improve" (WASC, 2014, p. 1).

Accreditation continues to be the number one driver for assessment across institutional types and, not surprisingly, it is the primary context for use (Kuh et al., 2014). Although the regional accreditors employ somewhat different models, NILOA has found no significant differences in the kinds of evidence being gathered and reported by institutions by region (Gannon-Slater, Ikenberry, Jankowski, & Kuh, 2014, p. 3).

Perhaps where accreditation is most distinctive in its evidentiary interests and needs is around the notion of a *culture of evidence*, a term that first took hold in the Western region but is now commonplace across the assessment community. The point is that good assessment is not about the amount of information amassed, or about the quality of any particular facts or numbers put forth. Rather, assessment within a culture of evidence is about habits of question asking, reflection, deliberation, planning, and action based on evidence. Determining whether a culture of evidence exists is no simple task, but the principle is one of the distinctive and most important contributions of accreditation, calling on campuses to pull together an integrated story of its efforts to provide students with a meaningful educational experience. Chapter 7 explores accreditation in much more depth.

Faculty

One of the enduring issues in assessment is faculty involvement in the process. Indeed, the need for greater faculty engagement was among the top challenges identified by provosts in both 2009 and 2013 (Kuh & Ikenberry, 2009; Kuh et al., 2014). However, a parallel survey focused on program-level assessment revealed a different picture, with more than 60% of respondents reporting that all or most of their faculty were already involved (Ewell et al., 2011, p. 11). In point of fact, it is hard to know how many faculty are really involved or exactly how. Whatever the answer, assessment will lead to improvement only when its evidence speaks to faculty and engages them. So, then, what do faculty want to know about their students' learning?

A cynical answer is that faculty don't want to know anything more than they know already, that they are set in their ways and not inclined to change. At too many institutions, faculty opine that if they had better students, their teaching would yield better results. But on campuses where faculty have become involved in assessment and related inquiry-based activities, they want rich, nuanced information about individual students in their courses and programs. For instance, participants in an initiative at Gonzaga University (linking assessment and the scholarship of teaching and learning) formulated a variety of complex, nuanced questions about what and how their students learn. A faculty member in English who wanted to help students become more active and critical readers investigated what students "think it means to 'read' and what they *do* when they read a written text, especially a literary text" in her 100-level literature course (quoted in Boose & Hutchings, 2014). A participant in religious studies worked to document the process of transformation that occurs (or does not) for students in her Inter-Christian Dialog course; her aim was to "repersonalize" education and to discover ways to respond more fully to the experience of individual students.

Nuanced questions like these reflect intellectual curiosity and an institutionalized ethic of care for students. But there are also pragmatic impulses in play. Many faculty today are trying new approaches in their classrooms and they want to know whether the hard work entailed in redesigning activities and assignments is worth the effort. As noted earlier, this kind of authentic, classroom-based assessment is gaining headway, spurred on in part by the vision of assessment that animates the Degree Qualifications Profile (Ewell, 2013a), which more than 400 campuses have begun to explore and implement.

Of course, faculty are not a homogenous group and, as suggested earlier, what counts as evidence may vary considerably by field. Language is telling here. The sciences and social sciences are completely comfortable talking about "data," but that is not a word one typically hears in the humanities, where evidence is largely qualitative. Accordingly, assessment in English departments may revolve around the close reading of student papers; in psychology, one may find more appetite for scores and statistics. Understanding and inviting these differences may be one of the best routes into greater faculty engagement with assessment (Heiland & Rosenthal, 2011; Hutchings, 2011). The essential role of faculty in assessment is explored more deeply in Chapter 5.

Campus Administrators—Chairs, Deans, and Provosts

Most campus administrative leaders were once faculty, and many of them understand and appreciate (and even reward) faculty inquiry into their own students' learning but they are often trying to answer questions from governing boards and policymakers as well. In short, chairs, deans, and provosts need evidence that brings the two levels together—bottom up and top down. As pointed out in Chapter 6, this middle ground is often where assessment can make its biggest difference, answering questions about how to utilize scarce resources, where to push forward new initiatives (a new first-year program? better sophomore advising?), and to what extent different groups of students are meeting institution-level outcomes. Their questions are more nuanced and contextualized than those of policymakers but broader and bigger picture than those of most faculty and staff members.

One notable development in this regard is the move to connect different levels of evidence by "aggregating up" from classroom-level information like exam scores and grades. Technology, as mentioned earlier, can be key here. This includes commercially available data management software (Hutchings, 2009) but also locally developed systems like All in One at Prince George's Community College and Kansas City Kansas Community College's interactive course mapping database, where faculty enter information about individual student work that is then analyzed around the institution's university-wide 21st Century Learning Outcomes (Hutchings, 2014a). Much of the early action on this front has been in for-profit, online institutions, and in the community college sector, but it is now catching hold in other settings as well.

The Public: Students and Parents

What counts as evidence for students and parents as they think about higher education? In truth, this is a question many are puzzling over. Traditionally, decisions about what college or university to attend have been based largely on reputation or on proximity and cost. But there have now been a number of efforts to develop and make available information that speaks to the quality of the experience provided.

For starters, it is worth saying that students are not only "prospects." When they enroll and become members of the campus community, they become partners in the assessment enterprise, as we argue they can and should in Chapter 5. This means involvement in course-embedded activities such as ePortfolios that provide them with evidence of their own learning and help them think about their *experience* as learners (an activity in which all students should participate). It also means opportunities (several campuses have moved in this direction) to gather, analyze, and discuss assessment evidence in ways that have helped make it more actionable.

Reaching prospective students and their families is harder. Chapter 1 briefly describes the effort by the Voluntary System of Accountability (VSA) to assemble and report information relevant to higher education's consumers and clients. NILOA'S review of the system in 2012 reveals that those who visited the VSA website spent a good bit of time on the cost calculator and on basic information about graduation rates, but they rarely if ever got to the actual information about student learning—and exited quickly when they did get to it (Jankowski et al., 2012). For the VSA, this speaks to the usefulness of multiple portals that are customized for different internal and external audiences. More generally, it underlines the overarching theme that what counts as evidence—what will be *consequential* in terms of interest and use—is a function of audience needs and interests.

To this point, the NILOA team worked with representatives from the 13 universities that at the time comprised the Committee on Institutional Cooperation (CIC)—otherwise known as the Big Ten and the University of Chicago. One outcome of these deliberations was agreement that different groups were interested to varying degrees in five categories of information about the quality of undergraduate education:

1. To what degree do students benefit from attending your university in terms of (a) academic achievement, content knowledge, and cognitive/intellectual skills; (b) practical competencies and personal development; (c) degree attainment; (d) employment; and (e) postbaccalaureate study?

2. What enriching educational opportunities are available, and how many students take advantage of them? What distinctive opportunities are provided to students?

3. What evidence suggests students are able to integrate and apply what they learned?

4. What are the net costs for the typical resident and nonresident student to attend this institution? What factors influence the cost for students?

5. What internal institutional processes assure the quality of student learning? How are the results of these processes used to enhance student learning?

To respond to these questions, each of the 13 research universities shared what it was doing to collect and share internally the information that would address these questions. While no institution had enough data to answer every question definitively, every institution was committed to doing more to better understand how and to what extent its students were benefitting from the undergraduate experience and how their learning could be enhanced.

Conclusion: Moving to What Matters for Improvement

Moving from a compliance model of assessment to one focused on improving students' educational experiences means putting a premium on evidence. It also means, we have suggested in this chapter, being smart about what constitutes evidence and how to use it effectively. What matters for assessment for the improvement of student learning is not the amount of information gathered, but its usefulness to the community—and usefulness, or actionability, is determined by a number of factors: the quality of the evidence; its technical properties; and its match with the interests, questions, and dispositions of those who will be using it. As St. Olaf College Vice President for Mission Jo Beld (2010) argues, what is needed for improvement are "assessment projects centered on 'intended uses by intended users'" (p. 6)—what Michael Patton (2008) calls utilization-focused evaluation.

This means thinking hard about purposes and audience—about who, exactly, wants (or needs) to know what, and why—and doing so at the beginning, as decisions about instruments and methods are made, as well as at the end, once results are available. The challenges of using evidence cannot be solved after the fact. It means thinking not only about traditional validity and reliability but also about consequential validity. And it means building a community of judgment and deliberation among key actors and partners whose perspectives are critical at various points along the way. Put differently, assessment is about evidence, but it is just as much about people.

3

FOSTERING GREATER USE
OF ASSESSMENT RESULTS

PRINCIPLES FOR EFFECTIVE PRACTICE

Jillian Kinzie, Pat Hutchings, and Natasha A. Jankowski

Be not simply good; be good for something.

—Henry David Thoreau

GATHERING INFORMATION ABOUT COLLEGIATE outcomes has a practical goal: using it to improve both student learning and institutional performance. Yet, as Chapter 2 suggests, reaching that goal is not easy. Actually *using* assessment results to make informed decisions that enhance educational quality has remained an unmet promise on many campuses. From its first manifestation in the 1930s (Ewell, 2002) to its more familiar forms today, assessment of student learning has been put to many and sundry uses. Some of this activity has led to productive improvements in the quality of student learning, yet more has resulted in the compilation of information solely to satisfy the needs of accreditation or annual data collection, with little consideration given to the implications and use of the results.

But this may be starting to change. In the last decade, accreditation requirements for institutions to demonstrate the use of assessment results have increased, and institutions must now show that learning outcomes are defined, articulated, assessed, and used to guide institutional improvement (Provezis, 2010). Moreover, as the challenges facing academic institutions have escalated, the need for and practical utility of evidence of student learning have become more apparent.

As assessment practice has expanded in higher education and the pressure to demonstrate accountability for student learning has intensified, interest from the field in how to do this work has grown. The many requests for examples of how to assemble evidence of student learning and identify institutions that are modeling best practice have generated several books on outcomes assessment in higher education (see, e.g., Maki, 2004; Suskie, 2004; Walvoord, 2010) and have provided a warrant for hosting conferences and other convenings on the topic (Banta, Jones, & Black, 2009). The hundreds of short case studies of campus assessment practice that appeared in two key resources, *Assessment in Practice* (Banta, Lund, Black, & Oblander, 1996) and *Designing Effective Assessment* (Banta et al., 2009), provide comprehensive resources for profiles of good practice. In addition to these foundational volumes, there are now more than a few publications describing effective assessment practice (Banta & Associates, 2002; Bresciani, 2007; Maki, 2004). Even more, the thousands of attendees over the past 20 years at the popular Assessment Institute in Indianapolis and the hundreds that participate in regional-based fora, such as the annual Texas A&M Assessment Conference, are testament to the high interest in learning more about how to assess student learning. Since 2005, the Council for Higher Education Accreditation (CHEA) has recognized 32 institutions or programs for outstanding work in developing and applying evidence of student learning outcomes to improve higher education quality and accountability (see http://www.chea.org/chea%20award/CHEA_Awards_All.html). More recently, participation in and results from NILOA's 2009 and 2013 surveys of provosts and follow-up focus groups reflect a persistent appetite for information on best practices in assessment and provide concrete examples of institutions using evidence to improve.

One of the most encouraging findings from the 2013 survey (Figure 3.1) is that reports of institutional use of assessment evidence increased between 2009 and 2013 across every category including regional and program accreditation, program review, curricular modifications, and institutional improvement (Kuh, Jankowski, Ikenberry, & Kinzie, 2014).

Student learning outcomes results were reportedly used for the purposes of accreditation by nearly all participating institutions, and 9 of 10 institutions reported using their results in program review. Other

Figure 3.1:   Comparison of Uses of Assessment Results in 2009 and 2013.

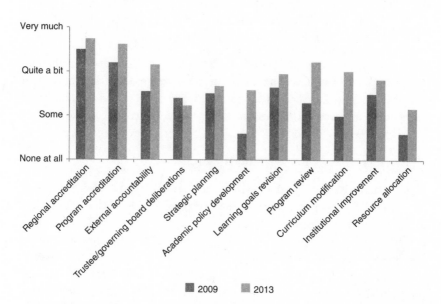

external accountability reporting requirements, for example, state performance metrics and initiatives like the Voluntary System of Accountability (VSA), were relatively frequent reasons for doing assessment, closely followed by curricular modifications, revision of learning goals, and instructional improvement. NILOA's earlier survey of program heads in two- and four-year institutions confirmed the picture painted by provosts, showing considerable assessment activity and use at the program and department levels (Ewell, Paulsen, & Kinzie, 2011). Clearly, this bodes well for those who would benefit from examples of productive use.

Despite all this activity, and considerable documentation of effective practice, there is still much to be learned about *how* to do this work well. Also, a nagging question persists: Does the availability and use of evidence of student learning make a material difference to improving student learning and institutional performance?

This chapter describes what productive use of assessment results looks like by drawing on a range of examples from diverse campus settings. Toward this end, the chapter is organized around the following questions:

1. What is the difference between *doing assessment* and *using assessment* results?

2. What approaches have been successfully employed on campuses that have achieved greater use of assessment results?

3. What principles might guide the field in furthering the use of assessment results to improve student learning?

Based on our attempt to answer these questions, we distill principles for guiding effective assessment use that point to ways to enhance student learning. To put our analysis in context, we briefly discuss the history of assessment practice and its lessons for productive use.

A Brief History of Assessment Practice

A glimpse of the history of assessment in higher education bares some of the roots of the notable variations in purpose, struggles with using results, and questions about how assessment is practiced that continue to characterize the movement today. Although the student learning outcomes assessment movement is often seen as beginning in the 1980s, assessment practice has a longer history, beginning in the 1930s as a practical and scholarly inquiry project to measure and understand cognitive gains (Ewell, 2002). A full 40 years later, work shifted to study the net effects of college and student persistence, and at the same time, some campuses, including Alverno College, placed greater emphasis on mastery learning and on assessing and certifying individual student accomplishments (2002). The work in these early phases of assessment greatly emphasized a practical and scholarly orientation, made methodological contributions to the emerging scholarship of assessment, and also helped institutions understand student learning.

Then, in the 1980s, the purpose of assessment in higher education expanded in response to pressures for accountability. At that time, the prevailing assumption was that assessment would serve the purposes of evaluation and accountability, usually at the level of program or institutional performance. Accordingly, assessment practice focused narrowly on the adoption of standardized tests to address concerns about educational quality expressed in high-profile public documents. One such report was the National Commission on Excellence in Education's 1983 report *A Nation at Risk,* which, although it focused on K–12 education, stimulated policymaker interest in assessment at the higher education level. Another, the 1984 report by the Study Group on the Conditions of Excellence in American Higher Education, *Involvement in Learning* (National Institute of Education), recommended assessment for the purposes of improving undergraduate education.

As the assessment movement grew, however, the emphasis on educational outcomes by federal and state agencies, accreditors, trustees and coordinating boards, and even students and parents, stimulated the adoption of a wider range of assessment activities and more nuanced evidence of what students know and can do as a result of their undergraduate experiences.

At the same time, the purpose of assessment was debated. Could assessment move beyond a process of measuring and collecting evidence for accountability and instead include the use of evidence in meaningful ways to improve? Barbara Wright (1997) asserted that assessment could serve both purposes and, most important, that assessment is a process that converts data into information that is used to improve student learning. In the practice of assessment, however, the dominance of accountability language and activities including testing, evaluation, measurement, and comparability can supplant language more frequently associated with student learning such as effort, growth, gain, mastery, and improvement. According to Peter Ewell (2009), since the early days of the assessment movement, assessment's two purposes have not rested comfortably together.

Alongside the growth in assessment activity and the emphasis on accountability and using evidence to improve emerged a natural curiosity about how assessment is accomplished—in particular, a desire for concrete examples about good practice. The rising demand from colleges, universities, and academic departments for help in learning the rudiments of assessment and for opportunities to exchange ideas about assessment practice and resources for continuous improvement prompted the establishment of several formal efforts to advance assessment practice. In 1986, the Fund for the Improvement of Postsecondary Education (FIPSE) supported two projects to develop expertise and resources on assessment and to publicize advances in the field: the University of Tennessee–Knoxville's Assessment Resource Center, and the Assessment Forum of the American Association for Higher Education (AAHE). These projects contributed major resources including books, research reports, studies of assessment practice, assessment bibliographies, international conferences, a consortium of campus-based leaders, and a national newsletter—*Assessment Update,* published by Jossey-Bass, the first newsletter dedicated to assessment in postsecondary education (Marcus, Cobb, & Shoenberg, 1993). Comprehensive resources on assessment, including *Assessment in Practice* (Banta et al., 1996), and step-by-step guides, such as *Assessment Essentials* (Banta & Palomba, 2014; Palomba & Banta, 1999), provided needed guidance for the growing field. Moreover, the examples included in these volumes confirm that good practice in assessment was occurring on hundreds of campuses across the country.

As this brief history of assessment practice suggests, the growth of institutional assessment practice corresponded with a shift of emphasis in assessment's purpose: a desire on the part of some to move away from compliance-driven data collection and toward the development of systematic ways to use evidence to improve the quality of undergraduate education. Engaging in assessment has become a condition of doing business for colleges and universities because of accreditation requirements and the need to show results (Ewell, 2009). Support for assessment from faculty and staff has increased with the growing emphasis on authentic and information-rich assessments more aligned with teaching and learning processes including portfolios, scoring rubrics, and surveys of student engagement that provide immediately useful feedback about instructional practice (Banta et al., 2009). In short, as noted in Chapter 2, campuses today have more and better evidence of student learning and the collegiate experience at the course, department, and institution levels. Yet compelling questions remain about how to effectively use results within levels and then to roll all this up into meaningful assessments of student learning and educational quality that broadly inform action. Unsurprisingly, practitioners are still clamoring for examples of effective *use,* illustrating that the link between assessment and improved student learning continues to be a challenge.

Doing Assessment Versus Using Results

The purpose of assessment is not achieved simply through the collection of vast amounts of valid and reliable data. Rather, assessment's purpose is to answer questions, shape better policies, make better decisions— all designed to improve student success and strengthen institutional performance. *Doing* assessment, simply performing assessment activities, is not the same as using assessment results. Considerable assessment activity can occur at a college or university—administering standardized tests to all students, documenting pass rates on licensure exams, writing reports about the results, for example. Until the institution uses the assembled evidence to answer questions about educational quality—about what students know and can do—and then uses the answers to guide change leading to improvement, it is just doing assessment. Assessment's true aim is using results, *harnessing evidence* to inform educational improvements. Linda Suskie (2004) put it plainly: "If an assessment doesn't help improve teaching and learning activities, why bother with it?" (p. 18).

Figure 3.2:   The Assessment Cycle.

The familiar visual depiction of the assessment process as an iterative sequence, represented as a six-stage cycle in Figure 3.2, illustrates the difference between assessment activity and use.

The first two stages of the assessment cycle—planning and identifying outcomes and gathering data—are usually associated with assessment *activity;* they are followed by the stages associated with use: analyzing and sharing results, identifying and implementing changes, and assessing the impact of changes; finally, in the model's most important feature, the cycle begins again. The first two stages of the cycle are generally considered easy, while analyzing and sharing results are harder, demanding careful interpretation and connections to units on campus—often requiring diplomacy, particularly when data do not comport with dominant beliefs. The final stages—acting on evidence, that is, implementing changes and assessing their impact—are the hardest in the cycle. All of the cycle's *use* stages require significant oversight and effort to complete.

The ease of assessment *activity* contributes to the widespread tendency to overemphasize the collection of data and ignore the use of evidence. In their analysis of why so little action followed the collection of extensive evidence in the Wabash National Study, a longitudinal study of student learning outcomes and experiences (http://www.liberalarts.wabash.edu/study-overview/), Charles Blaich and Kathleen Wise (2011) found that most institutions had more than enough actionable assessment evidence, including a range of national surveys, standardized outcomes measures, and student interviews—yet they had little experience in reviewing and making sense of the results and deciding what action, if any, might follow. They concluded, "The norm for many institutions is to gather data, to circulate the resulting reports among a small group of people, and then to just shelve them if nothing horrible jumps out—and sometimes even if it does!" (p. 12). Gathering data is far less risky and complicated than acting on the evidence in the data. The trick is to engage academics' interest in inquiry without triggering the familiar scholarly habits that would lead to gathering even more data and producing more reports.

The tidy notion of *closing the assessment loop* represents the stage of the cycle demonstrating the starkest difference between activity and use. The final stage of any assessment and improvement plan involves taking action on results and then going back to assess whether or not this action was effective. Institutions of higher education find it difficult to convert data into action and even more challenging to measure the impact of improvement initiatives (Banta & Blaich, 2011). Furthermore, while most assessment activity is associated with some sort of campus improvement or change, this is usually related to improving processes, such as better teaching methods, enhanced advising approaches, better faculty development programs, or more resources for a program, and usually not with direct evidence of improvements to student learning (Banta et al., 2009). Equal attention must be afforded to the difficult task of assessing impact on student learning.

Another stumbling block to using assessment results is getting caught up in creating the "perfect" research design. Blaich and Wise (2011) see this as a prevalent tendency among academics trained to strive for methodological purity and to distrust data collected through a less-than-perfect research design. Assessment must work with the best design possible—given what is practical, feasible, and most likely to produce reasonable results. The most feasible design must also answer a specific question of interest to campus leaders about educational quality or student learning. In assessment, as Barbara Walvoord (2010) observed, "You are not trying to achieve the perfect research design; you are trying to gather enough data to provide a reasonable basis for action" (p. 5). Notably, *enough data* is not about quantity—although one way to strengthen the usability of assessment results is to line up multiple points of evidence. Rather, data are *enough* when they provide evidence that is reasonably sufficient—perhaps good enough—to answer a specific question. When the doubt of methodological purists stalls assessment action, a possible way to redirect attention to data use is to invite the skeptics to participate in a thought experiment: Imagine that these data are true and that this is the best evidence we have. What should we do about it?

Assessment must, first and foremost, provide useful information to inform improvements and address questions of interest around student learning. Assessment is not about the technical adequacy of the design. Effective assessment requires persistent emphasis on utility and, as noted in Chapters 1 and 2, abiding concern for consequential validity—that is, for the impacts and consequences of the activity, the evidence it generates, and fitness of the evidence for the intended use. This means shifting the emphasis from collecting data to taking action and carrying out the commitment to measure the impact of actions taken.

Good Practice: Examples of Effective Use

Using assessment results is the most important and also the most challenging step in the assessment process. A central aspect of NILOA's work has been to document institutional examples of effective assessment work, with a particular focus on how evidence is used to advance improvements in students' learning (see http://www.learningoutcomeassessment .org/CaseStudiesInstitutions.html). Surveys and focus groups conducted with institutional leaders and assessment practitioners, nine in-depth case studies, and a cross-case analysis provide a rich picture of what effective practice in assessment use looks like (Baker, Jankowski, Provezis, & Kinzie, 2012; Kinzie, 2010). This section reviews the major findings of these inquiries with an emphasis on what accounts for effective use.

Distinct Levels of Use

Student learning outcomes assessment can be done at multiple levels— course, program, and institution. NILOA's case studies of effective practice highlight the use of evidence to improve student learning at all levels (Baker et al., 2012) and reveal that assessment is put to distinctly different uses at each level. This finding corroborated the results of NILOA's survey of provosts—showing a distinction between assessment at the institution level versus the program level, with the highest rate of changes in policies, programs, or practices based on assessment results in specific curricular requirements or courses and at the department or program level (Kuh et al., 2014). In this section, we discuss two distinct levels of use: institution and program/course. For the most part, course-level uses are closely aligned with program-level uses. Additional distinctions in course-level uses are highlighted in Chapters 2, 5, and 9 of this volume.

Institutional examples illustrating effective use of student learning evidence for institution-level improvement include strengthening connections between assessment and institutional goals by setting institutional priorities and strategic planning, informing institutional decision making, incorporating results into accreditation efforts, framing assessment at the institution level, revising institutional outcomes, improving student engagement and success, creating a culture of teaching and learning, enhancing faculty collaboration across campus, and reflecting on assessment processes and institutional practices.

A specific example of institution-level use is reflected in the approach that Texas A&M International University (TAMIU) adopted to frame assessment (Baker, 2012a). TAMIU's Project INTEGRATE (Institutional Network Targeting Evaluation, Goals, Resources, and Accountability Toward Effectiveness) involves participation from academic programs and administrative/educational support units in the assessment process. This initiative provides a structured framework for assessment at the institution by documenting the alignment of strategic planning, assessment activities, and resource allocation. Project INTEGRATE formalizes the policy, process, format, cycle, and documentation of the assessment process. The process is led by the University Assessment Committee, and all of TAMIU's academic programs and administrative/educational support units annually assess their programs or units, publicly report their findings, and designate academic degree program coordinators responsible for overseeing implementation of improvements.

In contrast, uses of student learning evidence for program- and course-level improvement examined by NILOA, including the following, are more closely connected to faculty, the curriculum, and student learning needs: setting faculty priorities; securing resources for professional development; improving student support services; revising curriculum, courses, and assignments; informing program reviews/departmental self-studies; aligning curriculum; and improving program outcomes.

Program-level uses in all NILOA institutional examples focus on specific problems or questions regarding student learning, emphasizing what is of most interest to faculty members. As noted earlier, focusing on the interests and questions of faculty members helps achieve faculty engagement with and ownership of assessment efforts, as well as leading more directly to assessment use to improve academic programs and courses.

One of the most robust illustrations of such program- and course-level use is at Carnegie Mellon University (CMU), which values and fosters diversity in how student learning outcomes assessment is undertaken within colleges and departments (Kinzie, 2012). Assessment at CMU is driven by faculty questions about student learning and effective teaching and is informed by departmental curricular interests, program goals, and disciplinary factors. The university's Eberly Center for Teaching Excellence provides assessment support and reinforces the link between implementing an assessment plan and program- and course-level improvement, employing a data-driven approach to help faculty improve the quality of teaching and learning and working closely with each dean, department head, and unit assessment faculty leader. The Eberly Center website documents student learning outcomes assessment at the department, program, and course levels and features dozens of assessment tools and course-level examples across disciplines including rubrics for assessing student work, worksheets to guide students' analyses, peer evaluation tools for group projects, and rating scales for oral presentations, among others (see http://www.cmu.edu/teaching/assessment/). Each course-level example is described using a common template including purpose, implementation, results, and faculty comments. Particularly instructive examples reveal instructor cautions and concerns, document what the faculty member changed in the course, and discuss the impact on students and their learning. Focusing on faculty interest in problems of teaching and learning and emphasizing the connection to centers for teaching excellence increase the likelihood that assessment results will lead to improvements in student learning.

Distinguishing the differences in assessment use between these two levels and the specific activities and approaches aligned with effective use is important as we strive to understand and improve campus assessment practice. Clarifying the intended level of use for assessment at the outset might help connect assessment activity more directly to use. TAMIU, for example, communicated at the outset of its assessment work exactly how assessment results would inform strategic planning and distinguished how results from program assessment reports would contribute both to institution-wide learning outcomes assessment and also to improved program-level outcomes. At the same time, consideration of distinct levels of assessment might also suggest different approaches as well as who and what actions might be most relevant to the work.

Begin with Use in Mind

Institutions that effectively use assessment results focus sharply from the beginning of any assessment initiative on how results will be used. The emphasis on utilization is strong in the related field of educational evaluation, and is formally expressed in Michael Patton's (2008) utilization-focused evaluation (U-FE) model, introduced briefly in the conclusion of Chapter 2. Unfortunately, as discussed further in Chapter 7, far too many institutions dominated by the need to respond to external entities, like state agencies or accreditors, approach assessment as an act of compliance, with the objective to measure something and end the activity as soon as data are reported. By laying the appropriate ground-work for use at the start of the assessment process, use of assessment results is more likely to occur.

In its simplest form, the emphasis on use could involve the develop-ment of a clear sense of purpose at the beginning stage of assessment. At Juniata College, the purpose of assessment and, in particular, the intended use of assessment data were regular discussion topics for the Institutional Effectiveness Council, a committee charged with getting data out of the institutional research office and into the hands of people who needed it (Jankowski, 2011b). An example of the positive effect of focusing on how data will be used at the outset of any assessment activity was demonstrated in the college's success in writing assessment and improvement. Juniata faculty members were concerned about the quality of students' writing and were curious about the effectiveness of the college's intensive writ-ing curriculum. Their College Learning Assessment (CLA) results showed that their students were not writing as well as expected; in addition, the writing activity items on the National Survey of Student Engagement (NSSE) revealed that their students were not as engaged with writing as were their peers at comparable institutions—confirming faculty percep-tions. Exploring whether simply including a lot of writing in the intensive writing curriculum was sufficient provided a meaningful reason for using assessment results. Faculty discussed the results and the curriculum in a forum convened by the Academic Planning and Assessment Committee and then took action to make changes to the writing seminar. Writing goals were added and course credit was raised from three to four hours so that additional writing components could be built into them. The changes also involved a commitment of institutional resources to provide workshops for faculty on the instruction and evaluation of writing. Speci-fying that assessment results would be used to explore student writing and improve the writing-across-the-curriculum requirement at the outset kept Juniata focused on taking action on results.

Patton's U-FE model, employed from the beginning of an evaluation project, formally focuses attention on what will ensure usefulness, what will affect use, and what practical changes will result. The utilization-focused/backward-design approach used in assessment at St. Olaf College, for example, helped departments keep focused on what they wanted to learn from the evidence collected (Jankowski, 2012a). By first considering the intended users and uses (Walczak, Harper, McClure, & Hisey, 2010), this approach treats results as a means to an end rather than ends in themselves and the process as incomplete until results are appropriately used. The backward-design approach, taken from classroom instruction, begins with the identification of the intended learning outcomes. Once these are determined, instruction and practice that support them as well as evidence that demonstrates them are identified with the purpose of facilitating students' movement toward the outcomes. The combination of these two models—the utilization-focused/backward-design model of assessment— begins with the question, "Who are the likely users of the evidence we want to gather, and how will they use it?" This approach is thought to increase the likelihood that faculty and staff will be able to act on the evidence of student learning they collect. Focusing on "intended uses by intended users" (Beld, 2010, p. 6) also leads to a variety of applications of results within departments including redesigns of gateway courses, different approaches to providing feedback on student writing, or even different sequencing of courses.

NILOA case study institutions have demonstrated that involving faculty formally, and in detail, in exercises designed to craft a set of specific teaching-related questions that faculty want answered can keep the focus of assessment on utilization. Front-end planning for utilization should also include expectations exercises: What do participants expect the data to reveal, or what might be the action or consequences of this or that result?

Leveraging External Processes

Although accreditation has a strong role both in the motivation for assessment and the use of assessment results, external influence on institutions' assessment use is also felt from institutional membership initiatives, national organization or foundation-supported efforts, and state mandates or other accountability initiatives. Even so, results from NILOA's provost survey revealed the most common use of assessment data is related to accreditation—trumping all other uses including informing strategic planning, improving instructional performance, and evaluating units or programs (Kuh & Ikenberry, 2009; Kuh et al., 2014). Nearly all campus leaders in survey focus groups described most of their assessment activity as related to accreditation, either in response to a reaccreditation recommendation about assessment practices or in preparation for an upcoming visit (Kinzie, 2010; Provezis, 2010). Although the compliance mentality typically adopted for accreditation can sometimes make assessment seem less meaningful, accreditation can be employed as a catalyst for assessment and improvement (see Chapter 7).

There are many cases of institutions using accreditation to leverage important changes on their campuses—or at least leveraging accreditation for meaningful campus improvements. When Roosevelt University started planning for their Higher Learning Commission (HLC) reaffirmation process, for example, university leaders and faculty intent on achieving a 10-year approval argued that the best way to achieve this would be to initiate their own meaningful assessments while ensuring that the activities and evidence satisfied HLC requirements (Kinzie, 2010). Signaling this at the outset of reaffirmation was important to the institution, as was the involvement of the president, associate deans, and senior faculty leaders who participated in the HLC Assessment Academy for further education and who structured support for translating HLC standards into institutional purposes.

Similarly, Augustana College (IL) started out implementing its assessment as an accreditation process (Provezis, 2011), but an important shift occurred when, during a faculty retreat, a follow-up accreditation report was shared that highlighted student transcript results, senior survey findings, and senior papers and projects. The faculty discussed the report with the view that, while the findings were acceptable, the institution could do much better. To that end, they formed 20 study groups, involving many faculty members, to examine various aspects of the college including the development of students' writing and critical thinking skills, understanding of the liberal arts, and multiculturalism and diversity. Accreditation served as a catalyst for this effort, but it was the investment of the faculty in study groups focused on meaningful improvement that helped most to advance these assessment activities at Augustana.

The increased emphasis by several of the regional accreditors on institutional improvement plans has also led to more meaningful use of assessment results. The president at Richland College of the Dallas County Community College District reported that, as the institution began its Southern Association of Colleges and Schools (SACS) reaccreditation process, the worry was that the process would take the institution off course. However, key leaders at the college took advantage of the flexibility of the Quality Enhancement Plan (QEP) process and of the opportunity it presented to tailor a project emerging directly from the concerns of faculty and staff (Kinzie, 2010). The process of developing the QEP and gaining feedback through the accreditation visit helped the institution stay committed to seeing their project through.

Georgia State University (GSU) also took advantage of the QEP process to hone in on a campus concern about student writing and critical thinking (National Survey of Student Engagement, 2012). NSSE data for GSU, when compared with results for other institutions with the same Carnegie classification, revealed that GSU's final-year students wrote fewer short papers and felt like their undergraduate experience contributed less to their critical thinking abilities. Members of the QEP team at GSU corroborated these findings with an internal survey of graduates' learning outcomes and academic program satisfaction. These findings informed the development of a QEP and targeted efforts at the university to improve students' critical thinking and writing skills in their major field of study.

Although accreditation still tops the list as the most important motivator for assessment activity and use (see Chapter 7), other external initiatives including national association projects and foundation efforts have also helped spur the use of evidence. Through its Outcomes and Assessment Grants, The Teagle Foundation has funded hundreds of institutions to use their assessment data to improve student learning (see http://www. teaglefoundation.org/Grantmaking/). Grants to Carleton, Macalester, St. Olaf, and many other institutions were identified as instrumental in bringing faculty together "to show them data about things they really care about" and to inform them "whether or not an innovation improved student learning and success" (Green & Bezbatchenko, 2014, p. 50). Augustana College has sustained its practices in assessment of student learning and liberal education and has maintained institutional action on assessment results (Provezis, 2011) with support from multiple Teagle Foundation grants, one focusing on growth in writing, thinking, and civic engagement; a second assessing the capstone experience; and a third exploring how to restructure faculty work to allow for more active, experiential learning strategies. Furthering this work has been the institution's involvement in the Parsing the First Year of College project, using instruments such as the ACT CAAP Critical Thinking Test and NSSE to understand the influence of institutional structures in supporting student learning and persistence. These projects have provided persistent pressure at Augustana to continue its assessment activities and have also added a national perspective to Augustana's efforts.

Other reference points and additional leveraging for assessment and the improvement of student learning have come more recently from two initiatives focused on what graduates should be expected to know and do to succeed in the economy, civil society, and their own lives—the Association of American Colleges and Universities Essential Learning Outcomes

(ELOs) and Lumina Foundations' Degree Qualifications Profile (DQP). Hundreds of institutions are using ELOs and the DQP to reinvigorate their work on learning outcomes, and many are testing the extent to which DQP proficiencies can be achieved, assessed, and reported. At Point Loma Nazarene University, for example, faculty use these proficiencies in culminating experiences to measure learning in the student's major field. Point Loma faculty also adapted the AAC&U Essential Learning Outcomes Rubrics in designing assignments for assessment (Fulcher, Bailey, & Zack, 2013b; Hutchings, 2014b).

As these examples demonstrate, institutions can further the effective use of assessment results on their campuses by taking advantage of required external initiatives—like accreditation—and reorienting the mandated work around what is meaningful to the campus. The examples also show that the prestige and credibility gained through association with foundations and grants can help advance assessment work, as can the visibility from connections to national projects. Most important, however, these institutional cases exemplify the critical shift from thinking about accreditation as something done solely to satisfy accreditors to using the opportunity accreditation provides to stimulate genuine inquiry toward needed improvement in student learning and institutional performance.

Linking Assessment to Internal Processes

One of the major findings from NILOA's focus groups and interviews with provosts about the challenges of assessment is the importance of normalizing assessment processes. Assessment activity and use becomes a regular part of work in the academy when assessment is woven into established structures and processes (see Chapter 4). Campus leaders described how some of the practices associated with getting more faculty invested in assessment and making assessment activities more widespread included making it part of standard institutional policies and procedures (Kinzie, 2010). When a department at The Ohio State University (OSU) updates its curriculum, for example, its documentation should include the department's goals for student learning outcomes and also descriptions of the methods to assess these outcomes. This approach has helped facilitate the gradual phasing in of required learning goals and plans for assessment across a variety of departments at OSU. Albany State University (ASU) adopted a similar approach by streamlining its required reports—program reviews and annual reports as well as assessment reports—all of which now must include information about student learning outcomes.

Moreover, one element of the required annual report from every ASU department and program is an explanation of how assessment findings were used. These institutions are demonstrating that by embedding assessment into existing processes they can reinforce the most important aspect of assessment: the use of results.

Creating organizational structures and positions for assessment within the institution has also made a difference. A director of institutional research at a community college reported that assessment really took hold on campus when an administrative position charged with assessment responsibility—associate dean for student learning—was created (Kinzie, 2010). To carry out this assignment, the associate dean works with committees composed largely of faculty charged with developing assessment plans. Two faculty members from one of the committees concentrating on career and technical education met with each program chair to talk about the program's learning objectives and to help the program develop clearly defined, assessable learning objectives. Each program at the college established a set of objectives, and chairs and faculty worked to identify how to assess student learning of those objectives. While crediting the revised organizational structure, this director also noted that the faculty members' visits with the program chairs had made an important difference in building collegial relationships among peers.

Another approach to structural adaptation for assessment was employed at the University of Missouri, where the director of the office of assessment has moved efforts forward by working with programs he perceives want support in assessment (Kinzie, 2010). On first meeting with program faculty, he asks, "What do you want your undergraduates to be able to do?" Working backward from there, he consults with faculty to revise curriculum and to identify appropriate measures and tools, also advising them how to use data to inform their improvement efforts. While this backward-design approach has worked well at Missouri, producing some elaborate assessment plans and processes in its programs, the completely voluntary nature of this approach—with some departments and programs indefinitely deferring participation—is a drawback.

At Colorado State University (CSU), assessment is built into a culture that values evidence and uses information to improve and strengthen student learning. Traditional institutional processes, including program review, strategic planning, peer review, and institution-wide assessment, have expanded to involve all academic departments and student affairs units and have been structured to provide mechanisms at regular intervals for considering assessment results and using data to improve (Kinzie, 2011). CSU's online system—known as PRISM (Plan for Researching

Improvement and Supporting Mission)—provides information on the university's performance in prioritized areas, uses a peer review system for feedback, and emphasizes the importance of documenting institutional improvements informed by assessment results. The PRISM system is a consistent, transparent platform for documenting and displaying results and improvement plans. Notably, the featured rotating examples on the PRISM website's homepage in "Spotlights on Program Improvements" illustrate CSU's emphasis on using results to improve. By all accounts, PRISM has intensified and normalized at CSU the use of assessment information in continuous improvement across all levels—in courses, programs, departments, and the university. Again, the development of standard processes for considering assessment results is key. CSU's assessment process requires faculty and department heads to review the strategic plan, curriculum, faculty productivity, learning outcomes results, and other measures recorded in the PRISM online system to assess effectiveness and to reflect on and update information in the system. The process has helped departments to make changes in the curriculum, to demonstrate scholarly productivity, and to make the case for curricular improvements particularly important to the department. The online system has fostered a shared understanding of assessment and learning by making it possible for all faculty and staff members to view the plans of other units and to explore best practices in assessment across divisions. Simply having access to past plans and other unit reports has accelerated collaboration on the creation of rubrics and interview protocols and on the use of data in planning and improvement initiatives. Access to institution-wide results and information has prompted greater use of data in planning and reporting.

Another important link between meaningful assessment practice and internal structures at institutions has been evident in the work fostered in centers for teaching and learning, a development we return to in Chapter 9. To bring faculty work in assessment into the spotlight, and to strengthen the connection between assessment and real improvements in teaching and learning, many institutions have found welcome connections between assessment and the scholarship of teaching and learning, or the work of centers for teaching and learning. A variety of institutions have set up the infrastructure creating more collegial approaches to assessment—for example, the Eberly Center for Teaching at Carnegie Mellon, the Center for Teaching at Augustana College, and other less formal campus-based arrangements organized by centers for teaching and learning. Assessment is likely most effective when it flows from standard processes of teaching, faculty development, and established reporting structures. While many advances in assessment use were in response to external requirements like accreditation, expansion also came and can still come from greater investments in the creation of structures and mechanisms to support and sustain assessment activities.

The Quest to Close the Assessment Loop

Completing the assessment cycle—that is, measuring the impact of the action taken to improve student learning and, the ultimate stage, gaining evidence of improved student learning—is assessment's nirvana, perhaps. As Trudy Banta and Charles Blaich (2011) report, few institutions have achieved that goal: realizing actual change in student learning after using assessment results to bring about change. However distant that goal may seem, assessment practice seems to demonstrate that a necessary condition of effective assessment use is the *quest* to close the assessment loop.

A heartening feature of the case study institutions is that they all saw room for improvement in their assessment efforts (Baker et al., 2012). In particular, they acknowledged that assessment is an ongoing process in which closing the assessment loop begins the assessment process anew. Commenting on the continual nature of the process of assessing student learning, leaders at case study sites indicated they did not see their work with assessment as complete but, rather, as continuing to evolve. No one was completely satisfied with their current use of assessment results and all wanted to learn more about their students in order to improve student learning. Recognition of the evolving cycle of assessment and interest in improving student learning at these institutions helped stimulate continuous effort for improvement.

Taking time to reflect on assessment results, documenting what changes were made, and most important, examining whether the implemented changes have been successful, are all vital steps. Case study institutions were committed to the level of reflection required for this and valued the time spent and the chance to make shared meaning of the results. For instance, LaGuardia Community College, a leader in the area of ePortfolios for a decade and with a well-established process for assessing student artifacts, still spends considerable time reviewing its process and considering what the results might suggest for new initiatives (Provezis, 2012). For example, after concluding its Benchmark Assessment Readings study, in which faculty from a variety of programs read samples of student work and evaluated the effectiveness of their rubrics, LaGuardia decided to conduct a more comprehensive study of student growth and learning (Clark & Eynon, 2011/2012).

Reflection on evidence and change based on improvement are woven into the assessment process at St. Olaf College. Every fourth year in St. Olaf's five-year assessment plan is reserved as a time for reflection—during which no new evidence of student learning is gathered (Jankowski, 2012a). Instead, evidence already gathered is studied for its potential to improve student learning—and used. This year of reflection, focusing on utilization, provides opportunities for departments to examine and reflect on institution-level results and to consider integrating those findings with departmental data. Reflection on assessment results is also a part of general education assessment at St. Olaf. Instructors of general education (GE) courses who agreed to assess one GE outcome in their course were asked to describe and reflect on their students' work in a brief General Education Student Learning Report, designed to be completed as soon as the instructor graded the work. Providing a structure with time for reflection on results, expectations for action, and intentional consideration of the impact of action taken can help move assessment activities through the full assessment cycle.

Seven Principles for Fostering Greater Use of Assessment Results

Gathering evidence of student learning in colleges and universities has matured over the last 35 years, in no small part because of increased pressure from external entities for institutions to know more about and be more accountable for what students gain from their undergraduate experience. Many institutions have worked assiduously to document effective practice and develop resources to guide further good practice. Many colleges and universities have well-designed assessment plans and are gathering evidence, and a smaller subset have used assessment results effectively. The examples of effective assessment use profiled in this chapter and in other publications point to seven principles for increasing the effective use of assessment results.

First, gauge the value of assessment work by the extent to which results are used. One measure of how well results are put to use is how the assessment cycle plays out in the campus assessment process. Are assessment priorities shaped by questions and concerns for student success that anticipate the productive application of results? Is work too often stalled in the data collection stage? Does the sharing-results phase tend to terminate the cycle? Where does the cycle get stuck, why, and what might free it up?

Second, identify the target for use of evidence of student learning when designing assessment work and sharing results. Evidence of student learning has multiple uses and may raise different questions and have different uses at different levels within an institution. Identify institution-wide or program-level goals and audiences that can be influenced by results. Document how results are used and trace the impacts on student success. The same assessment activity can have multiple uses at different levels at an institution. The challenge is to present assessment and the questions it explores in a way that persuades people that the results of the inquiry will have practical value in their work, at their level.

Third, begin assessment activity with the end use in mind. From the outset of any assessment process, consider the practical questions that are of greatest interest to potential partners—faculty, administrators, staff, and intended internal and external end users—and how the results could be used. Just as important, what do partners and end users expect to find? Exploring this question in an expectations exercise is a good way to stimulate concrete thinking about effective uses of assessment results.

Fourth, leverage the accreditation process for meaningful campus action to improve student learning. Ensure that the campus benefits from all the time and energy that accreditation requires by framing this work as more than an act of compliance—as a process to move the campus toward improvement in learning, teaching, and institutional performance.

Fifth, connect assessment work to related current national initiatives and projects. Membership associations, national organizations, foundations, and other collective initiatives provide a broader context in which to embed assessment work, learn from the work of other institutions, and to increase the impact, legitimacy, and value of assessment results.

Sixth, link assessment activity to campus functions that require evidence of student learning such as the program review process or a campus center for teaching and learning. Assessment, as outlined in Chapters 4 and 5, is more likely to lead to action and improvement if it is sustained rather than episodic; if campus structures and processes are in place to report results, discuss implications, and plan needed action; and if decision makers—faculty members, academic leaders, and others—are engaged in the process and guiding evidence-based change.

Seventh, work purposefully toward the final stage of the assessment cycle—assessing impact, closing the assessment loop—and remember that the assessment of student learning is a *continuous* process. Making decisions based on assessment evidence is important, but it also marks the beginning of a new cycle. What was the impact of the change? Did it lead to an improvement in student learning? Follow-through and taking time to assess the impact of evidence-based change is essential in fostering a culture that supports the meaningful use of assessment results.

Adhering to these principles to guide assessment work will help campuses make better use of assessment results that will, in turn, generate the amount and quality of evidence that provides a solid basis for action. With such evidence in hand, institutions will be better positioned to implement changes in teaching and learning on their campuses that will foster higher levels of student accomplishment.

4

MAKING ASSESSMENT CONSEQUENTIAL

ORGANIZING TO YIELD RESULTS

Jillian Kinzie and Natasha A. Jankowski

The trouble with organizing a thing is that pretty soon folks get to paying more attention to the organization than to what they're organizing.

—Laura Ingalls Wilder

THE ORGANIZATION OF ASSESSMENT on college and university campuses is as relevant to the work of higher education as it is varied in application. Assembled at national conferences, assessment leaders from academic and student affairs and directors of institutional research regularly debate the merits of different structures. Chief academic officers grappled with the same issue during a National Institute for Learning Outcomes Assessment (NILOA) focus group. Such conversations are useful in the sense that *how* assessment is organized can shape the relevance and application of the work.

Despite considerable interest, though, there is little agreement about best approaches to organizing assessment. In part, this lack of consensus reflects the various purposes assessment may serve and, thus, the varied forms and structures it may take. The deeper question, however, remains: Can institutions and programs organize assessment to yield actionable evidence and insights consequential to student learning?

The organization of assessment activities must take into account the need for multiple roles and tasks, including top-level leadership and vision for assessment, oversight responsibility for day-to-day assessment work, coordination of the various elements of assessment across an institution, and the actual implementation of assessment. For instance, one institution may assign oversight responsibility for all assessment activities to a vice president for institutional effectiveness, while another institution may embed coordination of assessment work into the provost's cyclical review of departments, while still another may place assessment planning and review in the hands of a campus-wide assessment committee. Other institutions may formally incorporate student learning outcomes assessment processes into faculty governance structures with some of the faculty members receiving release time for the work, while others are volunteer efforts. Still others may employ a distributed model for assessment, with separate administrative reporting lines for learning outcomes assessment in every department or program and across each functional area in student affairs, with little to no collective coordination or planning. Moreover, state higher education systems may envision assessment as a partnership among campus faculty and administration, faculty senates, and system administration. Whether the approach is highly organized and formally executed, distributed or decentralized, informal or reactive, the organization of assessment in higher education exists in many forms.

Institutional structures and culture (Kuh & Whitt, 2000; Peterson & Spencer, 2000) also affect how assessment may and should be organized in different institutions. A 1996 study of the ways institutions collect and use assessment information by the National Center for Postsecondary Improvement (NCPI) identified a wide range of institutional assessment practices and various organizational patterns in assessment processes but concluded that assessment management policies and practices to support assessment appeared haphazard (Peterson & Augustine, 2000). More recent profiles of institutional assessment practice suggest approaches still vary widely across institutions, although more intentional structural integration may be occurring (Baker, Jankowski, Provezis, & Kinzie, 2012; Banta, Jones, & Black, 2009). Yet, to be consequential, assessment work must be organized intentionally across an institution, with clear purposes and ends in mind for collected evidence. Given that consensus remains elusive about how to organize an effective assessment program, the focus of this chapter explores three questions:

1. What do we know about how assessment work is organized?
2. What is organized when we organize assessment?
3. How might assessment work be organized if student learning outcomes are to yield actionable evidence and inform changes in curriculum and pedagogy that enhance student accomplishment?

How Is Assessment Work Organized?

Assessment scholars generally endorse certain principles of good assessment practice including establishing learning goals; designing a thoughtful approach to assessment; involving a variety of stakeholders; implementing multiple data collection methods; examining, sharing and acting on assessment findings; and regularly reviewing the assessment process itself (Banta et al., 2009; Palomba & Banta, 1999). These overarching principles guide most of the conduct of doing assessment in higher education. However, how to enact these ideals—that is, how to organize the *doing* of assessment work on a campus—is less clear.

The importance of leadership for assessment, in terms of providing vision and purpose as well as delineating who should have oversight responsibility for assessment in colleges and universities, is well documented in the assessment literature. Catherine Palomba and Trudy Banta (1999) and Peggy Maki (2004) identified the importance of designating assessment leaders to coordinate institution-level efforts and to communicate the priority of assessment, policies, and results. Leaders may hold various positions within institutions, such as key administrators at the vice presidential level or faculty members charged with coordinating assessment efforts. Other organizational models for assessment leadership distribute responsibility for assessment to an assessment committee, populated by a variety of constituents including faculty, students, student affairs professionals, librarians, and institutional research staff, or a centralized assessment office to provide oversight of assessment. Over the last decade, most universities and large community colleges have established offices for assessment on their campuses charged with conducting and supporting assessment activities, while smaller institutions have at least identified an assessment director or part-time faculty coordinator of learning outcomes assessment activities (Kinzie, 2010).

Department- or program-level assessment may be similarly organized, with a chair appointing a faculty point person, or a director in student affairs, or a committee to conduct assessment, or a collection of each. Leadership for assessment exists at all these levels at St. Olaf College, starting with the college president, who is featured in a video on the institution website, speaking about St. Olaf's assessment efforts for friends of the college, and supported by an assessment director who has intentionally coupled administrative directives and faculty governance of assessment to spread assessment activities across campus (Jankowski, 2012a). Whether assessment is coordinated by an administrator, a faculty member, a central office, or a committee, some level of leadership and oversight of assessment is necessary for it to be consequential across an institution—yet the impact of assessment may be broader if the organization of leadership and oversight are integrated and supported throughout an institution.

Although identifying someone as an assessment leader is recommended by some as an important element of good assessment practice, agreement about how work is further organized and supported varies substantially from institution to institution. Maki (2004) argued for a view of assessment as a collective practice to pursue meaningful questions about teaching and learning. While no one model can be effective everywhere, she suggests that building a collective commitment to assessing student learning requires the establishment of shared responsibilities forged through new relationships among faculty across departments, crossing boundaries to establish connections between faculty and student affairs professionals, and putting in place systems that rely on evidence of student learning to inform institution- and program-level action. LaGuardia Community College president Gail O. Mellow, for example, demonstrates a strong collective approach to assessment by regularly reading all of the college's Periodic Program Reviews (PPRs), giving feedback and focusing support on projects that show impact on student learning and success (Provezis, 2012). Thus, this presidential leadership supports and heightens focus on assessment that is of consequence to students and their learning.

While leadership is critical, for assessment to be productive, embedding its work throughout an institution is equally critical. Barbara Walvoord (2004) emphasized the need to embed responsibility for assessment into existing institutional processes, such as cyclical reviews of departments and programs, strategic planning, general education curriculum reform, budget requests, the evaluation of teaching, and other student learning initiatives. Embedding assessment in existing processes can lessen concern about creating supplementary (and often redundant) structures and can reinforce the idea that assessment should be a routine activity across the institution—although even this approach still requires leadership for assessment. Developments at Colorado State University (CSU) illustrate this approach (Kinzie, 2011). Over the last dozen years, CSU enriched collaboration on assessment between academic and student affairs and expanded its continuous improvement system for managing information sharing to serve the decision making and reporting needs of various audiences. This system—known as the CSU Plan for Researching Improvement and Supporting Mission, or PRISM—provides information on the university's performance across all programs, uses a peer review system for feedback, and emphasizes the importance of documenting institutional improvements informed by assessment results. The system is organized around providing assessment evidence that is of consequence to improved student learning.

Support for assessment in the form of resource and budget allocation is another key organizational feature. Institutions vary in their traditional budget allocations for staff time, materials, professional development funds, and resources for assessment methods and tools (Cooper & Terrell, 2013). LaGuardia Community College invested significantly in assessment by using grant funds to plan and pilot their effort, and then designated institutional funds to scale up the college's now nationally recognized ePortfolio system (Provezis, 2012). In addition, the dean advances assessment by funding faculty and staff participation in conferences, by offering a range of assessment-focused campus workshops, and by making assessment a priority for all programs. LaGuardia's approach stands out as an exception to the finding by George Kuh and Stanley Ikenberry (2009) from a NILOA survey of chief academic officers that most campuses were undertaking student learning outcomes assessment with minimal budgets and only two or fewer staff dedicated to assessment. Similar survey results were found in program-level assessment, reinforcing the view that assessment is undercapitalized (Ewell, Paulsen, & Kinzie, 2011). Limited information exists on institutional spending on assessment (Cooper & Terrell, 2013). In their examination of the cost of assessment, Randy Swing and Christopher Coogan (2010) concluded that most institutions are left guessing how much to spend on assessment to achieve the best return on investment, but they advocate calculating the cost and benefits of assessment to initiate campus conversations about budgeting for and investing in assessment activities.

Professional development is a structural element that must be organized to ensure that faculty, staff, and others involved are properly trained to undertake meaningful assessment activities, especially since most faculty members and staff lack training in assessment approaches. This consistently tops the list of institutional needs in advancing assessment efforts

(Kuh, Jankowski, Ikenberry, & Kinzie, 2014). On most campuses, such training can be offered through an assessment office or a center for teaching and learning. The Eberly Center for Teaching Excellence at Carnegie Mellon University (CMU), for example, has advanced student learning outcomes assessment and faculty training at CMU by serving as the hub of support for faculty engaged in assessment, including department and one-on-one consultations (Kinzie, 2012). In addition, because assessment is driven by the questions raised by faculty about student learning and effective teaching, and is informed by departmental curricular interests, program goals, and the particular discipline, assessment at CMU is more closely tied to faculty work than is the case at other institutions, and it reinforces the link between assessment and improvements to student learning.

Looking across the various approaches described thus far, it is clear that institutions have organized assessment work differently and to different levels of success in designing assessment structures of consequence. Although NILOA 2013 provost survey results found that 71% of respondents reported that student learning outcomes assessment had substantial ("very much" and "quite a bit") support from their institution's organization and governance structures, it is clear that more can be done to ensure that assessment evidence available on campuses is used to guide institutional actions toward improving student outcomes (Kuh et al., 2014). Key to this effort is integrating assessment work into the institution's governance and organizational structures. Moreover, while organizational structures and institutional governance may be more or less congenial to assessing student learning, provosts identified specific ways assessment work could be advanced, including more professional development for faculty (64%), more faculty using the results (63%), and additional financial or staff resources (56%).

Institutions struggle with designing, developing and implementing a sustainable comprehensive approach to assessing student learning that leads to meaningful use of results. Jack Friedlander and Andreea Serban (2004), discussing assessment in community colleges, argue that an overall framework is needed for organizing and reporting learning outcomes at the course, program, and institution levels that allows institutions to compare changes over time that is responsive to the specific institution type and students served. The authors say the principal challenge lies in making assessment comprehensive enough to encompass various types of programs, staffing situations, course delivery modes, and student mobility encountered in community colleges so as to provide useful information for improving learning. In contrast, a survey of member research universities by the Association of American Universities (2013) indicated that 70% of respondents were moving toward centralized assessment activities with a specific office charged to develop, coordinate, and implement assessments—an approach that may not serve the same needs as the comprehensive system advocated for community colleges.

One way to consider the challenges of organizing for assessment is to systematically identify the factors related to organizing consequential assessment activities. Figure 4.1 indicates the various factors that may have an impact on the organization and design of assessment activities. External influences such as disciplinary associations, state mandates, and accreditation processes, for instance, may influence an institution's assessment processes and approaches. Further, institutional norms, the levels at which assessment occurs throughout an institution (such as general education, co-curricular, and program-level), and the purposes and focus of assessment activities may influence the organization of

Figure 4.1: Various Factors Influencing Organization of Assessment.

assessment. Moreover, institutional history with assessment, culture, and governance structures all may, in various ways, influence the view of assessment and how it is undertaken. Finally, the student population, size and setting of the institution, mission, and existing reporting lines and reporting structures may lead an institution to different ways of organizing assessment-related work. While each of these factors may constrain the organization of assessment activities, they reflect the influence of four critical institutional factors—philosophy, context, internal structures, and the wider context—on how assessment can be organized, and serve as boundary markers within which the organization of actionable assessment activities occurs.

The examples in this section suggest there are some common practices for organizing how assessment gets done. Leadership is essential. Building collective commitment to pursue meaningful questions about teaching and learning and linking assessment to other educational processes such as program and curriculum review, planning, and budgeting can help embed assessment, and more important, make the work consequential to enhancing student learning. Insisting that assessment information be provided in support of budgeting requests is another approach for linking assessment to decision making. Funding professional development and training faculty members and staff to work collaboratively to use assessment results to improve the conditions for learning provide strong organizational support for assessing student learning outcomes. Additional organizing essentials are aligning assessment activities with the institutional mission, integrating assessment work into the institution's governance and organizational structures and thinking more expansively about what is being organized and the structures needed for support.

Although more assessment evidence is available on campuses than ever before, information is not as widely shared as it should be and using it to guide institutional actions toward improving student outcomes is not nearly as pervasive as it could be (Chapter 10). As institutions mature in their engagement with assessment processes and activities and review current structures and organization of assuring student learning, various factors may impact the organization of assessment, and the diversity of organizational approaches to assessment work may not be a hindrance but a result of the diversity of institutions within the arena of higher education. For assessment to be actionable, meaningful, and embedded into everyday endeavors, however, it is worth asking serious questions about what specific activities are being organized. It is to this task we now turn.

What Is Being Organized?

Various aspects of the educational experience may be organized in relation to the assessment of student learning. In some institutions, for instance, the focus is on collecting and reporting assessment data and developing systems to process assessment results. Yet a focus on *reporting* may not include a direct connection with questions of student learning, or connect with teaching processes. Moreover, assessment that is organized around reporting may narrowly define learning as only occurring in courses and related academic affairs functions. Focusing on reporting may also lead to a compliance mentality in which assessment is seen as an add-on to regular teaching and learning processes and, thus, not consequential.

If, instead, the focus is on organizing *learning*, different organizational structures and approaches may emerge. For instance, assessment may be connected with centers for teaching and learning (Hutchings, 2011), possibly involving larger systematic views of where learning happens and how information about it might be captured. At the same time, to better understand when and where assessment activities may prove the most impactful, productive activities may include creating spaces for conversation and meaning-making around evidence of student learning and exploring how students navigate the entire institutional structure. A focus on organizing learning also leads to the view that assessment is not the purview or responsibility of a single office but, instead, is an activity that crosses institutional silos and offices in providing a comprehensive picture of student learning within various institutional structures and levels.

As assessment efforts shift from examining a sample of students at the end of their educational trajectory toward an embedded approach that explores student learning throughout the course of their educational experiences, assessment has been organized in different ways. Some of the more thoughtful models today involve the examination of curriculum design through backward-design approaches intended to ensure that the outcomes desired of students' achievement at the end of their tenure are built into coursework all along the way (Jankowski, 2012a) and to encourage collaboration between faculty and student development teams collectively exploring the effects of the curriculum on individual student learning, with an eye toward student support (Jankowski, 2011a). The shift to focusing on individual students and their learning has also supported approaches to organizing learning, such as competency-based education, that involve a move away from measuring learning by accumulated credit hours and course content to allowing students to move through material at their own pace while continually measuring progress and learning (Johnstone & Soares, 2014; Klein-Collins, 2013). In this context, assessment is intricately linked to prior-learning assessments, to larger conversations about the values inherent in educational experiences through such initiatives as the Tuning effort to define quality in higher education (Institute for Evidence-Based Change, 2012), and to a growing focus on an integrated educational experience that includes the co-curriculum. The University of California–Davis, for example, integrated a badging system for undergraduate majors in sustainable agriculture and food systems organized around experiential out-of-class learning (Fain, 2014a)—because when focusing on where students learn across an institution, it becomes important to collect and integrate data from different sources to capture that learning in various forms and provide meaningful evidence to various actors, including students.

How Should Assessment Be Organized If Improvement Is the Goal?

The extent to which assessment is effectively organized for learning partly depends on where it is housed within an institution, to whom the people responsible for assessment report, whether it is framed as satisfying accountability requirements or providing actionable evidence to improve, and the extent to which these efforts are connected. Reward and recognition structures also reinforce the organizational structure of assessment. These questions are not necessarily about what is being organized. Instead, they are focused on the structures and supports necessary or sufficient to ensure that what is being organized—student learning—is done in meaningful and consequential ways. Thus, there is the additional need to consider the organizational structures and supports for assessment-related work.

Depending on what an institution is organizing when designing assessment systems, several questions need to be considered in relation to the structures and supports needed to engage in the work. Among those questions are these: Who owns assessment? Who is directly responsible for assessing student learning? Who supports the work of assessment? Engaging in thoughtful conversation around these and similar questions requires exploring the specific roles of various offices and structural supports. The organization of effective assessment work should take into consideration *all* the places where learning occurs, ways to increase cross-campus collaboration and sharing of assessment plans and evidence, and approaches to link the stakeholders and end users of assessment work with assessment professionals and resources. It is only through conceptualizing assessment in this way that a system can develop that is of consequence to student learning across an institution.

Identify All the Places Learning Occurs

Viewing the organization of assessment efforts as an exercise in examining *all the places where students learn* leads one to consider the range of sites and players to involve in assessing student learning. One aspect of undergraduate education emphasized as an important site for addressing a comprehensive set of outcomes essential for all students is general education (Johnson, Ratcliff, & Gaff, 2004; Penn, 2011).

General education is an important place to look for students' achievement on learning outcomes that are core to undergraduate education and key to developing the knowledge, skills, abilities, and dispositions for all students. Yet, the knowledge and skills that general education is typically understood to develop—including writing and quantitative literacy and critical thinking—are areas in which graduates as a group are not performing at the most proficient levels (Pascarella & Terenzini, 2005). In addition, considerable evidence suggests that subject matter knowledge and academic skills are enhanced by curricular experiences that require integration of ideas and themes across disciplines. Such evidence includes that of Angela McGlynn (2014) who found that experiential learning beyond the classroom enhances student learning and engagement at community colleges. Thus, examining how the organization of general education fits into the larger picture of assessing student learning should be considered in conversations about organizing assessment activity.

In addition to general education, there are many other possibilities, some of them largely overlooked. An oft neglected arena for student learning that can be assessed is on-campus student employment (Bentrim, Sousa-Peoples, Kachellek, & Powers, 2013; Dundes & Marx, 2006; Fallow & Steven, 2000). Student affairs is another such arena. Christina Athas, John Oaks, and Lance Kennedy-Phillips (2013) administered a survey to assess outcomes about student employment within student affairs divisions and found that work experiences offered environments in which students could apply knowledge gained through academic work as well as acquire new competencies and integrate transferrable skills. Students further reported that the longer they worked in student affairs departments the more motivated they were academically to complete college and the clearer their academic and career goals became. Another example of assessing learning associated with on-campus employment is the Guided Reflection on Work (GROW) program, housed in student affairs at the University of Iowa (American Association of Colleges & Universities, 2014). Supervisors in that program engaged student employees in semistructured conversations about how their work is related to academic studies and to developing knowledge and skills. Participants in the program saw connections between their work and academic courses and reported that their work helped them clarify their goals as well as know how to talk about these experiences on their resume. These two examples of assessing learning in campus employment point to the potential for learning in multiple places across an institution—sites not necessarily captured in traditional assessment reporting structures.

Student affairs units are also critical sites for student learning and must be considered in approaches to organizing assessment work (Bresciani, Moore Gardner, & Hickmott, 2009). The Division of Student Development and Assessment at Denison University views assessment as a process of "identifying how we as a division contribute to student learning" because they are "committed to providing students with learning opportunities" (http://denison.edu/campus/student-development/assessment). Student affairs at Denison is viewed as intricately connected to furthering student learning across the entire institution, and its assessment efforts demonstrate this commitment. Additional illustrations of assessing where students learn are in the University of South Carolina's framework for data collection across multiple levels related to student learning and the role of student affairs in fostering learning opportunities (Fallucca & Lewis, 2013). Additionally, there are guides on undertaking assessment in academic advising (Aiken-Wisniewski, Campbell, Nutt, Robbins, Kirk-Kuwaye, & Higa 2010), career services (Makela & Rooney, 2012), and libraries (Gilchrist & Oakleaf, 2012), and various publications have been released on the relationship between assessment and student affairs (Schuh & Gansemer-Topf, 2010).

Foster Cross-Campus Collaboration Through Assessment Committees

A popular approach to organizing assessment work is through committees composed of faculty, staff, and students from across an institution. Assessment committees were identified by surveyed chief academic officers as one of the top organizational supports for assessing student learning, with nearly two-thirds of respondents indicating that committees were an effective means for sharing assessment results within the institution (Kuh et al., 2014). Assessment committees were important across all institution types, and the creation of new assessment committees was also cited as a source of optimism for enhancing student learning outcomes assessment.

Committees not only provide widespread oversight of assessment, but, when populated with representatives from across the campus, also can increase the sharing of assessment plans, methodology, and evidence. Cornell University's Core Assessment Committee, for example, which functions as the central organizational structure for leadership, oversight, and coordination of assessment activities across the university, is chaired by the vice provost for undergraduate programs, and membership includes an assessment liaison from each college and school, the university assessment manager, as well as representatives from the center for teaching excellence, the dean of students office, and the office of institutional research. The committee serves as an advisory and policy body, monitors and conducts periodic reviews of the university's educational goals and of assessment efforts within the colleges, schools, and other units on campus, and provides a vehicle for facilitating information sharing across units.

Assessment committees serve to coordinate and review assessment processes, with program or department level liaisons sharing back to the various levels. Union Institute and University has an assessment committee that includes representatives from the library, information technology, and the writing center. This committee approves policies, vets university-wide rubrics, coordinates assessment activities, and facilitates training to assess student work across the curriculum. The University of New Mexico created a college assessment review committee comprising faculty from each college, school, and branch campus to provide feedback on student learning outcomes, assessment plans, and annual assessment reports, and to grow institutional capacity for assessment among the faculty and departments. Some units provide a modest stipend for faculty involvement in assessment, and the committee works in concert with the office of assessment, which offers workshops for the committee and provides templates for review. While some institutions provide course release for faculty on assessment committees, others do not, and some are part of the governance structure while others operate outside of the academic senate. Committee responsibilities also vary greatly, as some committees provide feedback to programs, review student artifacts, and engage in cross-campus dialogue on evidence of student learning (Muffo, 2001; Paradis & Hopewell, 2010).

For assessment to be meaningful, faculty, staff, and academic leaders must have confidence in the quality of the work. Collaboration through committee work has the potential to provide a foundation of trust in assessment processes, and it also serves as a professional development opportunity through the review and commentary on assessment plans and reports. Faculty peer reviewers at the University of Nebraska–Lincoln, for instance, use a rubric to review program reports (http://www .unl.edu/ous/pearl/resources.shtml). Faculty members at the University of Houston–Downtown review and then have dialogue with peers, thus, serving a function of peer-to-peer professional development around assessment issues and fostering across-campus dialogue related to evidence of student learning.

Structures that support collaboration, information exchange, and training may also lead to enhanced transparency within the institution. Linda Krzykowski and Kevin Kinser (2014) found that campuses were more transparent when they "had one structure that provided oversight for faculty performing assessment (the provost's office or a governance structure that required assessment reports) and a separate one that trained faculty on assessment practices as well as explained and encouraged assessment" (p. 71). Thus, while one structure may be utilized to oversee and provide professional development for faculty engaged in the committee structure process, it is still beneficial to partner with other units that contribute to broader faculty involvement, such as centers for teaching and learning. Juniata College's Center for the Scholarship of Teaching and Learning, for instance, is a faculty-led center that provides support for course-level assessment activities focusing on questions of immediate interest to faculty. While Juniata's faculty see this center as a campus leader in assessment efforts and professional development, program reports are also provided to a faculty committee, the Academic Planning and Assessment Committee, which reviews and provides feedback on program assessment plans and results (Jankowski, 2011b).

Collaborative approaches to assessment are more naturally found in small institutions. In a case study of the conditions that support assessment practice within student affairs divisions at three small colleges and universities accredited by the Southern Association of Colleges and Schools Commission on Colleges and reaffirmed within the last three years, Beau Seagraves and Laura Dean (2010) found that the size of an institution may impact the organization of assessment efforts because smaller institutions have limited resources and staffing to conduct assessment. Smaller size allowed for more informal conversations and greater sharing of assessment responsibilities because most professionals wore multiple hats, worked collaboratively, and sat on committees together. Themes that emerged from the Seagraves-Dean analysis included a focus on the conditions promoting assessment including support from senior student affairs leadership, informal conversations around assessment, clear expectations and communicated value of assessment as a means to improve, and a collegial atmosphere that welcomed both positive and negative results. Informal conversations, regular collaboration on assessment-related initiatives, and a generally supportive environment for collective action, coupled with support from administration, allowed for more engaged involvement in assessment and use of results.

Link End Users of Assessment Work with Assessment Professionals

Reporting lines and connections vary among institutions between assessment professionals and the units, faculty, and staff expected to take advantage of assessment results. For instance, assessment may be occurring in student affairs but not be connected with the office of institutional research (IR), a centralized office of assessment, or centers for teaching and learning. In other cases, an institutional research office is the keeper of entering student placement data and surveys about the quality of undergraduate learning experiences, but the units that could make use of such information are unaware of the information or are not provided access to it. Having multiple and separate reporting lines for assessment activity, or failing to intentionally link assessment expertise with units that can take advantage of results, has the potential to create silos among units and limit the benefit of assessment efforts to improve student learning (Bers, 2008; Schmidtlein, 1999). With assessment occurring vertically and horizontally across an institution, it is vital to engage with various partners such as institutional research, centers for teaching and learning, and offices of assessment and planning.

To increase the effectiveness of student learning outcomes assessment work and to facilitate access to outcomes data as well as analytic tools and talents, it is essential to tighten the connections between institutional research and all departments, units, and committees charged with assessment. Institutional research offices have access to an array of data elements related to students and the undergraduate experience that may provide a more extensive picture of student learning. Yet, all too often, the role of institutional research is centered on reporting functions and little effort is directed to fostering partnerships with units to work together to address important questions about student learning. In a survey of institutional research offices, however, J. Fredericks Volkwein (2011) found that the role of IR has shifted over the years toward institutional effectiveness and student learning outcomes assessment. As such, not partnering with or involving IR in conversations about results, data flows, data audits, or meaning-making related to assessment evidence may prove detrimental to the organization of assessment.

Principles for Organizing Assessment

Michael Bastedo (2012) suggests that organization theory may improve student learning by helping us question how to better design institutions to promote learning outcomes. While different sets of principles for conducting assessment exist, the diversity in approaches to organizing assessment described in this chapter suggests such principles for organizing consequential assessment work have not been articulated. As institutions explore how to embed assessment within larger systems and work to "create a shared academic culture dedicated to assuring and improving the quality of higher education" (Angelo, 1995, p. 7), we offer the following principles for examining current organizational structures and considering how to improve the organization of assessment activities within institutions.

Organize with Purpose

The value and purposes of assessment should guide its organization. The why of assessment, what assessment can and cannot do, and the benefits of examining student learning need to be clear and shared throughout an institution. Patrick Terenzini (2000) stated that engagement with assessment involves reconsidering the purposes and outcomes of college by clarifying what students should know and be able to do as a result of attending. After establishing a shared understanding of the value and purpose of assessment, institutions need to engage in conversations on the various levels at which assessment occurs, to what end the collected evidence may (and may not) be used, and how an organizational system might be designed that can capture learning in all places and levels throughout the institution.

Organize for Systemic Learning

Assessment should encompass a systemic view of student learning in terms of involving the entire educational community in assessment as a collaborative and collective effort around students and their learning. Learning is holistic, cumulative, and shaped by a myriad of experiences inside and outside the classroom. As Linda Siefert (2011) observed when discussing the University of North Carolina–Wilmington's use of VALUE rubrics, "No one part of the general education curriculum, nor of the university experience as a whole, is solely responsible for helping students write well, think critically, or conduct responsible inquiry and analysis. These skills are practiced in many courses" (p. 2). In this sense, assessment has the potential to cut across silos and bring people together to focus on students and their learning, collectively. Thus, an effective assessment program takes a systemic view of when and where students learn and is implemented with consideration that learning occurs in multiple places throughout a student's educational journey, supported by assessment systems designed to capture learning across them all.

Organize for Distinction

Assessment activities should be aligned with distinctive institutional characteristics and conditions. When designing assessment processes and structures, an important consideration should be the alignment of assessment activities with institutional characteristics including the institutional mission and educational vision. Institution type makes a difference in how assessment is organized: Assessment looks different in an entirely online institution, for instance, and it takes different forms in a career and technical program within a community college than in a small bachelor's-granting college. While Serban (2004) and Nunley, Bers, and Manning (2011) discuss how community college assessment is different, Maggie George and Daniel McLaughlin (2008) offer a clear example of the power of institution type in their discussion of assessment in tribal colleges. They argue that assessment can be used to achieve tribal college goals by framing assessment processes and structures in relation to native philosophies and cultural sensibilities based on designing institutions and programs that work from and advance native knowledge. They argue that if assessment is framed as a tool for self-knowledge and self-discovery, it can be linked to native philosophies in ways that support the work of and learning about students served.

Organize for Flexibility

The assessment program should be flexible and should address institutional priorities and end-user questions about the quality of the student experience. As other chapters have mentioned, flexibility in measures and approaches to assessment is vital to sustain meaningful efforts. When discussing results from NILOA's various surveys of institution- and program-level assessment activities, Pat Hutchings (2011) observed that methods vary significantly from one field to another, just as the questions of interest may vary. This emphasizes the need to organize assessment data to capture and collect information that can accommodate the different views of disciplines and users about what counts as evidence. Such an approach may lead to more effective use of assessment results because these results are more meaningful to the respective audience. Hutchings further cautioned that an inflexible approach built on reporting may lead to a checklist mentality—especially among faculty—as contrasted with sustained engagement. The diversity of approaches to assessment is a help, not a hindrance, to improving quality in higher education.

Organize for Capacity

Develop sufficient organizational capacity to do the work. Some aspects of the organizational structure of assessment are foundational and involve examining institutional readiness to engage in comprehensive and sustained assessment work. James Bess and Jay Dee (2008a, 2008b) argue that higher education institutions are complex organizations confronting a range of challenges including how to coordinate the work of experts and build an organizational identity that still allows for uniqueness. They also stress that a key challenge of organizational design is to find ways to coordinate the work of differentiated units without interfering with the work of highly trained specialists. One possible vehicle to build organizational capacity is to engage in collaborations across units around questions of student learning, take advantage of connections with centers for teaching and learning, and broaden assessment efforts to include IR and student affairs. Dedicating funds to support professional development in assessment would help, as would greater sharing of information about students and assessment results about learning processes and outcomes across campus—and intentionally weaving this into collaborative processes to improve student learning.

Conclusion

While these principles can be useful in considering how to organize assessment work in a college or university, whatever organizational form is chosen, it is imperative that it adequately captures student learning inside and outside the classroom, on and off the campus. It is also essential that organizational structure, culture, values, and rewards reinforce collective and collaborative effort and eschew siloed activity. The manner in which assessment work is organized should focus on integrating, connecting, communicating, and ultimately supporting meaningful structures and processes that enhance student learning. This is not an exercise in compliance but a collective commitment to supporting and better understanding student learning to enhance and improve the educational experience.

If the question is how institutions should organize and support assessment of student learning, the answer is as prismatic as the diversity of institutions across the landscape of higher education. The common end to which all institutions should strive when organizing assessment, however, is thoughtful, careful, deliberate, integrated, and sustainable assessment systems that can provide actionable evidence to improve student learning.

PART TWO

WHO CARES? ENGAGING KEY STAKEHOLDERS

5

FACULTY AND STUDENTS

ASSESSMENT AT THE INTERSECTION OF TEACHING AND LEARNING

Timothy Reese Cain and Pat Hutchings

Outcomes assessment makes us seriously ask whether our undergraduates are actually learning what we are teaching.

—Gerald Graff (2010, p. 160)

A REOCCURRING THEME THROUGHOUT this book is the primary role of faculty in assessing student learning outcomes. Along with student affairs professionals, librarians, and others who regularly interact with students, faculty are key to effectively using assessment results to improve student learning. This is not a new argument. From the beginning of the assessment movement, assessment scholars, practitioners, and other stakeholders have acknowledged the importance of meaningfully involving faculty in assessment work. Faculty engagement has been recognized as an essential element in successful programs as it ties assessment to classroom practice, underscores faculty's central role in ensuring the quality of the educational experience, and has the potential to shift campus culture so that it supports and values the collection and use of evidence of learning. Yet if authentic faculty engagement is the "gold standard" in assessment, fostering and sustaining it remains one of the perennial challenges (Hutchings, 2010, p. 6).

Of course, faculty compose only one group at the intersection of teaching and learning. If assessment is, as we argue, about improving learning outcomes rather than meeting reporting requirements, students are necessarily central as well. They are not merely the compilers of portfolios, the subjects of standardized tests, or the objects of teaching and efforts to improve it. They are assessment's raison d'être, and, as such, key contributors to and participants in robust efforts at educational improvement— yet they are not as frequently or explicitly considered in assessment conversations as are the other important stakeholders in the process. This is a missed opportunity.

In this chapter, we examine the roles and responsibilities of these two key constituency groups, although many of the ideas apply as well to other professionals in close educational relationships with students. We consider how educators (whatever their formal roles) and students can interact with and support each other in achieving the goals of assessment, and we offer examples of institutions where this happens in promising ways. As is done throughout this book, we also draw from NILOA's 2009 (Kuh & Ikenberry, 2009) and 2013 (Kuh, Jankowski, Ikenberry, & Kinzie, 2014) surveys of chief academic officers to raise pressing issues and provide evidence of institutional challenges and changes. In so doing, we consider issues of disciplinarity and context, point to the potential for institutional culture change, highlight the importance of how assessment is talked about, and offer suggestions for building on the work that faculty already do and value while engaging students in improving their educational experiences and outcomes.

Faculty

The assessment movement as we know it today arose in part as a response to late twentieth-century concerns over quality and accountability in higher education, exemplified by national reports such as *Involvement in Learning: Realizing the Potential of American Higher Education* (National Institute of Education, 1984), *Integrity in the College Curriculum: A Report to the Academic Community* (Association of American Colleges, 1985), and *Time for Results: The Governors' 1991 Report on Education* (National Governors' Association, 1986). These reports—and the concern they both fed off of and extended—fueled widespread interest in assessment among both reformist educators and policymakers.

With a push from states and, increasingly, from accrediting agencies, assessment became linked to accountability, a link that helped spread the movement and propel campus participation but that led, simultaneously, to challenges from many faculty worried about assessment's provenance and purposes.

Despite pushback from many in the academic community, growing numbers of faculty were already engaged in their own conversations and efforts to document and improve teaching and learning in higher education. Indeed, even the 1985 Association of American Colleges (AAC) report, which was particularly critical of faculty (Muscatine, 1985), pointed to "a new area of research. . . directed toward how students learn (or fail to learn) specific subject matter, what difficulties they have with various models of abstract logical reasoning, what preconceptions or misconceptions impede their mastery of concepts or principles in the given subject, what instructional approaches and devices are effective in helping learners overcome the obstacles which are encountered, what exercises and feed-back accelerate the development of various desirable skills, and how best to make the best uses of instructional technology" (p. 12).

As part of this effort, which was one of several converging streams of work in what became known a decade later as "the scholarship of teaching and learning" (Boyer, 1990; Huber & Hutchings, 2005), professors engaged in a variety of activities to understand how and what their students learned. By this time, Alverno College had already adopted a competency-based curriculum, prioritizing students' abilities and learning over course completion. In the 1980s, the Writing Across the Curriculum movement focused faculty efforts on improving how their students wrote and thought. By the end of the decade many faculty had begun to engage with classroom-based assessment in new and important ways. With Thomas Angelo and Patricia Cross's (1993) *Classroom Assessment Techniques: A Handbook for College Teachers* as a defining early work, faculty were expanding the tools at their disposal and the techniques they were using in assuring that students were meeting intended outcomes of their college courses.

The faculty's central place in assessment is deeply embedded in its responsibility for the college curriculum. Although the historic power of the faculty in American higher education can be overstated—the early battles for control of colleges in the United States resulted in strong external control, rather than formal faculty authority—the delegation of curricular matters to the faculty became slowly ensconced in American higher education. As the *Statement on Government of Colleges and Universities* (1966), written under the auspices of the American Association of University Professors, the American Council on Education, and the Association of Governing Boards of Universities and Colleges (1966) claimed: "When an educational goal has been established, it becomes the responsibility primarily of the faculty to determine the appropriate curriculum and procedures of student instruction" (p. 2). Moreover, to the drafters of the statement, this faculty prominence extended to extracurricular activities with educational purposes. And even where this faculty authority has been challenged in recent years, the primary place of faculty in curricular discussions and decision making has remained a necessity. It is, indeed, a core academic value at the heart of American colleges and universities. As such, assessment for the improvement of learning outcomes is inherently a faculty-centric process that relies on their expertise, values their professional disciplinary judgment, and supports their efforts to focus on student learning on both the small and large scales.

Challenges

Faculty concerns about student learning outcomes assessment are manifold, encompassing worries over the reasons for and drivers of it, uncertainty about the ability to accurately measure learning, fears over the potential for the misuse of data, and concerns involving workload and work life in times of diminishing resources. The external push for assessment from states and the federal government, as well as the incorporation of learning outcomes into contemporary accreditation requirements, has caused many in the faculty to view assessment narrowly, in terms of accountability and compliance rather than in terms of student learning. It has also led to a belief that assessment is a fad that will soon pass. As one respondent to NILOA's 2013 survey of provosts indicated, "Many faculty see an 'assessment push' as another in a long line of academic change initiatives. If they just hold out long enough, the initiative will go away. . . ."

At the extremes, some faculty see assessment as one more encroachment of neo-liberal ideology into an increasingly corporatized university (Champagne, 2011; Martinez-Alemán, 2012; Powell, 2011). They highlight the top-down nature in which assessment can but does not have to be implemented, and they raise questions about the respect accorded to professional expertise. When viewed only through the lens of accountability, assessment can be seen as evidence of distrust and, as such, offensive (Linkon, 2005). It can also be viewed as a threat. Multiple 2013 survey respondents indicated that their biggest worry was that faculty resisted assessment out of fear that the results would be used for evaluative purposes, with potentially negative implications for individual faculty and specific programs. In the words of one respondent, "We have to do a lot of work. . . helping faculty see the value of assessment, which has been seen as an oversight and compliance activity. [It is] still challeng-ing getting faculty to find value [and] understand process, without feeling scrutinized or threatened."

This concern over the misuse of assessment for evaluation is layered and multifaceted. It is at the same time philosophical, protectionist, and indicative of the increasingly tenuous place of faculty in modern American higher education. It bears not only on the evaluation of faculty directly but on what Peter Ewell (2002) termed the *ineffability debate*—"the extent to which educational outcomes can be specified and measured at all" (p. 17). Some argue that the learning that takes place in higher educa-tion is so complex, and plays itself out over such a long period of time, that any effort to assess it will necessarily fall short. This is especially true when assessment is equated with standardized testing of finite skills that might be desired in the workplace. Some faculty, especially those in the humanities, associate assessment with less support for academic values and an emphasis on job training and market forces to guide decision making (Champagne, 2011). Such a coupling can have pernicious effects.

If, for some, assessment raises questions of values, for many, it equally raises questions of value. As institutions try to make changes guided by assessment results—completing the assessment cycle—faculty have questioned the associated opportunity costs of actively engaging. Doing assessment means not doing something else that might bring greater sat-isfaction or reward. More significantly, evidence of improved student learning as a result of assessment has been difficult to find, as is borne out in both the scholarly literature and the 2013 survey.

Trudy Banta, Elizabeth Jones, and Karen Black's (2009) solicitation of best practices in assessment resulted in 146 responses from across the nation that could be included in their book *Designing Effective Assessment*, yet only 6% of the respondents provided evidence that learning had actually improved as a result of these practices (Banta & Blaich, 2011, p. 22). More over, NILOA's case studies of promising practices in assessment highlight that even successful institutions do a better job identifying changes in prac-tice resulting from assessment activities than actual increases in student learning fostered by those changes (Baker, Jankowski, Provezis, & Kinzie, 2012). Faculty often possess little expertise in assessment, which discour-ages their participation in the first place, and without seeing clear evidence of the benefits of the process, they are understandably inclined to put their efforts into activities with clearer payoffs (Hutchings, 2010).

These faculty concerns are situated within larger ones involving the workplace and work life. Faculty often feel overburdened and pressed to fulfill increasing numbers of tasks and responsibilities. When viewed as additional work for external accountability, rather than as an embedded core activity, assessment can become one more drain on faculty time and potentially one more issue for the faculty union to negotiate. As a provost survey respondent from a liberal arts college wrote, "I am worried that an already overloaded faculty will rebel at what is perceived as 'more work' when the expectation is given within the next year that all faculty are expected to be involved in assessment work." Another noted, "Faculty carry heavy teaching and service loads; institution is understaffed. Both assessment and using the results of assessment compete with time for the basic functioning of the institution. . . . To put it another way: I worry that faculty are teaching too much to reflect on and change their teaching." Moreover, for tenure-line faculty, rewards systems rarely signal the value of assessment activities and, therefore, discourage faculty from taking ownership and engaging fully (Hutchings, 2010).

For the majority of faculty who are off the tenure track, the concerns can be even more pressing. They are frequently low paid, poorly supported, and excluded from faculty governance. When invited to participate in assessment activities, they may not be remunerated for doing so or, due to their tenuous positions, might not be able to freely and openly contribute. Even if they are, their very contingency makes continuity in participation more difficult and places extra burdens of training on assessment staff and permanent faculty—burdens they may not be equipped to handle.

Taken together, faculty are at times mistrustful of the drivers of assessment, concerned about validity of measures, worried about how the data will be used and misused, and operating in situations that disincentivize engagement. These attitudes and conditions can have ripple effects, as a survey respondent from a doctoral/research university noted:

> Even when assessment is integrated into other programmatic activities, it still takes time and energy. Faculty are stretched thin with heavy teaching loads. Even the faculty who are motivated and interested are at high risk of burnout based on the following challenges: (1) lack of time to do assessment in ways that provide information they value; (2) lack of buy-in from other faculty in their departments, which increases the workload for those who do see the value; (3) lack of reward structures within faculty evaluation for promotion and tenure (faculty decide what "counts" and if other faculty don't

value the work, it won't be recognized); and (4) feeling overwhelmed by the work required to design and make improvements when they discover something isn't working.

These faculty concerns are real and important; they speak to the contested workplace that is American higher education and highlight the tensions on individual campuses caused by the reach of assessment and its ties to accountability. Yet there is evidence of change among the faculty and across American higher education more broadly. According to Ewell (2009), "The majority of academics now realize that engaging in assessment has become a condition of doing business for colleges and universities because of accreditation requirements and the need to show results to taxpayers and potential customers" (p. 6). Moreover, the concerns of and about faculty expressed in the provost survey were paired with dozens of responses indicating great hope for and evidence of faculty buy-in and ownership. The same respondent who offered the lengthy quote in the preceding paragraph also pointed to a cultural shift among the faculty from questioning the purposes of assessment to questioning how it can best be done.

Contexts and Culture

When considering and promoting faculty engagement in learning outcomes assessment, culture, climate, context, and language all matter deeply. Culture is the long-standing way a group understands itself and its shared values (Kuh & Whitt, 1988). It involves beliefs and meanings that are deeply embedded and not easily changed. It implicates language, ritual, and the way an institution presents itself to itself and to others. Climate is more immediate and changeable. It involves feelings and understandings about organizational life (Peterson & Spencer, 1990). Both culture and climate inform how institutions operate and shape the experiences of those who act within them. Institutional cultures that value community and teaching, encourage collaboration and participation, and welcome faculty participation in local conversations are conducive to fostering faculty engagement with learning outcomes assessment. So, too, are cultures that emphasize innovation and improvement, such as that at Carnegie Mellon University (Kinzie, 2012). Carnegie Mellon's research culture facilitated its adoption of data-informed decision making, and its openness to reinvention allowed it to embrace assessment for institutional improvement. The university's assessment efforts were certainly furthered through systemic and intentional efforts, as described in Chapter 3, but the efforts were also rooted in the institution's culture, a culture that respects data and research as well as departmental and faculty control. With such an emphasis, the process at Carnegie Mellon was guided from the bottom up and relied on the faculty to determine the best approaches in their courses, programs, and departments. Similarly, at St. Olaf College, assessment was framed as a form of "inquiry in support of student learning" and, as such, built on the institution's cultural commitments (Jankowski, 2012a, p. 2). Yet just as institutional culture and climate can foster faculty participation, they can also impede it, as highlighted by the provost survey respondent who noted that the biggest worry about assessment was the "campus climate issues revolving around work scope, duties, focus on quality, and the general associated control issues between administration & faculty." Distrust between the faculty and the administration, whatever its roots, can derail assessment efforts before they even begin.

Of course, institutional culture and climate are informed by larger structural issues, and so is the assessment of learning outcomes. While assessment efforts need to be consistent with institutional and programmatic purposes at any institution, at a large, highly diversified institution or one with multiple campuses, for example, they may need to be even more complex, layered, and flexible, taking into account the multiple cultures that exist in such contexts. As such, assessment activities might need increased adaptability so that faculty at the program level are provided multiple avenues and opportunities to create and enact the practices that they value within much broader college and institutional frameworks. Moreover, the turnover that can occur anywhere, but especially at institutions relying on contingent labor, can forestall well-planned efforts and threaten sustainability. Structural support and faculty development, important anywhere, may be even more so at such institutions. Likewise important are the larger roles of faculty in institutional governance and the other avenues through which faculty exercise their voice. For example, although all three major national faculty collective bargaining representatives have supported assessment (Gold, Rhoades, Smith, & Kuh, 2011), on the ground, some provosts report that their faculty unions resist assessment as added work outside of their contracts. The ways in which faculty participate in governance and decision making matter, and these need to be addressed at the program, department, school, and institution levels.

Just as important as larger institutional identities are the disciplinary cultures in which faculty operate; together, in Burton Clark's (1997) terms, they are the "primary matrix of induced and enforced difference among American academics" (p. 22). They help to shape perspectives and practices of individual faculty, programs, and departments, and they contribute to the cultures and climates therein. As such, they also shape faculty views on and experiences of assessment. As noted previously, many of the harshest critiques of assessment have come out of the humanities. When then-president of the Modern Language Association Gerald Graff (2008) advocated for assessment at the organization's 2007 national meeting and again in writing the following year, he faced significant criticism and calls for resistance (Bennett & Brady, 2012). Many raised the issues of corporatization and ineffability previously noted. Yet other disciplines have been much more open (see, e.g., Steen, 2005, for work in mathematics), and even some that have been most skeptical are now showing some signs of engagement, such as the statement on outcomes assessment from the American Philosophical Association (2008). Not surprisingly, the literature is clear, too, about how much further along faculty in preprofessional and accredited programs are in their thinking about and use of assessment (Banta, 2009). This finding was echoed in the 2013 provost survey responses, where it was coupled with requests for information on how to bring liberal arts faculty along.

As noted in Chapter 2, disciplines matter in effective assessment practice because they can inform how faculty perceive and approach assessment. Whereas in one discipline, standardized exams might appropriately capture learning, in another, portfolios might best allow students to demonstrate their proficiencies across a number of intended outcomes. Moreover, disciplines influence how much and to what ends assessment results are used (Ewell, Paulson, & Kinzie, 2011). As the primary organizing scheme of the academic side of American higher education, disciplinarity must be central to assessment, allowing faculty to operate where they are most comfortable and to bring their field's distinctive questions, methods, and ways of thinking to the task of improving their students' learning (Hutchings, 2011).

Language must also be considered because the ways we talk about assessment are culturally significant and can influence how members of the academic community react to and interact with it (Deffenbacher, 2011; Ferren, 1993; Hutchings, 2010). Faculty can be "sufficiently put off by the lingo not to bother attending to the message" (Shapiro, 2014, para. 6), for example, or, in contrast, they can be welcomed through language that speaks to their interests and values. Terms such as *value added* that come from management, measurement, quality control, or accounting are not likely to make friends of educators (Ewell, 2002). But it is not just that institutions need to avoid language that might leave faculty out of conversations or that might activate their fears over corporatization. Institutions must also work toward shared understandings of the language that *is* used (Bennion, 2002). Clear, agreed upon definitions will help facilitate conversations, as they did at Loyola Marymount University where the director of assessment worked with departments to create assessment principles and terminology that could be endorsed and supported across campus (Goldman & Zakel, 2009). On a larger scale, the Degree Qualifications Profile (DQP) provided a common language that allowed schools in a Lumina-funded Southern Association of Colleges and Schools Commission on Colleges project to expand their conversations and come to new understandings across disciplinary boundaries (Jankowski, Hutchings, Ewell, Kinzie, & Kuh, 2013). Language makes a difference, and attention must be paid to how it works to promote or inhibit a culture of assessment.

Engaging Faculty

With the importance of context, culture, and language as a backdrop, what should institutions do to promote faculty engagement? There is no single answer that will work on every campus or even within each program or department at any single institution, yet some recommended practices can help institutions as they work to establish or further faculty participation and ownership.

LOCATE ASSESSMENT IN THE COMMITMENTS THAT FACULTY HOLD Framing assessment as improving learning moves the conversation away from accountability, corporatization, and assessment-speak and connects it to the educational values and work that attracted many academics to higher education in the first place. Likewise, tapping into faculty members' dedication to inquiry invites them to bring their habits and skills as scholars to questions about their students' learning and how to improve it.

RESPECT FACULTY CURRICULAR AUTHORITY AND OWNERSHIP Many faculty hold deeply embedded values regarding academic freedom and their roles in shaping curricular and educational experiences. For them to engage fully with assessment, they should be supported in their conversations about and efforts regarding assessment rather than directed to preset conclusions in a top-down manner. As a provost survey respondent argued, "We need strong faculty leaders to help drive this. If it remains an administrative initiative, it does not gain traction."

CULTIVATE THE FACULTY VOICE Rather than dismissing faculty questions and complaints as mere intransigence, respect the validity of their perspectives. Senior faculty may have been through previous iterations of assessment or related efforts, and that experience may inform how they view current ones. Or faculty concerns about reporting formats or other requirements may point to areas in need of improvement. As such, it is important not to let the long-standing narrative of faculty resistance diminish the respect that their very real concerns are afforded.

FACILITATE BOTH FORMAL DEVELOPMENTAL OPPORTUNITIES AND INFORMAL SPACES FOR FACULTY TO ENGAGE WITH, LEARN ABOUT, AND ENACT ASSESSMENT Even though faculty already do work critical to assessment, they often doing so without formal training or full consideration of the variety of approaches their efforts might take. Ongoing professional development opportunities at multiple institutional levels are crucial for promoting expertise, sharing information, and encouraging dialogue about student learning. They are even more so at institutions with high turnover. An assessment office or committee might well play a role in providing this kind of support, but it could come as well (and perhaps better) from other places in the institution—for instance, the teaching center, in conjunction with work on curriculum and course or assignment design. Also important, though, are the informal spaces— the "teaching commons" (Huber & Hutchings, 2005)—that provide forums for faculty to communicate with each other about wide-ranging pedagogical issues, questions, and insights. Indeed, as noted by multiple provost survey respondents and evident in NILOA's work with the DQP (Jankowski et al., 2013), this informal communication about student learning can both facilitate assessment efforts and be one of the most promising outcomes.

CREATE MECHANISMS TO SHARE INTERNAL BEST PRACTICES AND SUCCESS STORIES If one of the challenges is that faculty fail to see the value of assessment efforts, providing institutional examples of evidence-based improvements in learning is crucial. Building the teaching commons is one way to share such stories, but, as discussed in Chapter 10, there are other effective approaches to communicating with internal audiences—for instance, through written reports, websites, and special events. Taking advantage of these approaches can build shared values and affect institutional culture.

PROVIDE THE STRUCTURAL SUPPORT TO ENCOURAGE FACULTY TO TAKE ASSESSMENT SERIOUSLY Institutional values are communicated by what gets funded and what gets rewarded. If improving student learning through assessment activities is important to an institution, then incorporating it into the reward structure for faculty—both on and off the tenure line—is crucial. It serves both to indicate symbolically the importance of the work and to compensate faculty appropriately for their efforts. It bears thinking, too, about how such work is seen in the reward structure. Serving on the assessment committee, meeting monthly for a semester, might be appropriate evidence of institutional service. But more sustained intellectual engagements—say, the creation of new assessment tools and the published analysis of results—might warrant treatment as the scholarship of teaching and learning or as research. And for faculty who are incorporating more rigorous forms of assessment into their classrooms—designing new assignments linked to the DQP, for instance (see Ewell, 2013a)—assessment work should be seen as part of effective teaching.

BUILD ON DISCIPLINARY EXPERTISE AND PERSPECTIVES Even with pushes for interdisciplinarity and multidisciplinarity, most faculty are rooted in their discipline and conceive of their work through disciplinary lenses. Relying on those perspectives and on the expertise that faculty bring about and from their fields can foster ownership and make assessment more authentic. It can also promote discussions of shared understandings within programs and departments. At the same time, discipline-based conversations and activities can open doors to broader conversations and promote dialogue across institutions, allowing for the consideration of the shared and the divergent goals and outcomes of, for example, an education in history and one in nursing.

ALLOW FOR FLEXIBILITY WITHIN A SHARED FRAMEWORK Since faculty are embedded in their disciplines and cultures, and since many fear homogenization through assessment, there should be multiple paths for demonstrating student learning. These can and should be informed by campus-level conversations about outcomes—conversations in which faculty across the institution are highly involved—but rigid formats that promote standardization can both undercut faculty engagement and limit the potential of assessment efforts.

EMBED ASSESSMENT IN THE WORK FACULTY ARE ALREADY DOING AS EDUCATORS Faculty are already creating assignments, monitoring student progress, and adjusting syllabi and curricular plans. They are already evaluating their students' learning in courses and in majors by providing feedback on assignments and by giving grades. They are already deeply involved in informal and formal practices that can feed into assessment and improvement activities. As is discussed in Chapter 2, these faculty efforts were initially kept separate from assessment because they were seen as too subjective. Yet they need not be. In fact, such activities are crucial to assessment, and they can be captured, coordinated, and built upon, as campuses devise ways to aggregate information about individual student learning at the course level (information that exists in every course on every campus) up to the program and institution level (Ewell, 2013a; Hutchings, 2014a; Richman & Ariovich, 2013). Doing so not only honors and engages faculty expertise but also helps to address issues of workload, efficiency, and assessment fatigue (the topic of Chapter 9). Most important, connecting assessment to the ongoing, regular work of teaching and learning increases the chances that it will lead to changes that improve the education of students.

Students

Their classroom roles put faculty squarely in the center of the assessment process, but they are not alone in those classrooms. They are joined by their partners in the teaching and learning process—the students—who can also be partners in assessment. Explicitly bringing students into assessment activities strengthens that partnership and underscores the fact that assessment is about learning, not about reporting. In this partnership, students can reflect on what and how they are learning and can engage faculty more deeply by locating assessment in the work they do and the places they do it.

Providing students with information about the higher education experience has been a major industry for decades now. The *Fiske Guide to Colleges* ("the #1 bestselling college guide") is now in its thirtieth edition, and the most recent issue of *The Princeton Review* annual guide trumpets "The Best 378 Colleges." Both guides, naturally, have extensive websites where students and their parents can check out all manner of facts and figures about the institutions they are considering: Where are the wildest parties? The best engineering programs? The students with the highest SATs? For those with the resources, admissions counseling services can provide more tailored information matched to the interests and needs of aspiring students. The policy world has been busy gathering and organizing information as well, with booklets, hotlines, and websites—like the Voluntary System of Accountability (VSA) mentioned repeatedly in this volume—that provide data about student demographics, graduation (and attrition) rates, costs, and employment prospects to ensure that appropriate information is available for would-be students to make wise decisions.

Yet few of these efforts focus on what students are actually learning, and they spend even less energy helping students make sense of their educational experience once they are part of it. In this regard, we think of the University of Michigan senior quoted in Chapter 2. In a portfolio documenting progress throughout the tremendous variety of courses and opportunities offered by the institution, the student reflects, "I have had many amazing experiences but I didn't really know what they meant or how they all fit together. Now, I see patterns and themes. . . . There has been some direction to it all along" (quoted in Miller & Morgaine, 2009, p. 9). This student's portfolio can serve as rich evidence for those seeking to understand and improve the undergraduate experience. Just as important, though, it provides powerful evidence for the student who wrote those words: markers of how far he or she has come and of the ability to see and articulate that progress. In this sense, the portfolio is a reminder, too, that students are not just objects of assessment and sources of evidence. They are central actors in the learning process, positioned, as no other partner in the effort is, to bring personal experiences and voices to the assessment conversation. Moreover, their involvement (which can take a variety of forms, as we will see) can help to engage faculty more deeply in assessment. Most important, students can benefit directly, as learners—which is, after all, the purpose of assessment. What, then, is known about the role of students in assessment? And what are the possibilities?

Historically, this picture has been mixed, like that of faculty. In the early years of assessment, students were seen primarily as the objects of assessment. With policymakers arguing that it was "time for results" (National Governors' Association, 1986) and with grades held in low regard, the trend was toward externally devised instruments that yielded scores and numbers. Sampling techniques were the order of the day, and the experience of the individual student was really not the point of assessment as campuses scrambled to respond to state and system mandates.

But there were exceptions. At Alverno College, for instance, assessment meant a requirement that every student demonstrate proficiency on a carefully specified set of outcomes. Additionally, students were expected to develop the capacity for *self-assessment*—the ability "of a student to observe, analyze, and judge her performance on the basis of criteria and determine how she can improve it" (see http://depts.alverno. edu/saal/terms.html#sa). For more than 40 years, Alverno students have been required to assess their work before submitting it to their faculty members, who then assess not only the work itself but the students' own self-assessment. Over time students become increasingly skilled at monitoring and adjusting their own performance. Although this may not be a comfortable task at first, self-assessment gives students a central role in the assessment process. In some ways, one might argue, the assessment students do of themselves is the most important form of assessment, as it fosters a capacity to monitor and direct their own learning in life beyond college.

As noted previously in this chapter, the classroom assessment movement in the early 1990s gave faculty a new set of tools and techniques for exploring the learning of students in their own courses. But many of those tools and techniques were also useful to *students* in reflecting on and articulating their experience as learners. The one-minute paper, for example, asks students to identify what they understand or take away from the day's lecture or discussion and also what is as yet unclear to them—an exercise that focuses attention and one that students get better at over time. A more elaborate technique is the student representative group, in which students are invited to meet regularly with the faculty member (say, every two weeks) to discuss how the course is going, what they are learning, and how the experience might be improved (Angelo & Cross, 1993). The purpose of techniques like these is to gather evidence the teacher can use for immediate improvements, but a corollary benefit is increased thoughtfulness by students about their learning experience and themselves as learners.

Today, the use of portfolios, an approach of choice on many campuses, as noted in Chapter 2, clearly puts the student at the center of assessment. Portfolios provide an occasion for students to pull together their work over time, to step back from that work and reflect on its meaning and trajectory, and, with the aid of ever-cooler multimedia tools and affordances, to present themselves in ways that are distinctly personal and creative—with video clips, art work, links to other sites, photos, and the like. More than three-fifths of all undergraduate students today attend two or more institutions on their way to the baccalaureate degree—often starting, stopping out for a time, and starting again, perhaps in a different place (Peter & Forrest Cataldi, 2005). These swirling patterns of enrollment underscore the need for experiences that help students connect the various elements of their learning—across courses and disciplines, between the learning they do in the classroom and their lives outside, and over time (Association of American Colleges and Universities, 2002; Huber & Hutchings, 2005). Assessment that addresses this need, as portfolios do—and as carefully designed and scaffolded classroom assignments can do as well—are understandably gaining ground.

In short, one of the things that student involvement in assessment can mean—and has come increasingly to mean—is choosing assessment approaches that engage students in meaningful reflection about their learning, approaches that make them more thoughtful and self-aware as learners and that help them connect their experiences over time and across contexts. Portfolios are one example, but so are capstone experiences and assessments anchored in external community-based experiences; these approaches meet the test of consequential validity, discussed in Chapter 2, by bringing into play important consequences for the most important participants in the assessment process: students. This is student involvement in assessment "FOR learning" (Eynon, Gambino, & Török, 2014, p. 107), and it is on the rise as these kinds of approaches gain ground (Kuh et al., 2014).

Institutional Models

Some institutions have taken the notion of student involvement to another level, finding additional roles for students in the assessment process and seeing them as "an untapped resource as institutions seek ways to prove their value to both students and society" (Welch, 2013, para. 1).

One successful model of this approach is taking place at North Carolina A&T State University (NCA&T) and had its genesis in the institution's involvement in the Wabash National Study of Liberal Education, a multiyear effort to determine how much students change during their time in college. Looking for ways to translate the study's assessment results into ideas that lead to real improvement, the project's leaders came up with the idea of inviting students into the process. Participating campuses were asked to identify a "specific point of assessment data that would be more fully understood and actionable with student input" (Blaich & Wise, 2011, p. 1). Student–faculty and student–staff teams then worked to design different ways to reflect student perspectives—including surveys, interviews, focus groups, and town hall meetings. The approach turned out to be especially useful in interpreting results from standardized surveys and instruments, which are necessarily framed in general ways that do not capture the particular circumstances on any given campus, thus, masking problems but also missing important opportunities to build on what is working.

At NCA&T, the injunction to involve students led to the Wabash-Provost Scholars Program, established in 2008. Each semester, Karen Hornsby and Scott Simkins, faculty members who run the program, train 15 to 20 undergraduate students to conduct focus group sessions with their peers, to gather and analyze various kinds of assessment data, to develop written reports and recommendations, and to lead scholarly presentations on their work and experiences. In brief, the Scholars' task is to "dig deeper" (Baker, 2012b, p. 6) into the institution's assessment results—helping to make evidence more actionable. Their insights are shared with other students, faculty, and administrators, including the provost and chancellor, at a public presentation (2012). In addition, the Scholars have assisted with campus-wide national assessments, conducted surveys, and overseen a comprehensive week-long time-diary study including over 200 students.

Over recent years, Wabash-Provost Scholars have conducted campuswide student focus groups on the university's learning environment and classroom teaching practices, the impact of student-led versus facultyled supplemental instruction, ways to increase the intellectual climate on campus, strategies for increasing successful enrollment of transfer students, and student attitudes toward diversity and inclusion. In addition, they assisted NCA&T's math department in assessing the efficacy of a new Math Emporium pedagogical innovation.

Their work has been especially consequential in highlighting practices and policies that impede student success on campus—for example, outlining the characteristics of effective supplemental instruction practices and illuminating issues regarding students' use of out-of-class time. Results of their scholarship are being used to inform faculty, staff, students, and administrators of students' perspectives on academic and institutional concerns and to shape campus efforts to improve retention and graduation rates (Hutchings, Huber, & Ciccone, 2011). More recently, topics of investigation have focused on assessing the university's progress toward meeting its goals for expanding enrollment and diversity.

Allison Cook-Sather, Catherine Bovill, and Peter Felten (2014) highlight the close collaboration between students, faculty, and administrators in the Wabash-Provost Scholars Program and the sense of academic independence fostered by the program that have made the Wabash-Provost Scholars a valuable addition to the university's institutional assessment strategy but also a powerful high-impact learning experience for the students involved. As noted by a recent Scholar, "What has surprised me most about this program is how much of a role we play as a student. . . . From the forming of questions, to conducting the focus groups, and even to the summarization of the data and the final presentation, we truly were in charge of this research project. . . . I believe that I can use the skills I learned to not only develop better relationships with others but also to apply those skills to other 'real-world' situations and settings in my career" (p. 78).

The University of California (UC)–Merced is one of the university's newest campuses, but its program to involve students in assessment— Students Assessing Teaching and Learning, or SATAL—is now well established. In fact, the program played an important role in UC–Merced's initial accreditation. Many of SATAL's features are similar to those at NCA&T. Students design, collect, and analyze various forms of evidence— both qualitative and quantitative—to help faculty and programs improve their work through formative assessment. This might mean running a focus group with other students and producing a report on the results, interviewing a class and sharing what is learned with the instructor, or administering mid- or end-of-course evaluations and then tabulating and writing a summary report for the instructor. As this suggests, much of SATAL's work is focused at the classroom level, and the program's website includes an impressive collection of comments from instructors who have changed their practice as a result. But program-level assessment and research is also a prominent part of the picture. For instance, SATAL focus groups with students prompted applied mathematics faculty to rethink their senior capstone experience (Center for Research on Teaching Excellence, 2011). More recently, the program worked to aggregate data from interviews with students in first-year courses to ascertain what teaching methods are most effective; collaborative group work in various forms came out high across all settings, although showing differences in different disciplinary contexts (Chu & Renberg, 2014).

According to SATAL director Adriana Signorini (2013), the program operates on the assumption that "undergraduates are well positioned to provide supplemental classroom and curricular support." Students can talk with other students—for instance, in focus groups and interviews— in nonthreatening ways that lead to "authentic reflection on learning" (para. 3). Although SATAL is just part of UC–Merced's overall assessment effort, it gives value to the "voice and views of students and their educational development" in that process, and the indirect evidence gathered by students "coupled with more direct evidence, such as course portfolios and examinations, can provide a more holistic understanding of what's happening" (http://crte.ucmerced.edu/satal).

Typically, SATAL involves 10 to 15 students at any given time. In an exit survey when they leave the program, participants report high levels of impact on their research skills and their capacities for teamwork and leadership. According to Robert Ochsner, director of the Center for Research on Teaching Excellence (where SATAL is housed), "There's a real cohesiveness among these students. They spend a lot of time together and gain insights about education and themselves as learners." As a result,

Signorini adds, "They become a bridge between *all* students and faculty" (R. Ochsner & A. Signorini, phone interview, May 12, 2014).

Leaders of student assessment activities at both NCA&T and UC–Merced would probably agree with Josie Welch (2013), director of assessment at Arkansas State University (ASU), who said that "the key to effectively involving students in outcomes assessment is to intentionally match faculty need with student interest" (para. 1). Welch tells the story of ASU's theater department, for instance, which had years of self-evaluations submitted by students as part of the end-of-the-first-year bachelor of fine arts review. Following a recommendation by the university's assessment office, faculty began preparing evaluations to accompany each student's self-evaluation. A student intern interested in both the arts and statistics analyzed the data from these documents and wrote a report highlighting the importance of self-discipline for students concentrating in theatre. As a consequence, the program has seen improvements in student health, time management, and professionalism.

Often, students involved in such projects are enrolled in research methods courses, so assessment provides real-world applications of methods they learn in class. Four such ASU students worked together to double the response rate on senior exit surveys after they hypothesized that the problem was the mode of delivery. Another group, intrigued by data from NSSE and FSSE, "conducted an experiment that resulted in an evidence-based report to deans on just how much faculty [could] expect of first-year students if they 'saw us as we see ourselves'" (Welch, 2013, para. 3).

In short, Welch says, "When students serve as statisticians, interns, and researchers, this is a 3-way win for faculty, students, and directors of assessment" (para. 1). Faculty use the evidence gathered and analyzed by students in a variety of ways—in their own courses but also, for example, in presentations to curriculum committees. Students are able to showcase their work in graduate school applications and resumes. More broadly, the work they accomplish together advances the campus culture of assessment.

Students and Faculty Learning Together

The theme running through all of these examples is that students' most important involvement in assessment is as learners. Whether they are creating portfolios of their work over their college career, helping to interpret survey data at the campus level, or consulting with a faculty member about his or her classroom, they are bringing their perspective as learners—and also *deepening* that learning by reflecting on it, talking about it with other students and with faculty, documenting it, and in some cases developing new strategies for studying it and for asking questions about it. At times this can be unsettling, both for students and for the institution, as students take on new roles and authority and as they (sometimes) come face to face with less effective aspects of their educational experience. But the process can be powerful, giving students a greater sense of agency as learners and an opportunity to be part of something bigger—contributing to changes that will make the institution more effective for other students, now and in the future (Werder & Otis, 2010).

A nice parallel, pointed out earlier in this chapter, emerges here too: students' most important involvement with assessment is in doing what they do as learners, that is, learning; the most promising route to faculty engagement in assessment is in doing what they do as teachers, that is, teaching.

To put it differently, powerful assessment occurs when assessment becomes a regular part of the ongoing work of learning and teaching, rather than something added to or different from this. Indeed, as noted earlier, language can get in the way of real engagement, and therefore it may be useful not to focus on assessment per se but on the activities that achieve its purposes: interactions between students and those who interact directly with them—faculty, student affairs staff, librarians, and others in educative roles—undertaken in a spirit of inquiry, evidence gathering, reflection, deliberation, planning, and action.

Such activities can take many shapes. Excellent examples include the Teaching and Learning Academy at Western Washington University, which brings together some 100 faculty, students, and staff each term to explore educational issues on campus (Werder, Ware, Thomas, & Skogsberg, 2010); student–faculty course design teams at Elon University, whose work over a number of months results not only in new syllabi but also in important learning for both faculty partners and students, who gain "enhanced engagement and metacognition" (Cook-Sather et al., 2014, p. 68); a collaboration by students and faculty at Chabot College, which resulted in a video—*Reading Between the Lives*—that opened up a much-needed space for discussion of the challenges that students face as readers on that campus and many others (McFarland, Chandler, Patterson, Watson, & Williams, 2007); graduate students in chemistry at the University of Michigan who work in intergenerational teams with faculty and undergraduates on instructional development projects designed to prepare them for careers as professional educators (Huber, 2004; Hutchings & Clarke, 2004); a small grants program at Illinois State for teams of faculty and students (either undergraduate or graduate) who wish to undertake a scholarship-of-teaching-and-learning project investigating some aspect of students' involvement in research, scholarship, or creative work (http://sotl.illinoisstate.edu/grants/funding/small.shtml); the Ethnography of the University Initiative, founded at the University of Illinois, which sponsors and archives Institutional Review Board-approved, course-based research on and about students' colleges and universities and asks that students offer research-based recommendations for institutional improvement (Hunter, Abelmann, Cain, McDonough, & Prendergast, 2009).

None of these is called assessment (which, for those not drawn to assessment, may increase their appeal), but each entails educators and students coming together to explore some aspect of teaching and learning on the campus, to gather evidence about it, and to organize that evidence to be useful to and used by others. All reflect the notion of a culture of inquiry and evidence; all are motivated by an interest in the good things that happen as a result—not by a compliance mentality or a mandate.

Seen in this way, there may be more assessment going on—with more potential for impact—than is generally recognized. Important elements of it are not coming from assessment offices (although savvy assessment directors will find ways to support such work behind the scenes). And much of it comes out of existing communities of interest and practice where inquiry and the use of evidence find a natural home in the ongoing work of students and faculty.

Conclusion

Former Harvard University president Derek Bok's 1986 discussion of the importance of assessing outcomes in *Higher Learning* was seen as a bellwether of sorts, indicating that such an understanding was gaining traction. Almost three decades later, in *Higher Education in America*, Bok (2013) highlighted a crucial element for making assessment more than a matter of compliance: "Proposed reforms that offend [academic] values often meet resistance from the faculty and ultimately fail. What is less understood is that academic values can also be a powerful force for constructive change, since faculties will usually experience discomfort and agree to reforms once they are persuaded that existing practices conflict with the principles and responsibilities that help define their professional identity and shape the aspirations that give meaning to their lives" (p. 8).

For many years now, the need for more faculty engagement in assessment has been at or near the top of the wish lists of provosts and higher education leaders. Indeed, the response has become so routine as to seem obligatory and automatic. A different perspective on the challenge, such as that offered by Bok, is needed. Deeper forms of engagement, engagement for improvement rather than compliance, will only emerge when assessment is seen as a natural and necessary enactment of core academic values—and, indeed, when its absence is seen as a violation of those values. That kind of change will be incremental—and much slower than many of us would like—but it is useful to imagine what it would entail.

For starters, as argued in this chapter, it would mean putting assessment much more firmly at the heart of the educational process—in the classrooms, laboratories, studios, service-learning settings, playing fields, and other venues where educators and students meet. It would mean making students active participants in the work, inviting them to inquire about their learning and engaging them in answering those questions and acting on the answers. More broadly, it would mean seeing teaching and learning (and the educational experience more generally) as an arena that invites and even demands the skills and habits of inquiry that faculty value as scholars and researchers—and then rewarding that work.

As reported elsewhere in this volume, there is now some progress in this direction, with classroom-based methods gaining ground. Provosts now identify the rise of such authentic measures as one of the most promising developments in assessment on their campuses (Kuh et al., 2014). Indeed, many institutions are reporting a new depth of engagement and a new appreciation for assessments' role in teaching and learning. As one provost survey respondent noted, "Faculty are excited about helping students. It drives what we do and the ways in which we do it." Another explained, "The focus has shifted from assessment to student learning— what faculty are interested in talking about." Talk is not enough, of course, but finding ways to bring all those into the conversation who belong there is a prerequisite for assessment that makes a long-term difference in higher education's effectiveness.

6

LEADERSHIP IN MAKING ASSESSMENT MATTER

Peter T. Ewell and Stanley O. Ikenberry

When the best leader's work is done, the people say, "We did it ourselves."

—Lao Tsu

LEADERSHIP IS IMPORTANT IN ANY college or university endeavor, but it is especially critical for effective and meaningful assessment of student learning outcomes. While faculty engagement and buy-in are often emphasized as the most crucial determinants of successful assessment, the central argument of Chapter 5, these are rarely attained in the absence of visible, sincere, demonstrated support by the institution's leaders. This is true for a number of reasons. First, in any campus effort and at all levels, through use of their bully pulpit, institutional leaders set the tone for and articulate the values that drive the assessment effort. As earlier chapters in this volume have argued, the critical values in effective assessment eschew a culture of compliance in favor of a culture of genuine engagement for authentic improvement. If institutional leaders openly and personally champion assessment as a way for both academic programs and the institution as a whole to get better at every available opportunity, a more successful and enduring approach usually results. At the practical level, institutional leaders plan budgets and allocate resources—thus providing the material resources that nourish any initiative or program. And equally instrumental, because academe's coin of the realm is recognition as much as remuneration, leaders are in a position to highlight and reward the contributions of those engaged in assessment through awards as well as conference, travel, and publication opportunities.

For purposes of this chapter, *leadership* consists of four main incumbents. First, there are the members of boards of trustees, whose primary role is setting institutional policy at the highest level. Board members, however, do not typically discuss academic policy very much and consequently fail to perceive their fiduciary responsibility for maintaining and assuring an institution's academic quality—just as important as ensuring the institution's fiscal solvency. Chief executive officers (CEOs)—presidents and chancellors at both the institutional and system level—constitute the second set of actors. These individuals are in the best position to set the basic tone of the assessment enterprise and to use the bully pulpit to build a supportive and improvement-oriented assessment culture. The third set of actors consists of chief academic officers (CAOs), whose direct responsibility is to oversee and improve the institution's academic programs. CAOs are charged with assessment governance and carry out this responsibility by establishing and managing an appropriate committee structure and system of academic program review. They also manage academic budgets, determining whether or not sufficient financial resources are available through either direct allocation or faculty release time. The fourth set of actors consists of deans and department chairs (D&DCs) as well as leaders of student affairs units, who provide the crucial midlevel management of the institution's programs and, consequently, their assessment efforts. It is a well-known axiom of the academy that faculty members owe primary allegiance to their disciplines, so success at the school and department levels will usually determine the extent to which any institutional assessment effort is effective and sustainable.

Given this array, this chapter discusses the role of each set of actors in creating and maintaining an effective and improvement-oriented assessment infrastructure and its surrounding culture. The assessment responsibilities of each of these actors are described along with their operational activities and the specific challenges each must deal with. As in previous chapters, much of the evidential base for the discussion is provided by the 2009 and 2013 NILOA surveys of provosts and CAOs and the 2011 survey of assessment at the department and program level (Ewell, Paulson, & Kinzie, 2011; Kuh & Ikenberry, 2009; Kuh, Jankowski, Ikenberry, & Kinzie, 2014).

Governing Boards

Governing board members occupy a prominent but carefully delimited place in the assessment of student learning outcomes. On the one hand, they are ultimately responsible for an institution's assets and activities. This means they are obliged to examine academic quality and are the only authority—save that of the state in the case of public colleges and universities—that can compel the institution's president to pay attention to something. On the other hand, the powers that boards possess must be exercised with restraint. Too much intrusiveness—especially in academic matters—obstructs effective governance and can constitute a significant threat to the quality of teaching and learning. In practice, this delicate balance between action and restraint means that boards generally act indirectly in the realm of assessment policy by asking questions and ensuring that the basics of academic quality assurance are in place.

Roles and Responsibilities

The governing board has two basic responsibilities to the institution with respect to assessment. The first is a fiduciary responsibility for academic quality that is just as important as its better-known fiduciary responsibility for the financial affairs of the institution. Just as it is a violation of its fiduciary obligation for a board to allow an institution to fail financially, it is a failure of board responsibility to allow an institution to graduate students who do not meet accepted standards of quality with respect to what and how much they have learned. Boards clearly recognize the former when they authorize and receive the results of a financial audit—a process that certifies for a given period the credibility of the institution's financial statements. The academic counterpart of the financial audit is the accreditation review—a process that periodically certifies the soundness of the academic awards the institution confers with respect to content and quality. When members of the governing board literally stand behind a graduating class at a commencement ceremony, they symbolically bear witness to this fiduciary obligation.

The second responsibility of governing boards with respect to assessment is consistent with the obligation that any governing authority has to the organization over which it presides: to ensure that the organization's leaders possess the tools needed for effective management. For colleges and universities, one of these tools is assessment—whether it is embodied in the direct assessment of student learning outcomes or in the indirectly through surveys or program review. A central duty of the board, therefore, is to ensure that such information-gathering processes are in place and, especially, that the results of these processes are used to dispassionately evaluate teaching and learning—with an eye toward their continuous improvement. Another part of this responsibility is the board's role in selecting or periodically evaluating the performance of the institution's president. A significant consideration here is the effectiveness with which the president champions assessment and its use as a management tool. To emphasize this matter, some institutions use a set of performance indicators that include assessment results as part of an annual presidential evaluation. Truman State University in Missouri, for example, has followed this practice for more than two decades.

These two board responsibilities thus encompass the double role that assessment typically plays at any academic institution. The first is summative and embodies the role that assessment frequently plays in external accountability, largely through regional or program accreditation. The second is formative and embodies the role of information-based quality improvement that effective assessment should also play. Governing boards must foster both.

Operational Activities in Assessment

The board's principal operational activities in assessment are to ensure that basic assessment processes are in place and that the institution's leadership is using the results to monitor and improve the teaching and learning process. This first requires basic knowledge of what these processes are and how they operate. One widely cited source on this topic (Ewell, 2013b) lists these processes in the form of five basic questions that can be asked about any business: How good is our product (learning assessment)? How good are we at making our product (retention and student flow)? Are our customers satisfied (surveys of students and employers)? Do we have the right mix of products (program review)? Do we make the grade (institutional accreditation)? Board members should know that each of these information functions is in place at the institution and should broadly review their results.

Ewell (2013b) also lists a number of principles that should guide board engagement in assessment. The first emphasizes a posture of indirect engagement by enjoining board members that running the curriculum is the faculty's responsibility; the board's role is to remind them of that responsibility. The second principle admonishes board members to keep discussions of assessment results focused on strategic issues like maintaining academic quality and new program directions and to refrain from getting tied up in the details of academic management. The third asks board members to expect and demand a culture of evidence in which anecdotes are minimized and assertions backed with evidence-based argument. The operational imperative of all of three principles is that boards should ask academic leaders probing questions about the meaning and action implications of any assessment evidence they present. They then should listen carefully to the answers these leaders provide to assure themselves that matters of academic quality are being properly attended.

Two final aspects of the governing board's operational engagement with assessment require brief mention. First, many of these activities will properly take place in the academic affairs committee of the board, which usually comprises a subset of board members, academic leaders, and faculty members. Even in cases like this, conclusions and key issues must be aired for the full board at the next available opportunity. Second, many public institutions have multi-institutional governing boards as part of a state college or university system. Exercising proper oversight of academic quality through a system board can be a major challenge in large systems because the opportunity for question and answer between board members and academic leaders is so limited. In such cases, board members need to remain especially focused on ensuring that crucial quality assurance and improvement processes like accreditation and program review are attended to and where each institution in the system is in the rhythm of these processes.

Principal Challenges and Responses

Institutions frequently encounter two challenges when governing boards address assessment. One of them arises because the professional and career backgrounds of board members mean they are typically more familiar with money and organizational strategy than they are with curriculum and pedagogy. This can lead to considerable reticence on the part of boards to grapple with topics like assessment of student learning—topics with which many board members may not feel comfortable or competent, even though they may have valuable perspectives to contribute to the discussion. Several approaches can be effective in meeting this challenge. The most important is to avoid the use of the arcane language and terminology that unfortunately typifies much discussion about assessment and academic quality. Most of the real content in a discussion about findings and methods can be readily translated into more understandable terms, much as Ewell's five basic questions, noted previously, represent a business-like reframing of basic academic quality practices. Another way to address this challenge is to ensure more frequent direct contact between board members and faculty members, particularly through the academic affairs committee. Greater familiarity through more frequent contact—particularly informal contact—will help diffuse the barriers that board members may have imposed on themselves when it comes to discussing matters with which they feel less comfortable. Finally, increased familiarity will be a by-product of ensuring that discussions of academic quality are held regularly, as advised earlier.

A challenge opposite to the one discussed above is encountered when board members choose to intervene proactively in the operational management of academic affairs. In assessment, this may take the form of immediately recommending direct action to fix a deficiency that assessment results appear to have uncovered without sufficient faculty discussion or respect for academic governance. Worse, it may mean mandating a particular assessment approach (like a standardized test) without consulting academic leaders or the faculty. In their professional lives, board members are often accustomed to direct action and tend to be impatient with the much slower pace of academic decision making. More substantively, some board members may have deeply held—even ideological—positions on what and how particular subjects should be taught. Both of these conditions threaten to undermine the delicate balance of previously discussed strategic oversight. Clarifying the limits of appropriate board concerns through board handbooks and the orientation of new board members can be helpful here, but the most essential behavior to cultivate is that of asking good questions.

Presidents and Chancellors

As chief executive officers of the institutions they lead, presidents are ultimately accountable for everything an institution does. While overseeing academic matters like the assessment of student learning is more properly the direct responsibility of the institution's chief academic officer, presidents play a major role in ensuring that assessment receives the resources that are necessary and that assessment results are used productively. Presidents are a major factor in raising assessment's visibility in the eyes of both the institution's internal constituencies and its external stakeholders. Many of the institutions that have emerged as leaders in assessment have enjoyed long periods of vigorous and visible support from their chief executives. Prominent examples include Truman State University, the University of Charleston (WV), James Madison University, and Miami-Dade Community College (Banta & Associates, 1993).

Roles and Responsibilities

One of the most important oversight responsibilities of any president is to ensure that the institution is meeting all applicable requirements to remain accredited, because losing accreditation means losing access to the federal financial aid funds upon which the survival of many institutions depends. Assessment of student learning constitutes a critical component of the regional accreditation process, so it is central to the process (see Chapter 7). Indeed, the most recent NILOA survey of institutional assessment activities shows that regional and program accreditation are the top drivers of assessment activities on all kinds of campuses (Kuh et al., 2014). Presidents must know where the institution is in the accreditation cycle and what the institution is doing to meet its obligations to provide evidence of student academic achievement. This is particularly important because assessment is not something that can be started or restarted overnight. Sound processes of gathering evidence—particularly if they are authentic and genuinely embedded in the regular processes of teaching and learning—take a long time to put in place and can be quickly forgotten through inattention and lack of support. All of us have worked with colleges and universities that have allowed their assessment activities to atrophy, with a consequent struggle to restore lost interest and capacity when it is time for reaccreditation. It is ultimately the responsibility of the chief executive to make sure this situation does not occur.

Consistent with points made in the previous section, a second central presidential responsibility is ensuring that the governing board is kept informed about assessment. As the administrator directly responsible to the board for the conduct of the institution's business, this responsibility is undeniable but does not need to be discharged personally by the president. Indeed, it is most frequently accomplished by the CAO and other academic leaders. But the president needs to anticipate what questions are going to be asked by the board and then to enlist appropriate people to respond.

Finally, presidents bear the continuing responsibility to run their institutions in the most effective and efficient manner, consistent with the institution's mission and current strategic plan. Consequently, presidents should be aware of the role and potential of information drawn from assessment in identifying areas that need improvement inside the institution and of the opportunities for communicating assessment results to external stakeholders. Again, presidents frequently do not do this directly themselves but, more often indirectly, through academic administrators and public affairs officials.

Operational Activities in Assessment

The most important of the operational activities in assessment is the president's role in supervising the institution's CAO and the office of academic affairs, because this is where responsibility for assessment is located at a majority of campuses. Through one-on-one management meetings and reviewing the regular activities of the CAO, the president is in the best position to make sure that academic affairs is devoting sufficient and significant attention to assessment and is getting the support it needs. This supervision is as much attitudinal as it is physical. That is, the president must visibly signal that he or she regards assessment as a priority for the institution and will intervene to champion it whenever this is warranted.

Similarly, the signature presidential initiative on many campuses is the strategic plan. Indeed, the launch of a new strategic plan frequently accompanies the inauguration of a new president, and the plan is often intended to signal the new administration's priorities. Because of this, the strategic plan offers a president an excellent opportunity to formally incorporate assessment and to communicate that she or he considers the assessment of student learning a priority. Equally important, if assessment is already a priority, a new strategic plan can make this priority more visible and reinforce commitment to it. At the same time, the president can work with the strategic planning committee to make sure that appropriate elements of the plan are empirically grounded—that is, with clear and concrete evidence of need and with empirically measurable outcomes.

While the prior two activities are of great consequence, probably the most critical activity for presidents with respect to assessment is visible and effective use of their bully pulpit to champion assessment at every available opportunity. This is what especially distinguishes the institutions named at the beginning of this section as having had particularly effective presidential leadership in assessment over a long period of time. With respect to internal audiences—especially faculty and academic leaders—the president should exploit every opportunity to point out that assessment processes remain an institutional priority and to mention particular assessment results as either matters to celebrate, if positive, or areas needing improvement, if negative. Indeed, presidents committed to assessment may cite assessment results in support of major decisions that they and the board have taken, even though these results may have played only a supporting role in making the decision. With respect to external audiences, especially funders and those to whom the institution owes accountability, the president should be transparent about assessment results indicating what students are learning and how graduates are faring after leaving the institution. Such results—especially about recent graduates—often provide presidents with the most powerful messages to demonstrate that the institution is fulfilling its educational mission, and they can prove particularly effective in making a case in fundraising.

All of these points also apply to the activities of presidents of multi-institutional systems, although at a somewhat higher level of generality. System presidents must champion assessment symbolically as well as through policy, planning, and resource allocation, but they generally rely on institutional chief executives to lead and support assessment efforts more visibly because proximity is a major key to an effective CEO role in this arena. System heads are also in a good position to judge the extent to which institutional presidents are discharging their responsibilities with respect to assessment and to take appropriate corrective action of they are not.

Principal Challenges and Responses

A first important challenge facing presidents with respect to assessment is to provide the resources necessary to fund assessment activities and infrastructure and, at least as critical, to fund or otherwise support improvement efforts undertaken to address deficiencies identified through assessment results. Presidents face many competing claims for support—all of which are important and many of which are urgent. In the face of these claims, it is easy to let those related to assessment—which are usually less time dependent—move to the back burner. This not only is bad for assessment materially but also sends an unmistakable message that the president does not really support assessment as a priority. Money behind presidential words will always trump presidential words alone.

A way that presidents can address this challenge is to clearly know—relative to what peer institutions are doing—how much their institution is spending on assessment as well as other kinds of support they are providing. There are few known or established conventions about how much an institution ought to spend on these functions (Ewell & Jones, 1985), but good opportunities to pick up such information are at meetings of presidential associations like the American Council for Education, the American Association of State Colleges and Universities, the Association of Public and Land Grant Universities, the Council of Independent Colleges, and the American Association of Community Colleges. NILOA's periodic surveys on this topic also provide some information about extent of assessment support for different kinds of institutions.

A more far-reaching action that presidents can take is to establish a permanent improvement fund to support improvement efforts in teaching and learning that assessment results have suggested. Under normal budgetary conditions—nearly always bad these days—improvement efforts are generally funded with skimpy and fluctuating budget leftovers. Establishing a permanent improvement fund to support such efforts helps mitigate this tendency and simultaneously sends an undeniable message underscoring presidential support. A fund of this kind does not have to be big to be noticed, but its existence is extremely important in sustaining a campus effort.

A second prominent challenge for presidents is to make the assessment process and its results accessible to external stakeholders and the wider public. Higher education has entered an era of unprecedented interest in accountability, and accountability is increasingly based on institutional results. Making results of assessment public is within the institution's obligation to address both the explicit requirements of accreditors and also the more implicit twenty-first-century expectation for transparency of their critical stakeholders (Chapter 10). Because the expectation for transparency has increased so quickly and recently, presidents are not always fully aware of its importance. For generations, the data an institution reported to its accreditors were protected by confidentiality. Most presidents also have an understandable reluctance to report data that reveal institutional weaknesses or defects. To be sure, accreditors are working hard to strike a proper balance between disclosure and confidentiality by developing explicit mechanisms to report accreditation findings.

One way presidents can respond to such circumstances is to publicly commit the institution to becoming more transparent about student and institutional performance and widely disseminating the institution's obligation. This obligation, of course, will be somewhat stronger for public than for independent institutions, but to some degree it applies to all. A second action a president can take is to direct the institution to conduct a formal transparency audit—a structured review of the institution's public communications on various topics, concentrating especially on its Web presence. NILOA has developed a methodology for conducting such a review that is easily applicable to different kinds of institutions, and many have undertaken this process to their benefit (Chapter 10). Finally, a number of institutions have created public interest websites to communicate the benefits they confer to their stakeholders. These contain a wide range of information of interest to the public but are largely centered on learning results, student survey results (for example, NSSE), alumni employment and graduate school attendance, and the benefits of applied research. The NILOA website contains several examples of such websites including Slippery Rock University and Juniata College (see http://www.learningoutcomesassessment.org/FeaturedWebsitePast.html).

A final challenge is the fact that presidents at all types of institutions tend not to stay at the institutions they lead for very long. According to American Council on Education (ACE, 2012a) statistics, the average time of chief executives at American colleges and universities is seven years. This is in contrast to the institutions with especially strong presidential support for assessment mentioned earlier in this section, whose presidents had tenures of almost 20 years during the time they built their assessment programs.

Presidents can do several things to combat the consequences for assessment of changing incumbents. One is to work with the governing board to establish a job description and selection criteria that emphasize support for assessment when a succession becomes imminent. Truman State did exactly this, for example, for the last two presidential successions. More important, the president should work with academic leaders to build a strong and deeply rooted assessment culture among midlevel academic leaders (deans and department chairs) and faculty leaders. Although strong and exemplary presidential champions of assessment are critical in establishing an effective assessment process, presidents should consciously work to establish at their institutions a deeper culture of this kind that transcends any nascent cult of personality. To return to the example of Truman State, successive presidential tenures since the 20-year service of assessment's founding president at that institution have been significantly shorter, with no loss of commitment to assessment or momentum in carrying it out.

Provosts and Chief Academic Officers

CAOs have the central leadership role in assessment at any college or university. The CAO is ultimately responsible for the quality of the academic program and, thus, has a direct interest in monitoring its outcomes in the form of student learning. More important, the CAO is responsible for revising curricula and enhancing pedagogy across all academic programs—a process that is aided by relevant information about student performance. Like the president, moreover, the CAO can demonstrate decisive support for assessment by providing needed resources in the form of positions and budgets. Although midlevel academic administrators like deans and department chairs exercise direct and independent leadership in assessment matters—especially in programs or disciplines that must undergo specialized accreditation—it is difficult for them to run effective assessment efforts without significant backing from the CAO's office. Responsibilities are broadly similar for the institution's top leadership in student affairs but are necessarily focused there on activities in that realm of institutional functioning.

Roles and Responsibilities

Consistent with the more general obligations for the integrity of teaching and learning mentioned already, CAOs have three basic responsibilities with respect to assessment. The first is to ensure that the institution has in place a well-specified set of learning outcomes for each academic program, developed by the relevant faculty in partnership with academic administrators and consistent with a parallel set of learning outcomes for the institution as a whole at each degree level offered. This responsibility goes beyond just making sure that a document is in place. It also encompasses an obligation that faculty be aware of these outcomes and align course materials and learning experiences with them as fully as possible.

The second responsibility is to ensure that mechanisms are in place to gather robust and reliable evidence about the extent to which students are attaining these outcomes that can be disaggregated by student population. Such evidence can be of many kinds but should represent well-established principles of sound evidence such as validity (including consequential validity, as pointed out in Chapter 2) and reliability. The evidence also should be verifiable and replicable, relevant to real-world teaching and learning situations, representative of the populations or settings for which specific learning takes places, and capable of informing action intended to improve outcomes (WASC, 2002).

Third, and absolutely critical, the CAO is responsible to see that the resulting evidence is analyzed and used by faculty and academic administrators. As will be discussed more fully, this may entail establishing and overseeing campus-wide assessment committees, incorporating assessment results into strategic planning or program review, and making sure that commitment to assessment is a part of faculty recruitment and hiring criteria as well as promotion and tenure review. All of these responsibilities may be even more important in student affairs, where learning goals may not yet be formally established or visible to the wider campus community.

Operational Activities in Assessment

As they discharge these responsibilities, CAOs engage in a number of specific operational activities in assessment. Probably the most important of these is discussing programmatic assessment plans, activities, results, and action implications of programmatic assessment at dean's meetings on a regular basis. It is up to the CAO to receive regular reports on these matters in order to make sure that faculty members in all departments and programs are engaging in assessment and using its results. Because of the importance of specialized accreditation, moreover, the CAO should consult with deans to keep current on the assessment implications of upcoming accreditation reports and review visits. She or he should also meet regularly with the institution's assessment committee to review the extent to which programmatic and institutional evidence gathering is proceeding on schedule and to determine whether or not intervention is needed.

CAOs also oversee the institution's program review process—arguably its central vehicle for monitoring and improving academic quality. When reviewing program review reports, CAOs should ask questions about the depth and quality of a given program's assessment evidence and what that evidence suggests about curricular or pedagogical implications. If a report asks for additional resources or positions at the conclusion of a review, CAOs must look carefully at the evidence presented to see if it is sufficiently persuasive. Again, part of the reason for this is symbolic. Deans and department chairs will quickly learn that, absent appropriate evidence, new money will probably not be forthcoming. A similar logic dictates that CAOs require assessment plans when plans for new programs are submitted. Such plans should include not only the kinds of evidence of learning that will be collected, but also the target levels of performance that should be expected within three to five years of the program's launch. This is equally true for student affairs programming.

A third important arena of action for CAOs is establishing policies for academic personnel including faculty hiring and reward structures. With regard to the former, CAOs should first ensure that candidates for open faculty positions are broadly familiar with assessment or that they are at least willing to learn and be part of it. Going further, they might also insist that selection committees review engagement in assessment at a former institution or in graduate school. Also, questions about familiarity with and support for assessment should be a mandatory component of any interview protocol for new faculty. Turning to reward structures, engagement with assessment activities should be an explicit criterion in institutional- and program-level promotion and tenure guidelines, and there should be evidence that candidates present such material and that promotion and tenure (P&T) committee members consider it explicitly. Finally, CAOs can make a weighty symbolic point by granting promotions to faculty members who are active in assessment but who might otherwise be passed over—although this action should be infrequent and used with caution. As argued in Chapter 5, treating assessment as intellectual, scholarly work, and rewarding it as such, is a route to more and deeper faculty engagement.

Principal Challenges and Responses

A first prominent challenge facing CAOs with respect to assessment is avoiding uneven development of assessment activities across schools and departments such that some of them engage in regular assessment activities while others do next to nothing. This can easily occur because the incentives for engaging in assessment can be so different for different fields. Because learning outcomes assessment is an accreditation requirement, programs and departments in fields with specialized accreditors will naturally have more assessment activity than others (Ewell et al., 2011). Assessment activities will also vary among academic programs simply because departmental priorities, faculty interests, and inherent characteristics of programs differ. Because learning outcomes in professional fields are often easier to specify and relevant evidence more apparent than in traditional arts and sciences disciplines, the latter are generally less eager to engage in it.

One step that CAOs can take to counter uneven development is to require well-articulated multiyear assessment plans from all academic units. These should contain enough detail that CAO staff, together with the assessment committee, can meaningfully judge the seriousness with which a given department or school has thought through the details of setting learning goals and gathering or interpreting evidence. In addition, CAOs can also establish formal approval processes, either through their own office or through the assessment committee, such that plans that lack sufficient detail or contain unsatisfactory actions are sent back for revision. Approved plans should also be made available internally so that all units can see them—an approach that is likely to spur more unit-level attention than if units can conceal lack of effort. CAOs can also ensure an equitable distribution of financial and personnel resources across units through supplementary allocations. Not only will such additional allocations directly support more activity, but distributing and accounting for them also can result in higher levels of leadership engagement. Finally, CAOs need to make extra efforts to resist attempts by more junior academic administrators they know to end around assessment requirements through special treatment. All too frequently, CAOs are approached privately and informally to cut special deals on the basis of close relationships presumed not to apply to other unit leaders. Obviously, such corruption in leadership should be assiduously avoided.

A second important challenge facing CAOs is somewhat similar: to ensure that as much attention is paid to assessing the outcomes of the general education component of the curriculum as is devoted to program-level assessment. Insofar as they invest energy in assessment at all, faculty members are much more likely to dedicate themselves to investigating learning in their own discipline or department than to examining the broader objectives of general education. In most institutions, moreover, direct responsibilities for developing and overseeing general education are diffuse. It is often claimed, for example, that general education is everybody's business but nobody's explicit responsibility. Indeed, the nearest thing to direct responsibility for general education established at most institutions is the CAO herself, often exerted through an associate vice president.

CAOs can take a first step to address this challenge by simply exercising more visible leadership over general education assessment. One way to do this is to establish and empower a general education council with broad responsibilities for overseeing and determining the effectiveness of general education courses. Doing so helps counter the typical situation under which the individual courses comprising a general education curriculum remain owned and staffed by academic departments. If a general education council is in place to approve (and, more important, disapprove) particular courses as part of the general education offering, there is more institutional commitment to investigate course effectiveness. It is also useful for CAOs to recognize that the methods used to conduct any assessment of general education proficiencies have a notable impact on the attention faculty and academic leaders devote to the topic. If an assessment approach is used independently from instructional delivery, for example, through a standardized examination, it is not likely to have wide support (and may not even be recognized as relevant) by faculty at large. If, on the other hand, a course-embedded approach to assessing these proficiencies is taken, faculty may be much more interested because such signature assignments will be an integral part of the classes they teach (Ewell, 2013a).

A third significant challenge for CAOs is ensuring that faculty members have sufficient knowledge of the details of effective assessment approaches to implement and learn from them. According to the most recent NILOA survey of CAOs, more professional development for faculty and staff and more faculty using results have risen to the number one and number two positions, respectively, on the list of what CAOs see as the highest priorities for assessment. Given their appropriate preoccupation with scholarship in their own discipline, most faculty are not regularly exposed to best practices in gathering evidence that students have learned what they are supposed to have learned across multiple classes. Rather, they engage in this activity largely within the confines of a particular class they are teaching and, even there, tend to employ one-time judgment-based grades. At most colleges and universities, as a result, the actual work of assessment is borne disproportionately by only a small subset of faculty, who are either interested in the topic or are assigned a role by virtue of a departmental position or committee membership. This means that actual faculty knowledge of how to practice effective assessment remains shallow and sporadic, a condition that deans and department chairs explicitly recognized in the NILOA unit-level survey (Ewell et al., 2011).

A strategy CAOs can use first to address this challenge is to work with the campus center for teaching and learning to establish an ongoing, well-supported program of faculty development activities in assessment. This program should address all the major aspects of student learning assessment including how to craft powerful and appropriate statements of intended student learning outcomes, how to collect direct and indirect evidence that students have attained proficiencies, how to interpret and analyze assessment results, and how to use the resulting learning to improve curricula and pedagogy. The center should also acquire and make available to faculty a set of published references and Web links to resources about various aspects of assessment (including http://www.learningoutcomesassessment.org). The CAO should not only ensure that these resources are in place but also direct every department to have at least one faculty member with assessment-related experience and provide the necessary support or course releases to enable this. The CAO can also require all new faculty members to participate in such faculty development activities in their first year or two as a condition of service. Chief student affairs officers should develop parallel activities focused on student affairs personnel.

A fourth prominent challenge for CAOs is to ensure that the results of assessment are used to actually make improvements in instruction or in academic policy. Both of NILOA's surveys about assessment practices showed that utilizing results remains one of the top challenges with respect to assessment that CAOs report (Kuh & Ikenberry, 2009; Kuh et al., 2014). One relatively straightforward way for CAOs to try to meet this challenge is to diligently examine regular program review reports to determine examples of changes made or proposed on the basis of assessment findings. In addition, CAOs can establish broadly participatory faculty-staff forums during which individuals drawn from different departments and functions can meet in small groups to brainstorm the specific action implications of particular assessment findings. Most institutions do not use assessment results largely because they lack appropriate structured opportunities for faculty and staff to discuss what these results might mean. Institutions that have created such opportunities have found that engagement and action are enhanced if the CAO has established a modest enhancement fund to follow up on any good ideas that emerge from these discussions. For example, Southern West Virginia Community and Technical College holds a data day each year for faculty and staff to consider and act upon assessment evidence in just this way.

A final challenge for CAOs is to make sure the institution's assessment approaches are reviewed and updated so that they are informed by the latest and most effective practices available. Once a set of assessment approaches has been adopted at a given college or university—often with considerable effort and investment—there is an understandable faculty and staff reluctance to change them. Assessment is a rapidly developing field, however, with new methods and approaches constantly evolving and being disseminated. For example, NILOA's surveys are showing a trend away from standardized testing toward more curriculum-embedded methods based on faculty assignments (Ewell et al., 2011; Kuh & Ikenberry, 2009; Kuh et al., 2014). Getting stuck with a set of practices that are never critically examined or updated is not healthy for an institution. CAOs can address this condition by establishing a regular process to assess assessment after a given number of years to determine what is working, what is not, and what changes ought to be made. For its well-known performance funding approach, for example, the Tennessee Higher Education Commission committed to a formal review of its program from the outset and has made a number of significant changes to it as a result (Banta, 1986). CAOs can also support small groups of faculty to go on learning journeys to campuses recognized as leading practitioners of assessment by having earned CHEA Awards in assessment or by having appeared in the assessment literature. A less expensive way to accomplish this goal is to encourage faculty members with an interest in assessment to serve as peer reviewers on accreditation visits.

Deans and Department Chairs

By virtue of their positions as academic middle managers, D&DCs are much closer to the actual practices of assessment than are the leaders covered previously. That said, their roles and responsibilities largely parallel those of CAOs but correspond to their more circumscribed spans of authority for the academic programs they oversee. The same can be said for unit directors in student affairs.

Roles and Responsibilities

Like CAOs, D&DCs are responsible for ensuring that the basics of assessment are in place for the programs under their supervision. This first responsibility means making sure that all programs have in place learning outcomes statements or goals that are created by their faculties and that are broadly known by both faculty members and students. The second part of this responsibility is particularly significant. It is common for learning outcomes statements—established largely for accreditation purposes—to be on the books but for faculty to have little apparent knowledge of them. The same can be said for student affairs staff.

A second responsibility is to ensure that all programs have in place methods for regularly gathering evidence of the extent to which enrolled students are mastering these established proficiencies. Again, evidence gathering can be of many kinds, ranging from third-party standardized examinations through portfolios and capstones to course embedded signature assignments created by teams of faculty. While a variety of methods is desirable, D&DCs should see that they are appropriate to the basic goals and character of each program. For professional programs in the health professions or education, for example, it would be questionable if results on licensure examinations were not considered. Both learning outcomes statements and assessment approaches, moreover, will normally be documented in the form of a program assessment plan, so another responsibility of D&DCs is to regularly review these plans—perhaps along with school or department assessment or curriculum committees—to make sure they are up to date and complete.

Finally, D&DCs are responsible for establishing and overseeing mechanisms to regularly discuss assessment findings for the programs for which they are responsible and developing recommendations for improvement. As is the case for CAOs, this responsibility may be most effectively discharged through program review.

Operational Activities in Assessment

More detailed activities consistent with the basic responsibilities of D&DCs, first, include designating within each academic program that the D&DC oversees an individual responsible for coordinating assessment. This position, often called *assessment liaison*, takes the lead on implementing the unit's assessment plan. Activities here include managing the process of creating and modifying the program's learning outcomes statements, locating and documenting assessment instruments or approaches, scheduling and coordinating processes for gathering evidence, preparing reports on what is found, establishing mechanisms for discussing the action implications of assessment findings, and following up on action recommendations once they are made. D&DCs should meet regularly with their assessment liaisons to remain abreast of developments in assessment and to determine if any intervention is needed. The same is true for student affairs units, where outcomes assessment may be less prominent.

A related activity is reviewing and monitoring program review reports from the various programs to determine if information on student learning is prominently included and to intervene if it is not. As noted earlier, because of its ties to action recommendations and resource requests, the program review process is probably the most visible tool for translating assessment information into program improvement efforts that most institutions have at their disposal, so D&DCs should take particular care to look at these documents regularly. Another thing for D&DCs to examine when doing this is whether and how assessment findings are linked to recommendations for new resources (positions, equipment, or dollars) or for changes in curriculum. Finally, D&DCs should ensure that the assessment plans of the units they lead are aligned with those of the institution as a whole.

D&DCs should also take care to stimulate the discussion of information derived from assessment in appropriate venues where faculty members gather to discuss curriculum and pedagogy. As noted earlier, institutions typically have very few opportunities to do this—one of the reasons assessment results are underutilized. Moreover, as discussed in Chapter 5, leaders at all levels need to make assessment integral to all discussions of teaching and learning. D&DCs can address this in at least two ways. One is convening a meeting of representative faculty and staff soon after the findings of a significant assessment is released to discuss their implications. Another is making discussion of assessment and assessment results an explicit topic of conversation in at least one faculty meeting each semester. Whenever possible, moreover, these discussions should include adjunct faculty.

Finally, D&DCs are responsible for monitoring the assessment requirements of any specialized accreditors that may review the academic programs for which they are responsible and for ensuring that the assessment activities carried out are consistent with these accreditors' requirements. Frequently, this involves getting access to third-party data such as state licensing authorities, because licensure examination scores and pass rates are a prominent data requirement of many specialized accreditors.

Principal Challenges and Responses

Probably the most important challenge D&DCs face with respect to assessment is building broad faculty engagement with the process. This challenge is also relevant to CAOs, of course, but its impact on D&DCs is much more immediate and direct because they are much closer to the action of essential faculty-driven components of assessment such as setting goals, gathering evidence, and interpreting and applying results. Many faculty members are not initially drawn to assessment—at least in the faintly administrative flavor in which they usually first encounter it. In fact, active engagement in assessment in most schools and departments is borne by only a few faculty members who are genuinely interested in the process or who have been assigned to it, and the balance of faculty members, while not actively opposed to assessment, are more than happy to let those few currently responsible do the job. Consequently, unsurprisingly, the people responsible for assessment in these situations are subject to burnout and unlikely to stay for long in these positions. A more important broader consequence is that most faculty members sit out assessment entirely.

One way to begin to respond to this challenge organizationally is to establish a formal succession plan to govern who serves in department or program assessment liaison positions over time. Doing so presumes that assessment liaisons are, in fact, in place in most departments and student affairs units, but establishing such positions should be a priority for D&DCs and student affairs unit heads, in any case. The existence of a formal succession plan not only helps address the practical problem of getting new blood into assessment, it also symbolizes that the effort is ongoing and requires a permanent infrastructure. Such succession plans usually include overlapping membership, in which the current assessment liaison stays on board for an additional year while the successor serves a first year. Such arrangements help promote continuity because so much of the business of serving as an assessment liaison involves personal, face-to-face contact.

Another way to deal with this challenge is to tap into the growing presence of assessment as part of the scholarship of teaching and learning (Hutchings, Huber, & Ciccone, 2011). The International Society for the Scholarship of Teaching and Learning, established in 2004, annually brings together hundreds of faculty from across the full spectrum of fields who are engaged in systematic investigations of student learning. Although it has been a long time coming, a number of disciplinary associations are now featuring sessions on assessment as part of their annual meetings, and some have produced edited publications on how to approach it. Examples include the American Political Science Association (Deardorff, Hamman, & Ishiyama, 2009) and the American Accounting Association (Gainen & Locatelli, 1995). These represent natural opportunities for regular faculty to obtain recognition for efforts in assessment, efforts that would otherwise not count as legitimate scholarship. D&DCs should become aware of these opportunities and inform relevant programs and departments of them. They might also consider establishing modest scholarship or support programs to defray the expenses of faculty members who choose to involve themselves in assessment in this way. Best of all would be to work with the CAO to find ways for the institution's promotion and tenure process to recognize such contributions.

A second challenge faced by D&DCs is that faculty members in the programs for which they are responsible have only a limited knowledge about the nuts and bolts of gathering and interpreting assessment evidence. For understandable reasons, individual faculty cannot be expected to regularly access the literature on assessment, especially since the bulk of it is unrelated to their disciplines. D&DCs can begin to address this challenge by disseminating links to resources, like NILOA, with information on assessment technology as well as announcing the efforts of disciplinary associations active in assessment. They should also instruct assessment liaisons to keep track of periodicals like the online monthly *NILOA Newsletter* and *Assessment Update* and notify their program faculty members when anything relevant appears in them. Additionally, as noted earlier, D&DCs should work with the CAO and other staff to develop appropriate training programs through the institution's center for teaching and learning. In doing so, moreover, they should be sensitive to the fact that different disciplines may use very different assessment approaches consistent with their distinctive cultures of inquiry (Ewell et al., 2011).

Finally, one of the most effective ways to directly involve more faculty members and to develop their knowledge about assessment is to engage their natural desire to become better teachers. For example, more and more campuses are adopting Lumina Foundation's (2014b) Degree Qualifications Profile as a basis for organizing curricular alignment and improvement efforts. In the realm of assessment, moreover, faculty-made assignments and examinations embedded in the curriculum represent the best way forward. Provosts in the most recent NILOA survey also considered assignments the most valuable evidence available of what students have learned (Kuh et al., 2014). While most faculty members lack the knowledge needed to create properly specified prompts that can serve as the basis for signature assignments, they sincerely want to know how to write better assignments. Again, D&DC and CAO efforts to build the necessary faculty development capacity to support faculty in this endeavor should pay noticeable dividends.

Aligning Positions and Messages Across Multiple Roles

In this chapter, we reviewed the responsibilities and activities for assessment for each leadership position independently, which are summarized in Table 6.1. We conclude by looking at how these positions work together to yield an effective institutional assessment approach. The central dilemma with respect to leadership in assessment is achieving this kind of alignment. Two specific challenges arise here. First, we know that the different perspectives embodied by leaders at different levels means that they have differing levels of information about what is happening in assessment and, consequently, different levels of concern. For example, notable differences in perceptions and knowledge about assessment between CAOs and department-level respondents were apparent in the three surveys that NILOA has conducted since 2009 (Ewell et al., 2011; Kuh & Ikenberry, 2009; Kuh et al., 2014). Second, the fact that the department-level survey revealed so many different kinds of assessment methods and motives across disciplines poses the challenge of telling a consistent story about assessment for the institution as a whole. Nevertheless, experience has demonstrated the efficacy of several approaches to coordinating and aligning assessment, described in Table 6.1.

Internal Channels of Communication

Aligning what appear to be disparate assessment activities requires informing the various parties involved in assessment about what is happening in real time (Chapter 10). Many campuses have a dedicated website for communicating overall assessment results consistent with the requirements of their accreditors, but such sites generally face outward and are rarely consulted by internal audiences. They can easily be reconfigured to do so, however, and can be used to communicate useful information to a multitude of units either practicing assessment or interested in assessment findings. The problem, though, is inducing people on campus to visit the site when it is updated with new information. One way to deal with this is to use a regular email contact list to alert the

Table 6.1 Various Responsibilities, Activities, and Challenges of Academic Leadership

Leadership	Responsibilities	Operational Activities	Principal Challenges	Responses to Challenges
Board of Trustees	• Public Accountability • Oversee quality improvement	• Ensure basic assessment processes are in place and institution's leadership is using results	• Professional and career backgrounds of board members • Excessive intervention	• Cultivate the habit of asking good questions • Clarify the limits of appropriate board concerns
Chief Executive Officers (CEOs)	• Meet accreditation requirements and ensure systems for assessment are in place • Inform Board on assessment	• Partnership with the institution's CAO and the office of academic affairs • Empirically grounded strategic plan • Champion assessment to various audiences	• Provide the necessary support structures • Public demand for transparency of assessment results • Presidential turnover	• Know cost and return on investment of assessment • Establish a permanent "improvement fund" • Make assessment activity and results fully available on campus • Direct the institution to conduct a formal transparency audit • Work with academic leaders to build a strong and deeply rooted assessment culture

(Continued)

Table 6.1 (Continued)

Leadership	Responsibilities	Operational Activities	Principal Challenges	Responses to Challenges
Chief Academic Officers (CAOs)	• Ensure that the institution has learning outcomes for each program and mechanisms to gather reliable evidence • See that resulting evidence is analyzed and used	• Discuss and share programmatic assessment plans, activities, results, and action implications • Solicit regular reports on assessment work • Make sure faculty members and academic leaders are engaged with assessment and using results • Consult with Deans to keep current on the upcoming accreditation reports and review visits • Establish policies for academic personnel, including faculty hiring and reward structures that address assessment	• Avoid uneven development of assessment activities across the institution and that attention is paid to assessing general education outcomes • Ensure that faculty have sufficient knowledge of the details of effective assessment approaches • Ensure results of assessment are used to make improvements • Review and update the institution's assessment approaches	• Require multi-year assessment plans from all academic units • Make plans available internally for review and consultation • Avoid any special treatment for administrators • Exercise more visible leadership • Work with the campus center for teaching and learning • Establish faculty-staff forums to discuss implications of particular assessment findings • Establish a regular process to continually "assess assessment" • Support small groups of faculty to go on "learning journeys" to other campuses • Encourage faculty members with an interest in assessment to serve as peer reviewers on accreditation visits

Deans and Department Chairs (D&DC)	• Ensure academic programs have learning outcomes statements that are known by faculty and students • Establish mechanisms to discuss assessment findings and recommendations for improvement	• Designate "assessment liaisons" • Review and monitor program review reports • Stimulate the discussion of information derived from assessment • Monitor the assessment requirements of any specialized accreditors	Foster broad faculty engagement in the assessment process	• Establish a formal succession plan for assessment personnel • Tap into the growing presence of assessment as a part of the scholarship of teaching and learning • Disseminate links to resources like NILOA • Work with the CAO and other staff to develop appropriate training programs through the center for teaching and learning • Harness faculty members' desire to become better teachers

relevant parties when new information is posted. A better approach is an electronic newsletter issued periodically that contains the requisite assessment information with easily accessible links to it.

Department- and program-level assessment practitioners, as well as their counterparts in student affairs, may also want to learn how other programs are approaching assessment. The best way to do that is through links on the assessment home page to program- and unit-level material, which can be indexed or sorted by various characteristics like type of assessment used, the point of time in the program at which the assessment is administered, incentives to induce student participation, and so on. To pique interest in looking at program- or unit-level assessment in detail, some assessment websites rotate a webpage of the month featuring sites exhibiting various good practices.

Most important is to remember that assessment is about people. Leaders at all levels must do everything possible to create more occasions for faculty and student affairs professionals to talk face to face about teaching and learning and to make meaning of assessment results to improve both. Consistent with Chapter 5, moreover, leaders at all levels should ensure that students are included in these discussions.

Program Review

Program review is featured in several of the strategies to address particular challenges for several leadership positions in the preceding sections because, like strategic planning, it is a particularly effective vehicle for involving leaders at different levels and for linking assessment information with palpable action. At the broadest level, program review is led by the CAO, who may have an associate vice president in day-to-day charge of the system who sees to logistics and scheduling. Most of those involved, however, are the leaders of academic programs and department chairs directly responsible for producing the requisite self-study documents and large numbers of faculty who analyze the assessment data and use them to develop recommendations for action. Faculty members are also involved through the program review committee and as third-party peer reviewers of a program's materials. Where nonacademic programs are included under program review, professional staff members play similar roles. People involved in program review thus cut across the leadership spectrum of the institution, prompting conversations about the meaning of assessment results that would otherwise not occur.

Program review is one of the few mechanisms at any institution that links information, curriculum and pedagogy, and money. Program review also encompasses the complete assessment cycle, from gathering evidence to action-oriented improvement. By accomplishing both of these, it converts the otherwise dry process of collecting evidence on student learning into a far more vivid and meaningful faculty and staff activity. Institutional leaders at all levels, therefore, should use the opportunity that program review provides to make assessment real enough that faculty and staff genuinely want to invest their time.

Key Investments

Preceding sections have touched on the importance of establishing an institutional assessment office and an associated assessment committee to coordinate and review the assessment process. They have also emphasized the importance of creating and supporting unit-level assessment liaison positions. This topic is useful to bring up here as well, because these positions provide a significant vehicle for keeping assessment activities aligned with one another and focused on improvement. Assessment offices and associated assessment committees, of course, are already prominent at most institutions; indeed, they are among the top three most important supports for assessment reported by CAOs in the most recent NILOA survey (Kuh et al., 2014). Their presence does not mean, however, that they are well funded or effective. Assessment committees, in particular, can play a strong role in assuring the consistency and alignment of myriad diverse approaches to assessment at the program or unit level. Most of their members are faculty who are drawn from many disciplines and who, therefore, can bridge the typical silos of department structure to communicate best practices in assessment. The actual roles played by institutional assessment committees also matter a lot in their effectiveness in promoting consistency and alignment. For example, if assessment committees are part of the institution's governance structure or are granted real authority to approve program-level assessment plans and reports such that they can send deficient plans back for revision or weigh in on interpretations and resource implications in program assessment reports, they will increase the seriousness with the process is taken by program chairs and faculty members as well as unit heads and professional staff in student affairs.

Assessment liaisons are almost as common among academic programs, according to the 2011 NILOA survey, but they are also apt to be part-timers with little support; respondents to this survey also reported staffing to be one of the most prominent challenges facing program-level assessment (Ewell et al., 2011). Because the distribution of resources across programs is likely uneven, CAO involvement may be needed to ensure that assessment capacity is adequate for all programs because program directors and department chairs may not have that capacity. Together, the interaction among the campus-level assessment office and program assessment liaisons is crucial to promoting the consistency and alignment of assessment activities at all levels. This interaction should reinforce and reflect parallel dialogues among the CAO and the various D&DCs about how to systematically improve teaching and learning.

Institutional Mission

Finally, leadership at all levels can exploit the potential of the institution's mission to fuel interest and involvement in assessment and continuous improvement. The mission represents the highest-level directive and the espoused priorities that should be visible throughout the institution's programmatic and organizational initiatives. More concretely, the mission touches the assessment of student learning outcomes in two significant ways.

First, most mission statements broadly characterize the attributes that graduates are supposed to have acquired in the course of attendance. While these are usually cast extremely broadly—too broadly, in fact, to serve as operational definitions for assessment—they do provide a launching point for discussions about what constitutes effective teaching and learning. Second, implications within the mission statement frequently have concrete entailments for assessment. If taken seriously, these can be followed up on empirically to see if the implied behaviors are actually in evidence. For example, the mission statement may imply that the institution values frequent informal out-of-class contact between faculty and students or fosters student leadership through programming in student affairs. Administering NSSE or CCSSE, which have items on these behaviors, to representative samples of students can help determine the extent to which the attributes characterized in the mission statement, in fact, are cultivated at the institution. A discrepancy between what the mission says and what is empirically determined can also stimulate broader discussion of the dimensions of the phenomenon and what the institution ought to do about it.

Conclusion

Consistent, aligned support from leaders at all levels, from members of boards of trustees to program directors, is a necessary condition for a successful assessment program at any campus. While faculty and staff members directly involved in teaching and learning are the institution's principal actors in assessment—setting learning goals, gathering evidence of learning, analyzing the evidence, and drawing implications for action—they need institutional leaders to signal that these activities are important and to allocate resources to support their efforts. Leaders at each level, appropriate to their span of control, have specific roles and responsibilities in their institution's assessment endeavor, but all of them share the responsibility to visibly champion the processes and day-to-day uses of assessment. Through consistent and continuous engagement, leaders can help move institutional efforts in assessment beyond mechanical accountability to external authorities and routine data collection at the behest of others toward the far more generative activities of exploring the implications of assessment evidence for curriculum and pedagogy and taking collective action to build on strengths and to rectify deficiencies.

7

ACCREDITATION AS OPPORTUNITY

SERVING TWO PURPOSES WITH ASSESSMENT

Peter T. Ewell and Natasha A. Jankowski

Quality means doing it right when no one is looking.

—Henry Ford

THE VALUE OF ACCREDITATION is often questioned by institutions that see its process as challenging and costly with few clear returns (Cottrell et al., 2009) and by policymakers that see its product as self-serving, ineffective, excessively focused on minimum standards, and insufficiently transparent (Banta & Palomba, 2014; Gaston, 2014). While accreditation in general and its student learning standards in particular may be widely misunderstood and poorly communicated, meeting accreditation requirements—to assure the public of the quality of the educational experiences they are providing their students—is institutions' most important response to the demand for accountability (Pathways to College Network, 2012). Yet quality assurance, or accountability, is only part of the accreditation picture. As noted by Barbara Brittingham,

Patricia O'Brien, and Julie Alig (2008), accreditation is also about institutional improvement:

American regional accreditation serves two basic functions: quality assurance and quality improvement. Through its public function of quality assurance, accreditation signals to prospective students, parents, employers, and others that the institution meets fundamental standards of quality. Through its private function of quality improvement, accreditation supplies institutions with a useful engine to foster improvement. (p. 69)

Both purposes for accreditation—quality assurance and quality improvement—are essential, but the tension between these purposes can quickly become problematic for accreditors and institutions striving for improvement while also responding to external demands (Ewell, 2009). The narratives of these competing purposes have played out in various ways, but most of the discussion on this topic has centered on how accreditors—not institutions—navigate the tension.

This chapter examines issues of institutional responsibility in relation to accreditation, beginning with a brief overview of accreditation followed by an examination of accreditation as a driver of assessment. It also addresses the mutual responsibilities of accreditors and institutions in undertaking, implementing, and sustaining a meaningful examination of student learning. Most important, the chapter proposes how institutions can navigate the tensions between internal improvement and external demands. If institutions' assessment programs focus on important academic questions, if various groups across campus are actively engaged, and if these groups discuss and use the results, then accreditation is no longer an act of compliance distant from teaching and learning. Nor is it the additional reporting burden so many perceive it to be. In short, it is possible to work for *both* purposes—accountability and improvement—through the same mechanism.

Accreditation: The Context

The first regional accreditation association, the New England Association of Schools and Colleges (NEASC), was established in 1885 as an answer to the question, "What is a college?" (Ewell, 2008; Gaston, 2014). Today, there are seven regional accrediting organizations that focus on the quality of institutions in six designated geographic areas of the United States and selected institutions in other countries (see following list, or map of areas, at http://nsse.iub.edu/images/usa_map.jpg).

1. Higher Learning Commission of the North Central Association of Colleges and Schools (HLC–NCA)

2. Middle States Commission on Higher Education (MSCHE)

3. New England Association of Schools and Colleges (NEASC)

4. Northwest Commission on Colleges and Universities (NWCCU)

5. Southern Association of Colleges and Schools Commission on Colleges (SACSCOC)

6. Western Association of Schools and Colleges Accrediting Commission for Community and Junior Colleges (WASC–ACCJC)

7. Western Association of Schools and Colleges Senior College and University Commission (WASC–SCUC)

In addition to these regional accreditors, there are about 50 specialized accreditors in professional fields such as medicine, business, and engineering (see list at http://www.chea.org/Directories/special.asp). Specialized accreditors focus on department-, program-, or school-level quality assurance with somewhat greater attention to the assessment of student learning. Specialized accreditors' requirements may include pass rates on licensing exams and may also establish specific competencies in alignment with professional needs. There are also six recognized national accrediting organizations (see list at http://www.chea.org/Directories/index.asp), some of which accredit faith-based institutions and some of which accredit for-profit programs and institutions (mostly in the field of business).

Accreditation is nongovernmental and voluntary, although with the expansion of federal student aid programs and the linking of student aid eligibility to accreditation, accredited status has become a practical necessity for institutions. Accreditation is based on peer review (Schmidtlein & Berdahl, 2005). Its main components are preparation of a self-study by an institution or program, one or more site visits by peer reviewers, followed by an accreditation action by the accrediting commission that establishes accredited status. Institutions accredited by institutional accreditors (regional and national), which are recognized by the U.S. Department of Education through a process called gatekeeping, are eligible to receive federal financial aid (Werner, 2004). Some specialized accreditors are also recognized as gatekeepers if they accredit free-standing special-purpose institutions. This provision, of course, renders accreditation essentially mandatory for institutions.

Historically, accreditors used quantitative criteria applied to inputs like numbers of faculty and numbers of books in the library. Over time, these review criteria were largely replaced by broader mission-based requirements and the provision of evidence of institutional effectiveness. Finally, prompted in part by federal requirements for accreditors to examine student academic achievement in the late 1980s, as well as a rise in the prominence of assessment in higher education, accreditors began asking institutions to provide information on student learning (Linn, 2006).

Accreditation as Assessment Driver

Accreditors have not always been interested in student learning outcomes. Prior to a focus on assessment as a mechanism of quality assurance and institutional improvement, accrediting organizations predominantly examined processes and inputs (Banta, 2001; Ewell, 2001). In the 1980s, when pressure was building for institutions to assure educational quality, then secretary of education William Bennett issued an executive order that included a notice to accreditors to examine the educational achievements of students as part of their institutional review processes (U.S. Department of Education, 1988). Additional specificity in the Department of Education's directives to accreditors regarding quality assurance processes came with the 1992 reauthorization of the Higher Education Act (HEA) (Banta, 2001; Ewell, 2008).

The Southern Association of Colleges (SACS) was the first regional accreditor to adopt *institutional effectiveness* standards, in 1984, followed quickly by the Western Association of Schools and Colleges (WASC), with the Higher Learning Commission (HLC) joining in the 1990s (Ewell, 2008). By the end of the 1990s, all higher education institutions in the United States were required by accreditors to conduct some form of student learning outcomes assessment (Ewell, 2001). Although they all require that institutions collect data about student learning outcomes, accreditors do not prescribe specific strategies for assessment. They instead insist that faculty at each institution take the lead in developing and implementing assessment approaches.

Over the years since Secretary Bennett's 1988 order and in each successive HEA reauthorization, accreditors have revised their standards and review processes to include more explicit requirements for the assessment of student learning. As a result of this history, accreditation has become a powerful impetus for assessment activity at most institutions. In two recent national surveys of provosts conducted by the National Institute for Learning Outcomes Assessment (NILOA), regional accreditation was listed as the primary driver for assessment work and the number one context for using assessment results (Kuh & Ikenberry, 2009; Kuh,

Jankowski, Ikenberry, & Kinzie, 2014). Moreover, in focus groups with campus leaders, respondents identified accreditation as the major catalyst for undertaking work on student learning outcomes (Kinzie, 2010). Further, in a NILOA study of assessment information posted on institutional websites, institutions accredited in the past two years were more likely to post information about assessment, including examples of the use of assessment results, than those not accredited within the past two years (Jankowski & Provezis, 2011).

Individual academic programs also reported accreditation as one of the top drivers of assessment work on a survey of program-level assessment, and programs that were accredited were engaged in more assessment activities than those that were not (Ewell, Paulson, & Kinzie, 2011). Supporting this, Trudy Banta (2001) argues that approaches to assessment in accredited disciplines are likely to be more fully developed than is the case elsewhere in the academy. For instance, in 1996, ABET, the accreditation agency for programs in applied science, computing, engineering, and engineering technology—which has long-standing involvement in supporting assessment of student learning—adopted a new set of standards shifting the basis of accreditation from inputs to what is learned. The criteria specified 11 learning outcomes and required programs to demonstrate student achievement in each of these areas. A study of the impact of ABET's outcomes-based accreditation criteria on programs and their graduates found that programs that implemented the revised criteria had higher levels of faculty support for continuous improvement, greater emphasis on professional skills, and more active learning than those that did not (Lattuca, Terenzini, & Volkwein, 2006). Graduates of these programs also reported better preparation for postgraduate challenges than their counterparts.

Accreditors help institutions undertake the actual work of assessing student learning by providing principles, statements, workshops, academies, assessment conferences, and resources (Banta, 2001; Council of Regional Accrediting Commissions, 2003, 2004a, 2004b, 2004c; Ewell, 2008; Maki, 2010; Wright, 2013). An examination of one of these technical assistance efforts, WASC's Assessment Leadership Academy, found that participants were more fully and effectively engaged with assessment when they returned to their institutions (Allen, Driscoll, & Booth, 2013). Despite assisting institutions in doing assessment work, accreditors are increasingly citing institutions for lack of progress in this area (Provezis, 2010).

Accreditation has undoubtedly stimulated more examination of student learning at more institutions than would have occurred without it, but responses by institutions and programs have been uneven. Randall Cottrell and associates (2009) observed that programs in the health professions face multiple competing demands for accreditation-related assessment information. Further, they argue that despite the fact that specialized accreditation in the health professions has been involved in assessment for many years, it has yet to be universally embraced. Thus, while accreditors have been drivers of assessment and have provided resources to help institutions and programs engage in the process, they do not actually do the work. Accreditors ask institutions to develop and sustain a culture of evidence-based decision making and improvement (Leimer, 2012), but the primary responsibility for quality assurance lies with the institution (Dill, 2014). They also ask institutions and programs to shift from an emphasis on creating assessment processes and infrastructures to using the information generated to make improvements (WASC, 2013). Yet, all too frequently, institutions and programs describe the assessment of student learning as if its main purpose is to meet accreditation expectations (Powell, 2013).

The Role of Accreditation in Assessment

If accreditation is driving assessment efforts on campuses and will almost certainly continue to do so, what exactly are accreditors asking institutions and programs to do? National and regional accreditors expect institutions to engage in the assessment of student learning in a systematic manner across the entire college or university—to establish learning outcomes statements, to collect a variety of evidence to determine if students attain these outcomes, and to demonstrate that this evidence is used to improve teaching and learning (Ewell, 2001; Wright, 2002).

Institutions frequently perceive accreditation as driven by accountability demands instead of as a process they can channel toward improvement (Ewell, 2009). In reality, accreditation is more a hybrid of improvement and accountability because the process of self-study provides institutions with a valuable opportunity to reflect on current teaching–learning and assessment practices and to identify areas for improvement. Accreditors ask institutions to look holistically at students and their learning without mandating how institutions should go about the process. What accreditors really want is for institutions to undertake internally driven efforts to examine student learning and to use the results to improve specific teaching and learning practices (Maki, 2010).

Accreditors may not have clearly or convincingly communicated to institutions and programs the value and purpose for undertaking this work, however. Charles Powell (2013) conducted a series of interviews with accreditors and reported that they struggle to help those outside the academy understand accreditation. Yet institutions struggle too. There are recurring critiques of accreditation that no matter how often they are put to rest seem to rise again (Gaston, 2014). These enduring narratives about how colleges and universities implement accreditation can lead to assessment processes divorced from teaching and learning. Accreditors want a system that accurately captures evidence of learning within institutions of higher education. They strive to ensure that institutions have the capacity to assess learning and have properly resisted calls for a standardized approach. Furthermore, accreditors have asked institutions to align assessment with their missions and to adopt meaningful mechanisms through which success can be evaluated and its results used to improve (Brittingham et al., 2008, p. 74). All too frequently though, institutions look to accreditors to tell them what to do and to provide specific descriptions of the kinds of evidence that will meet their expectations.

Yet, with the considerable variance in the ways institutions conduct student learning outcomes assessment, accreditors provide a common ground. In a report examining the 2013 NILOA survey results by accreditation region, the similarities in assessment practices outweighed the differences (Gannon-Slater, Ikenberry, Jankowski, & Kuh, 2014). Within the past decade, regional accreditors have expanded disclosure of accreditation findings and decisions, improved efficiency through more frequent and more automated institutional reporting, clarified the distinction between their priorities on accountability and institutional improvement, and developed less intrusive and more flexible protocols (Fain, 2014b; Krzykowski & Kinser, 2014). Even so, some observers see accreditors as blocking innovation, stifling institutional autonomy, and forcing institutions to assess student learning against their will (Dill, 2014). Gaston (2014) notes that while accreditors have made significant progress, adapted to changing times, and been responsive, important areas for improvement remain. These include consensus and alignment of standards and terminology across accreditors, credibility, efficiency, agility, creativity, decisiveness, transparency, and a shared vision. These are areas that institutions would be well served to engage with as well.

A review of 10 years of HLC involvement in the assessment of student learning, prepared a decade ago (Lopez, 1999), found that institutional assessment efforts were not yet systematic and that while institutions' awareness and understanding of assessment practices had increased, lagging behind were their implementation of these practices and action on the basis of their results. Review team and self-study reports revealed frequent misunderstandings of the purpose and nature of assessment, resistance to assessment by faculty and others, and a lack of skills to undertake assessment. On the other hand, institutions where assessment was successful were found to understand assessment's value as a mechanism to focus attention on learning, to have developed ways to facilitate implementation of assessment efforts, and to assume HLC's motivation in asking for this work was to help them improve. The same situation is probably still true today. This highlights the symbiotic relationship between assessment and accreditation. Without accreditation, would colleges and universities do assessment work on their own? On the other hand, would accreditation be in any way meaningful without assessment?

In the 1980s and 1990s, many institutions failed in their initial attempts to implement an assessment program in response to new accreditation requirements. Most institutions struggled because they scrambled to get assessment processes in place without engaging in a larger dialogue as to the purpose and value of the undertaking. The accreditation process provides institutions with a framework for starting and maintaining institution-wide discussions about assessment. These discussions will occur, however, only if academic leaders and those who do assessment work reject undertaking accreditation as an act of compliance and instead intentionally use the process to systematically review opportunities for collecting and using evidence of student learning.

Institutional Roles and Responsibilities

Colleges and universities and the programs within them are well aware now—although they have not always been—that gathering and using evidence of student learning is a priority for accreditation (Maki, 2010). Most institutions have responded accordingly. Yet not all institutional and programmatic responses have led to *meaningful* assessment activity. Conversations around accreditation as a driver of assessment have mainly focused on the roles of accreditors, but few of these discussions have looked explicitly at what institutions and programs need to do to make assessment a valuable activity.

Institutions approach assessment from different perspectives, some of which are in conflict with one another. For instance, in a case study of a reaffirmation process that included a requirement for follow-up on assessment practices by the accreditor, Wayne Schmadeka (2012) referred to the process as one of "a battle to control the terms of assessment" (p. 1). In this situation, accreditors were seen as being forced by the federal government to require the institution to examine student learning.

The institution, in turn, was responding to this requirement because it feared the loss of financial aid. Both responses were about compliance, not about genuine engagement. The suggestion for resolution presented in the case study was that accreditors should specify exactly what the institution should do to meet the letter of the requirements and the institution should simply follow these directions. This is not a helpful suggestion. In the same vein, Robin Blom, Lucinda Davenport, and Brian Bowe (2012) found in a study of why programs seek specialized accreditation that while program directors saw accreditation as a means to enhance the reputation of their programs and attract better students, only 18% of them considered the self-study process itself to be useful for program improvement. Representatives of programs that chose not to be accredited remarked that this choice was made because program accreditation was costly, burdensome, and of little value.

Should the institutions and programs in these examples be held responsible for not utilizing the self-study process as an opportunity for improvement? Or do these examples represent failures by accreditors to communicate with institutions and programs about what they really want? While the answer may be a combination of both, too little attention has been paid to the importance of institutions themselves taking responsibility for assessing student learning and implementing accreditation processes in ways that build on and support internal improvement efforts. This may partly be due to a compliance mentality among institutions, but it may equally be a function of how administrative leaders react to what accreditors ask them to do.

Some participants in a NILOA survey focus group of presidents and provosts reported that the results of assessment generated in response to accreditation were rarely used in campus improvement efforts; other participants, in contrast, commented that they used accreditation as a lever to advance assessment work on campus (Kinzie, 2010). Some participants reported that accreditors' negative comments about the institutions' assessment efforts stimulated more assessment activity on campus but also that this activity was mostly to deliver what the accreditors want instead of a deeper or more reflective response. In the 2013 NILOA national survey of institutional assessment activity (Kuh et al., 2014), many provosts mentioned accreditation when asked about what they are most hopeful for and most worried about in terms of student learning outcomes assessment. More than a few expressed hopes that accreditation would be a vehicle to help faculty understand the value of work on assessment. Provosts' worries related to accreditation were concentrated in three areas: that assessment work might not be sustained following the accreditation visit, that faculty would continue to see assessment as an add-on, and that assessment work would be undertaken to meet external expectations for accountability rather than to improve teaching, learning, and institutional effectiveness. This begs the question: Under what institutional circumstances does accreditation yield meaningful assessment?

One approach to effective assessment work that is proving successful is experimenting with the Lumina Degree Qualifications Profile (DQP) and accreditation. Four regional accrediting organizations—the WASC Accrediting Commission for Community and Junior Colleges (WASC-ACCJC), HLC, SACSCOC, and the WASC Senior College and University Commission (WASC-SCUC)—recently completed institution-based projects related to the DQP. Institutions participating in these projects reported that engagement with the DQP led to campus-wide conversations about curriculum and pedagogy, many of which led to a reconceptualization of their assessment processes (Rogers, Holloway, & Priddy, 2014; Southern Association of Colleges and Schools Commission on Colleges, 2014). The DQP provided institutions with an opportunity to engage in useful conversations about teaching, learning, and assessment without feeling rushed to prepare for an upcoming accreditation visit or to get an assessment data collection system in place quickly. DQP participants were able to effectively examine why assessment work is done, what it can do for the institution and its students, and how they want to go about doing it. These are topics that are key for both effective assessment and for successful accreditation.

Point Loma Nazarene University used the DQP, for example, to plan and execute a new model for assessing five basic proficiencies required by the WASC Senior Accreditation Commission (Fulcher, Bailey, & Zack, 2013a). McKendree University used the DQP in a top-to-bottom revision of its assessment initiative (titled Assessment 2.0) that involved creating a crosswalk between the DQP, McKendree's student learning outcomes, and AAC&U LEAP outcomes. McKendree is also using the DQP to identify specific gaps in its own learning outcomes statements and to reconfigure the construction of some challenging learning outcomes such as appreciation of diversity (Eggleston, 2013). Both institutions will include this work in their upcoming reaccreditation reviews.

Other institutions have used accreditation as a mechanism to further internal improvement. North Carolina Agricultural and Technical State University (NCA&T) used the SACS accreditation process to cultivate a culture of evidence through the creation of the Institutional Effectiveness Council and internal assessment systems (Baker, 2012b). Moreover, NCA&T faculty who participated in the reaffirmation process found it useful in their specialized accreditation reports and were able to streamline reporting to specialized and regional accreditors. Capella University used its participation in the HLC Academic Quality Improvement Program (AQIP) to focus on continuous improvement through the required action projects, such as integrating assessment data into decision-making processes, documenting subsequent actions taken, and tracking the impacts of those actions (Jankowski, 2011a). The efforts of NCA&T and Capella were designed to answer the question, "Are students learning what you say they are going to learn and what the profession or discipline demand they learn for success?"

Finally, in a study of student affairs offices in several small private institutions, Beau Seagraves and Laura Dean (2010) found that accreditation was utilized as an opportunity to refine assessment practices and to better connect the student affairs division to institutional mission and goals. Accreditation served as an opportunity to illustrate previous work with assessment and as a resource to others in the institution, thus creating mutually reinforcing assessment efforts.

Some Principles for Using Accreditation in Assessment

This analysis suggests five principles that enable institutions to effectively use accreditation as an occasion to collect and use information about student learning to inform decision making and to guide institutional improvement efforts.

The Institution's Own Assessment Philosophy and Information Needs Are Critical to Meeting Accreditors' Expectations

Campus leaders too often frame assessment as a mandate imposed by accreditors and organize the work independent of regular institutional structures and processes. If faculty are told by administrators about accreditors' requirements for collecting and using assessment results, they will subsequently view this work as unconnected to their own teaching and learning responsibilities (Ewell, 1988, 2001). Campus leaders must create supportive environments for faculty to develop assessment processes that are genuinely informative and that frame the value and purpose of accreditation in terms of real questions of interest at the campus about teaching and learning.

The Accreditation Review Process Is Continuous, not Episodic

Peter Ewell (2008) argued that accreditation self-studies—done meaningfully—provide regular opportunities for institutions and programs to examine their performance. To avoid restarting assessment anew every time an accreditation review is scheduled, institutions and programs should use these opportunities to establish and maintain continuous engagement in assessment and evaluation. For institutions that value assessment work and use assessment results in their decision-making processes, accreditation is an opportunity to review and reflect on evidence gathered over many years.

Assessment at Its Best Contributes to Both Accreditation and Internal Institutional Processes

According to Trudy Banta and Catherine Palomba (2014), accreditation processes are primarily for external review; thus, they cannot substitute for meaningful, regular internal evaluation. Both accreditation and internal processes such as program review, however, require evidence of student learning to achieve their respective purposes. Equally important, faculty and staff must meaningfully engage in these processes for them to be effective (Ewell, Ikenberry, & Kuh, 2010). Engaging in assessment work only a year or two prior to the accreditation site visit reinforces impressions that assessment is fundamentally a compliance function, disconnected from core teaching and learning activities.

A Variety of Stakeholders Are Actively Involved in the Accreditation Process

Many institutions develop assessment systems to meet accreditation requirements, but the sustainability of such efforts requires building a culture based on shared values and principles (Ndoye & Parker, 2010). Instead of being the purview of one office, multiple constituencies from across campus need to be involved including faculty, students, student affairs staff (Seagraves & Dean, 2010), institutional research, and external stakeholders. If the sole object of assessment is to develop a reporting system to feed accreditation, disengagement with the process will likely result because few members of the wider academic community will see the exercise as important.

As with Assessment Work, the Accreditation Process Is a Means to an End

Accreditation can be used by institutions and programs as a lever to stimulate wider campus conversations about teaching and learning (see Chapter 3). Banta and Palomba (2014) present inspiring stories of institutions that used negative accreditation reviews as opportunities to reflect on and redesign their assessment processes. Among the NILOA case studies of institutions that successfully used assessment results to improve, several are accounts of institutions turning assessment efforts around or, motivated by an upcoming accreditation review, developing meaningful campus-focused processes (Baker, Jankowski, Provezis, & Kinzie, 2012). The lesson here is that while accreditation may serve as a catalyst for assessment, how individuals within institutions and programs frame the specifics of what they do in response to this catalyst will decisively affect the success of their assessment efforts.

Concluding Thoughts

Would assessment work be as varied and widespread in U.S. colleges and universities today without accreditation, both regional and specialized? Almost certainly not. The history of institutions and programs engaging in assessment to date has predominantly been a story about responding to external forces. Assessment has yet to gain broad traction as something other than what is done just before accreditors arrive and forgotten soon after they leave. Yet institutions that engage in assessment because they genuinely see value in understanding student experiences and student learning are able to supply evidence to satisfy accreditation requirements *without* sacrificing internal improvement efforts. Such institutions are able to move beyond a posture of compliance by implementing assessment in a manner that is genuinely useful. The lesson is simple but profound: institutions that begin with improvement in mind get information that can simultaneously serve accreditation, while those that begin with accreditation in mind do not usually get information that is useful for improvement.

Accreditation is a partnership. If institutions and programs do not communicate the benefits of the process, accreditors on their own will be unable to respond to the many charges of ineffectiveness that have been leveled at them. Accreditors also need to acknowledge that institutions and programs want to be recognized by accreditors for their efforts to implement assessment. Many institutions just now encountering assessment through accreditation find they are not doing enough fast enough, so they need reassurance from accreditors to proceed with confidence. If institutions are not given this kind of reassurance and the time needed to develop a more genuine culture of assessment, they can easily slip into short-term responses dominated by compliance. Thus, the way forward does not involve pointing fingers either at institutions and programs or at accreditors. It instead requires finding ways to work together to build the knowledge necessary to enhance teaching and learning.

8

THE BIGGER PICTURE

STUDENT LEARNING OUTCOMES
ASSESSMENT AND EXTERNAL ENTITIES

Jillian Kinzie, Stanley O. Ikenberry, and Peter T. Ewell

For what you see and hear depends a good deal on where you are standing; it also depends on what sort of person you are.

—C.S. Lewis, *The Magician's Nephew*

SOCIETY HAS GOOD REASON to be concerned about the quality of higher education. What citizens know and can do is crucial to a robust economy, a strong democracy, and the well-being of individuals, local communities, and the larger community. For this and many other reasons, entities external to the campus—we focus on four—have vested interests in the quality of U.S. higher education institutions.

The two external entities we look at first in this chapter are state governments and the federal government. Governments have a huge stake—economic and otherwise—in the higher education enterprise. We discuss next an external entity comprising a variety of associations and organizations that emerged over the last century to represent the interests of various higher education sectors and to facilitate collaboration among colleges and universities. These organizations help shape education policy, especially at the national level. Last, we discuss philanthropic organizations, a fourth external entity with long-standing, legitimate interest in seeing that the nation and a broad range of stakeholders are served well by colleges and universities.

Depending on the issue, these four external entities frequently work independently to pursue their interests. Occasionally they collaborate. Sometimes they find themselves at odds with one another. Whether performing solo or as a troupe, over time, they have directly and indirectly influenced why and how colleges and universities engage in student learning outcomes assessment.

The influence of these external entities has ebbed and flowed over time, but in recent years their interests have coalesced around college completion, college costs, and educational quality. The most persistent pressure is for colleges and universities to be more accountable for college outcomes, although there is no clear consensus as to what these should be. One effort toward this end is the Obama administration's attempt to create a new federal system for rating colleges that features persistence and graduation rates, college costs, gainful employment, and loan repayment (Golden, 2013). Meanwhile, congressional hearings and the next reauthorization of the Higher Education Opportunity Act may fundamentally change the role of accrediting agencies that find themselves at the hazardous intersection of shifting government policies and expanding campus interests and academic priorities (Chapter 7). Colleges and universities are also feeling the push from philanthropic organizations such as the Bill and Melinda Gates Foundation and Lumina Foundation, among others, which have intensified their efforts to promote access and completion.

For more than a decade, these external forces have prompted higher education institutions and organizations to search for alternative ways to gauge student learning, quantify other college outcomes, and convey this information more effectively to government agencies and the public. Indeed, as noted in Chapter 1, these forces—led by accreditation—have exerted substantial influence on the forms and functions of learning outcomes assessment work on most college and university campuses. In doing so, however, these same forces have engendered a compliance mentality on the part of institutions that has hampered the use of evidence for internal problem solving. A sharp increase between 2009 and 2013 in the number of student learning measures that campuses use (Kuh, Jankowski, Ikenberry, & Kinzie, 2014) suggests an intentional effort on the part of hundreds of colleges and universities to obtain—through more data—a richer, more nuanced picture of student learning in response to persistent and mounting pressure from critics. Results from the National Institute for Learning Outcomes Assessment (NILOA)'s 2013 survey of provosts show that important assessment drivers—especially for public and for-profit institutions—are external pressures from government officials, statewide coordinating boards and state and federal mandates, and state-level funding formulas, foundation grant priorities, and institutional commitments such as the Voluntary System of Accountability (VSA).

This chapter discusses the role of these four external forces in shaping the student learning outcomes assessment agenda. We begin by reviewing the history of state policy related to assessment since 1987. This historical perspective is important because states have changed direction many times during this period and will almost certainly do so again. The second section of the chapter provides a parallel history of the evolution of federal policy up to the present. While most federal influence has been indirect through institutional accreditation, far more intrusive initiatives remind institutions that these forces can emerge with little warning and can have significant impacts on institutional practice. The chapter's third section considers the role of higher education organizations including those known as the Big Six: the American Council on Education (ACE), the American Association of Community Colleges (AACC), the Association of Public Land-grant Universities (APLU), the American Association of State Colleges and Universities (AASCU), the Association of American Universities (AAU), and the National Association of Independent Colleges and Universities (NAICU). In addition to these, many higher education membership organizations have been influential in areas related to assessment and educational quality, including the Association of American Colleges & Universities (AAC&U), the Council on Independent Colleges (CIC), and the Association of Governing Boards of Universities and Colleges (AGB), to mention just a few. In the chapter's fourth section, we explore the role of philanthropic organizations in advancing assessment work on campuses. We close the chapter by summarizing what institutions can do to respond to the broad array of government, association, and private foundation initiatives in ways that heighten student success and institutional performance.

The State-Level View

The first state assessment mandates emerged in 1987 largely in response to an influential report issued the year before by the National Governors Association (1986)—*Time for Results*. While the recommendations contained in this report affected only public institutions and were influential only for about a decade, they provided important stimulus and support for campus-based assessment at a time when its practice was just taking off (Ewell, 2002, 2005; Ewell & Boyer, 1988). Leading the responses from most states were policy proposals for common outcomes testing for college students that drew on states' K–12 testing experiences. Reinforcing this tendency was the fact that the few extant state assessment programs for public colleges and universities at the time—while having different characteristics and purposes—were test based (Ewell, 2002). Florida's College Level Academic Skills Test (CLAST) was a rising junior examination put in place largely to manage transitions from community colleges to public four-year institutions in a state that had invested heavily in a two-plus-two approach in the 1970s. Tennessee, then a pioneer in this area, had a performance funding system that based some portion of resource allocations to public institutions on learning outcomes (along with other dimensions of performance). Mandatory student writing assessments in such systems as the Georgia Regents and the California State University, meanwhile, offered additional contemporary examples of common assessments administered in public university settings. These precedents made it likely that state authorities would open any conversation about assessment with a testing proposal—not so much because they felt this approach was appropriate for accountability in higher education as because it was the only approach they knew.

During this time, college and university leaders were gaining experience with a reasonable alternative to state mandated assessments in their emerging work with assessment for improvement—advocated in *Involvement in Learning,* the final report of the blue ribbon Study Group on the Conditions of Excellence in American Higher Education (National Institute of Education, 1984). If public institutions were to undertake serious local assessment programs, use the results to make visible improvements, and report publicly on what they found, surely the state's need for learning-based accountability could be met in tandem with these activities. In the relatively benign accountability climate of the mid-1980s, such a bargain seemed like a good idea to many public officials. Sometimes, state leaders themselves proposed such initiatives. In Virginia and Missouri, for example, the initiatives came from the State Higher Education Executive Officers (SHEEO) agency, while in states like Colorado and South Carolina, they were written directly into law (Ewell & Boyer, 1988). Sometimes, too, they were the result of protracted negotiations, as in the state of Washington where an original testing proposal was converted to a full-scale pilot and was then dropped when it became clear that the resulting program was neither useful nor cheap (Ewell, 2005a).

Whatever their origins, by 1990 such *institution-centered* state assessment initiatives had been adopted by some two-thirds of the states (Ewell, Finney, & Lenth, 1990). Virtually all of them first required public institutions to prepare assessment plans for approval by the governing or coordinating board. Within these plans, institutions were to (1) develop statements of student learning outcomes for general education and for each major program, (2) propose concrete evidence-gathering mechanisms on student performance aligned with these goals, (3) create organizational pathways to use the resulting information to improve curriculum and pedagogy, and (4) prepare a public report summarizing both assessment results and what was done with them. Over time, about half the states adopting this approach established additional funding to pay for the process.

By the early 1990s, however, the states were facing increasingly challenging financial conditions and could no longer afford the levels of funding and staffing needed to support mandated assessment. Another reason for disinvestment was the fact that regional accreditors, partly in response to federal pressure, were increasingly adopting requirements for institutional assessment of learning (Ewell, 2005a). Since then, the pattern of state influence on assessment work in higher education has shifted. In most states, with adoption of the institution-centered paradigm for policy, although assessment requirements remained nominally on the books, in practice, states rarely knew whether these requirements were fulfilled because they no longer had the staff capacity to review institutional reports. Meanwhile, some states changed their approaches multiple times. In the late 1980s, for example, South Dakota began a statewide program of testing in generic skills and the major field (modeled on the pioneering institutional assessment program at Northeast Missouri State University), abandoned it in the mid-1990s for an institution-centered approach, and then reestablished a testing program that is still in place. The current pattern of state assessment requirements, revealed in a 2010 NCHEMS inventory of state policies (Zis, Boeke, & Ewell, 2010), all of which apply only to public institutions, is the result of these shifts.

Five states (Kentucky, Oklahoma, South Dakota, Tennessee, and West Virginia) have policies that require standardized testing (Zis et al., 2010). Various tests are used including the ACT Collegiate Assessment of Academic Proficiency (CAAP), the ETS Proficiency Profile, and the Collegiate Learning Assessment), as well as some ETS Major Field Achievement tests.

Although they all require testing, the five state programs are quite different. Oklahoma and Tennessee, for example, allow institutions a choice of standardized tests. Furthermore, Tennessee uses test scores, together with some two dozen additional measures, to drive its performance funding system. South Dakota is unique in that all students must achieve a given level of performance on the ACT CAAP as a condition of graduation. The other two state programs operate purely as a reporting mechanism but have no consequences for institutions for poor or exemplary performance. Similarly, six states (Georgia, Kentucky, Minnesota, Rhode Island, South Dakota, and Tennessee) have mandated student survey requirements. All use the National Survey of Student Engagement (NSSE) or the Community College Survey of Student Engagement (CCSSE), except for Minnesota, which allows institutions a choice of surveys. Tennessee, which also requires surveys of alumni and employers, uses the results of all surveys to help drive performance funding. Finally, 15 states employ common tests for placement in developmental instruction in writing and mathematics, and a dozen of these have established common cut scores designating "college-ready."

A total of 21 states have policies in place that do not rely on institutions adopting a common assessment instrument. Instead, they allow institutions to choose their own methods and, in most cases, to establish their own student learning outcomes as well. Following the classic institution-centered approach, all require public reporting at either annual or biennial intervals. In many cases, these requirements are embedded in a broader state statute or policy governing planning or program review. Once again, there is a great deal of variety here. Virginia has established a common set of statewide student learning outcomes statements, and the policy strongly suggests that institutions adopt a value-added approach; however, the choice of assessment method is left to institutions. The Missouri Department of Higher Education requires institutions to collect data benchmarked to the 50th and 80th percentiles on a nationally normed generic skills examination (as well as reporting scored on licensure examinations and pass rates on national examinations in the major fields), but the choice of instrument is left to institutions.

State higher education coordinating boards and systems also enacted performance funding schemes that induced campus assessment activity. As an approach to encourage colleges and universities to focus on the extent to which students are achieving desired outcomes at acceptable levels or rates and to fund institutions accordingly, performance funding has gained greater support from numerous state legislatures, from governmental organizations such as the National Governors Association and also from the Obama administration (Cavanaugh & Garland, 2012). Various models exist, but most are imposed by policymakers to increase transparency and accountability and to steer institutional behavior in ways state authorities deem in the public interest. Most performance funding approaches are designed to apply a fairly limited number of measures—for instance, persistence or completion rates—to all institutions in a system. The Pennsylvania State System of Higher Education (PASSHE) adopted a flexible approach that recognized differential missions and strategic directions. All 14 PASSHE universities share 10 required indicators that reflect core principles, including that students complete the intended credential; that students, faculty, and graduates reflect the racial/ethnic and economic diversity of the Commonwealth; and that private dollars are raised to increase universities' ability to meet their missions. Additional performance measures focus on institutions' missions and strategic plans, testing results (e.g., CLA, CAAP, or ETS Proficiency Profile scores) and student experiences with diversity and inclusion (as reflected in combined scores on applicable NSSE items). According to John Cavanaugh and Peter Garland (2012), under PASSHE, the targeted outcomes improved and accountability was strengthened.

Probably the most ambitious current state-sponsored initiative in assessment began in 2013. The Multi-State Collaborative (MSC) to Advance Learning Outcomes Assessment, sponsored by SHEEO and AAC&U and supported by the Bill and Melinda Gates Foundation, involves nine states (Connecticut, Indiana, Kentucky, Massachusetts, Minnesota, Missouri, Oregon, Rhode Island, and Utah) and is centered on creating state- and institution-level benchmarks for selected student learning outcomes including written communication and quantitative reasoning. MSC's approach avoids the use of standardized tests by scoring authentic student artifacts (student responses to actual classroom assignments) at participating institutions in each of the nine states using AAC&U Valid Assessment of Learning in Undergraduate Education (VALUE) rubrics. The initiative is based on a prior demonstration project in Massachusetts completed in 2013 and is undertaking a full-scale pilot involving almost 70 institutions. Each participating campus is expected to select a minimum of 75 to 100 de-identified artifacts per outcome drawn from students who are nearing the end of their undergraduate programs, spread as widely across faculty and disciplines as possible to ensure representativeness and scored by teams of faculty members from participating institutions trained on the VALUE rubrics. The MSC initiative is clearly "rooted in campus/system collaboration, authentic student work, and faculty curriculum development and teaching activity" (http://www.sheeo.org/projects/multi-state-collaborative-msc-advance-learning-outcomes-assessment). Eschewing reductive measures and ratings systems, MSC draws on faculty judgments of students' work and aggregates results in ways that allow for benchmarking across institutions and states. Moreover, consistent with the theme of this volume, MSC is designed to provide data for external accountability—but in a manner that faculty value and with externally benchmarked assessment results that can be used for internal improvement.

Some states have also been interested in seeing that institutions in the state develop a greater capacity for assessment work. Consistent with the institution-centered approach that requires public institutions to engage in assessment using their own goals and methods, a number of states have established organizations and conferences to develop technical capacity. Among the most active of these statewide organizations are the Virginia Assessment Group (VAG), the Washington Assessment Group (WAG), and the New Mexico Higher Education Assessment Association (NMHEAA). These associations, and their sponsored conferences, not only help develop institutional assessment capacity to meet state requirements but also help institutions meet the increasingly demanding requirements of their regional accreditors. Through association initiatives like these, states have come to recognize explicitly that accreditors will induce institutions to engage in assessment in a manner that comports well with state policy. Accordingly, states like West Virginia and North Dakota have within the last decade engaged third-party assessment consultants to help prepare their campuses to meet the assessment requirements of their regional accrediting organization (Ewell, 2011).

As is apparent from this review, current state assessment initiatives show considerable diversity. Moreover, states reverse or change policies related to assessment fairly frequently, requiring institutions to be flexible in responding to changing external requirements.

The Federal Policy Perspective

Unlike the states that fund and govern public institutions and thus have a direct incentive to see that graduates meet or exceed established levels of knowledge and proficiency, the interests of the federal government are much more diffuse. In 1987, the U.S. secretary of education called for accrediting organizations to place primacy on ensuring that the institutions they accredit collect valid and reliable evidence of student academic achievement as a condition of being recognized by the Department of Education as a gatekeeper for institutional eligibility to receive federal financial aid funds. This declaration was an important stimulus for all colleges and universities to pay attention to assessment (Chapter 7). From a financial point of view, the federal interest is ensuring that federal investment in student financial aid is effective by enabling students to graduate on time, obtain employment, and earn salaries that will permit them to contribute to the national economy and, not coincidentally, pay off the student loan debt that they have incurred. This is at least one obvious reason that gainful employment has always been a centerpiece of federal policy. Indeed, the central authorizing language of the Higher Education Opportunity Act (2013)—Part H, Section 496 (a) (5) (A)—does not mention learning at all, only performance on state licensing examinations, course completion, and job placement rates. The Obama administration's interest in a rating system focused on persistence and graduation, employment, and loan repayment is consistent with this traditional focus.

Nevertheless, Part H does establish the conditions for federal oversight of institutional accreditation, which is the instrument that the federal government uses to influence standards of quality for student academic achievement and, more directly, to establish eligibility for federal student financial aid. This language, and its predecessors in earlier reauthorizations from 1987, set the basic framework that has shaped the expectations of recognized accreditors since that time.

One recent attempt to extend federal influence came in 2006, in the wake of the Spellings Commission report (Commission on the Future of Higher Education, 2006)—which, although it did not explicitly recommend standardized testing, prominently featured as effective ways to demonstrate quality through a number of standardized examinations, including the CLA, the ACT CAAP, and the ETS Proficiency Profile. Under Spellings' leadership, the U.S. Department of Education began efforts to establish new federal rules requiring more explicitness about assessment requirements from recognized accreditors. Such haste in rulemaking was unprecedented because the Higher Education Act (HEA) had just been reauthorized a few years before and the Department of Education generally begins regulation well after a change in the law. This attempt to establish new HEA rules in the middle of a rulemaking cycle was ultimately unsuccessful, but it did signal a new and more aggressive accountability stance, which did not go unnoticed by regional accreditors and institutions of higher education.

Still, the impact on college and university campuses was evident. Some higher education institutions voluntarily put in place at least some of the measures that the Spellings Commission recommended in the form of a VSA—a report card initiative that included making public standardized test score results using a choice of one of the three examples noted in the Spellings Commission report.

While federal influence on learning outcomes assessment has been largely through the regulation of regional accreditation, federal action has occasionally ventured into other areas. By 1990, the U.S. Department of Education's Fund for the Improvement of Postsecondary Education (FIPSE) had invested in nearly 30 projects on student learning outcomes assessment (Marcus, Cobb, & Shoenberg, 1993). Two major projects funded in 1986, the University of Tennessee, Knoxville's Assessment Resource Center and the Assessment Forum of the American Association for Higher Education (AAHE), significantly expanded expertise and resources on assessment by contributing essential resources and opportunities for convening assessment leaders at conferences. Other projects supported by FIPSE resulted in insights about the limitations of standardized tests and the value of embedded assessment, the potential for a national cooperative test-development project, a statewide consortium approach to meeting a legislative mandate for assessment, and approaches to assessment within academic disciplines and in general education (Banta, 1991; Marcus et al., 1993). FIPSE projects explored the utility of a variety of assessment strategies and instruments and ultimately contributed to making outcomes assessment a common feature of the higher education landscape.

One concrete federal proposal about learning outcomes was nearly approved in the 1990s. The assessment ramifications of adopting the National Education Goals came just short of creating a federal learning outcomes testing program (Ewell, 2002). Formed in 1990 by the states' governors and the George H. W. Bush administration, the National Education Goals Panel (2002) established the nation's first objectives for collegiate learning and called for the development of valid and reliable assessments to track progress in critical thinking, communication, and problem solving. Adoption of the goals also signaled the beginning of a significant, although short-lived, period of aggressive moves by the U.S. Department of Education in the realm of postsecondary accountability, marked by initiatives such as the Student Right-to-Know Act (1990), which required the first public reporting of graduation rates.

Because a central tenet of the National Education Goals was to measure progress in attaining these goals over the next decade, a reliable standardized way of assessing these collegiate objectives was needed. To explore the operational specifications of assessment of communications and critical thinking skills, the National Center for Education Statistics (1992) convened a series of Study Design Panels that ultimately resulted in a call directed at the nation's test makers to build such an assessment. In early 1993, however, a new majority-Republican Congress saw this initiative as big-government overreach and ended it. Since then, similar calls for (and fears of) a national test for higher education have periodically arisen, providing an unsettling reminder that accountability, in one form or another, has been intimately entwined with assessment from its birth and is very likely to be so entwined in its future. Higher education's fundamental challenge in assessment remains essentially the same now as when the assessment movement began—that is, how to reconcile demands for compliance and accountability on the one hand with institutions' primary focus on the other hand being to harness evidence of student learning in ways that enable students and institutions to thrive and improve (Ewell, 2009).

The National Organization Picture

According to Alexis de Tocqueville (1835), America is a nation of joiners. His observation holds true of American colleges and universities as well. A large majority of faculty members and academic leaders from colleges and universities with similar academic missions, academic programs, and challenges join higher education associations that reflect the needs and priorities of their dues-paying members while at the same time helping them respond to federal policy requirements and the shifting national agenda. These organizations provide convenient venues for members to share perspectives and best practices as well as early warning systems for learning about and responding to national issues and demands. Most important from a policy perspective, national associations enable colleges and universities to collectively address common challenges and influence federal policy. The many higher education associations and interest groups offer multiple avenues through which the nation's highly decentralized, diverse higher education enterprise can attempt to reconcile institutional programs and values with broader national priorities and accountability demands.

In recent years, educational quality and student learning outcomes assessment have consistently appeared in higher education association conference agendas, publications, press releases, and special topic meetings. The earliest involvements of these associations in student learning outcomes assessment were in response to federally sponsored reports calling for education reform, including the National Commission on Excellence in Education's *A Nation at Risk* (1983), the National Endowment for the Humanities (NEH) report *To Reclaim a Legacy* (Bennett,

1984), and the National Institute of Education's *Involvement in Learning* (1984). Collectively, these reports made claims about needed curricular content and educational processes and the need for improved quality of teaching and student learning. The reports also urged faculty and academic administrators to agree on and disseminate statements of the knowledge, skills, and attitudes required for graduation and to assess systematically whether expectations for student learning were met. In general, higher education associations accepted these reports' emphasis on the need to improve undergraduate education, and several issued reports of their own on the subject and attempted to guide member institutions in their efforts to assess student learning outcomes.

An example of an early call for attention to educational quality by a national higher education association was the 1985 report by the Association of American Colleges (AAC; now the AAC&U) *Integrity in the College Curriculum: A Report to the Academic Community*. It described the work of AAC's Project on Redefining the Meaning and Purpose of a Baccalaureate Degree, conceding the lack of integration, coherence, and rationale in the curriculum and issuing a call to action to colleges and universities to examine the structure of the curriculum and to commit to assessing student learning and improving the quality of teaching. In *College: The Undergraduate Experience in America,* the Carnegie Foundation for the Advancement of Teaching, and its president, Ernest Boyer (1987), endorsed AAC's view and identified more specific problems weakening the curriculum—including inadequate conditions of teaching and learning and misplaced faculty priorities—and called for greater accountability for what and how students learn.

Another higher education association involved in the early stages of the assessment movement was the AAHE, which with the National Institute of Education (NIE) cosponsored the First National Conference on Assessment in Higher Education, held in Columbia, South Carolina, in fall 1985 (Ewell, 2002). Discussions at this conference focused on the recently issued reports and what colleges and universities ought to learn from the press for accountability and improvement. The assessment of learning was presented in these discussions, interestingly, as a form of scholarship— that is, faculty were expected to engage in assessment as an integral part of their everyday work, using tools from educational measurement to establish valid ways to gather information to improve curriculum and pedagogy. The conference discussions exposed the dearth of appropriate assessment tools, a weak foundation of assessment definitions, and a lack of institutional experience about how to carry out assessment practice. The acknowledgment of gaps in assessment experience resulted in the formal establishment of assessment conferences including, with support from the Fund for the Improvement of Postsecondary Education, the annual AAHE Assessment Forum (from 1987 to 2005), which provided regular convenings for scholarly presentation, professional networking, idea sharing, and promotion of student learning assessment. AAHE also issued a range of publications on assessment, from conference papers to resource guides (AAHE, 1997).

In 1992, AAHE released "Nine Principles of Good Practice for Assessing Student Learning" (http://www.learningoutcomeassessment.org/Principle sofAssessment.html), developed by 12 prominent scholar-practitioners of the movement, proposing a set of foundational principles for conceiving and executing assessment programs in colleges and universities. Notably, these principles have recently been reviewed in light of current assessment practice and have been found still relevant (Hutchings, Ewell, & Banta, n.d.; Kinzie, Jankowski, & Provezis, 2014.) Since these early responses to national reports about assessment, accountability, and improvement, most higher education organizations have consistently encouraged their member institutions to actively engage in student learning outcomes assessment and educational improvement.

The American Council on Education is probably the country's most visible higher education association, in part because it brings together and speaks on behalf of an unusually large and diverse academic community. ACE's more than 1,800 member colleges and universities enroll about 80% of the nation's college students. As the organization representing the presidents of U.S.-accredited, degree-granting colleges and universities—including two- and four-year institutions, private and public universities, and nonprofit and for-profit entities—ACE brings together college and university representatives from various sectors to tackle common challenges including questions of academic quality and integrity. Defining the purposes and aims of education, gathering evidence of student and institutional performance, and finding ways to use that information to strengthen performance are also part of ACE's agenda. More directly, ACE provides a national platform for discussion and debate on learning outcomes assessment and the appropriate use of evidence. In 1995 and again in 2012, ACE convened national conversations on the present condition and future directions of institutional and academic program accreditation in the United States and issued reports recommending the strengthening of the processes of accreditation and the quality of evidence on which consequential accreditation decisions are reached (ACE, 2012b). ACE also coordinates the Washington Higher Education Secretariat (WHES; also called the Secretariat), a voluntary forum for chief executive officers of nearly 50 national higher education associations serving different significant sectors or functions in postsecondary education. College costs, learning outcomes, and assessment were regular items on the Secretariat's 2013–2014 agendas (http://www.whes.org/meetings.html).

Activity in higher education associations around student learning outcomes assessment heated up with the release of the Spellings Commission report (Commission on the Future of Higher Education, 2006), which warned that colleges and universities were failing to prepare students for the twenty-first-century workplace and called for urgent attention to issues of access, affordability, quality, accountability, and innovation. The associations responded by trying to frame the dialogue around the challenges confronting undergraduate education and the need for change. *Addressing the Challenges Facing American Undergraduate Education. A Letter to Our Members: Next Steps* (http://aetl.umd.edu/NASULGC%20 Challenges_%20092106.pdf), issued jointly by the Big Six, enumerated seven challenges confronting higher education, including the imperative to improve student learning and the expectation of accountability for education outcomes, and specified how the associations would help their member institutions address these challenges. The most demonstrable aid came from AASCU and APLU in the form of the VSA, which provides online, accessible, understandable, and comparable institutional information (http://www.voluntarysystem.org/index.cfm). NILOA's evaluation of VSA, referenced in Chapter 1, found that people who visited the VSA website spent a good deal of time looking at the cost calculator and graduation rate data but not much looking at student learning outcomes information (Jankowski et al., 2012). This finding underscores the challenge in institutional transparency efforts to make student learning outcomes meaningful and understandable to a variety of end users (Chapters 1 and 10).

Among the sector-based presidential associations, APLU and AASCU have been the most direct about the need for gathering evidence of student learning and sharing it publically to strengthen public confidence and support, as evidenced by sponsoring VSA. Similarly, members of the American Association of Community Colleges at two-year campuses across the nation have been involved in launching AACC's own voluntary institutional report card—the Voluntary Framework of Accountability (VFA). In a 2013 survey of assessment practice at member institutions, AAU found that research universities employing a wide range of methods to assess undergraduate learning provided examples of how such information has been used to improve student learning (http://www.aau.edu/WorkArea/DownloadAsset.aspx?id=14849). Although AAU and NAICU have been far more cautious about declaring the need to gather and make public information on student and institutional performance, they have worked with their members to grapple with issues and challenges related to student learning assessment.

In July 2013, the Big Six higher education associations partnered with regional accrediting organizations to endorse new "Principles for Effective Assessment of Student Achievement" (http://www.wascsenior.org/files/principles_for_effective_assessment_of_student_achievement.pdf), an outcome of a meeting of presidents of regional accrediting commissions and provosts of public and private universities. The endorsement emphasizes the need to assess student achievement in ways congruent with institutions' missions and specified the importance of providing evidence of student learning through academic performance evaluations and post-college outcomes. Institutions are encouraged to use the principles to evaluate their assessment policies and procedures and accrediting commissions are encouraged to evaluate their assessment standards—with the aim of using the shared principles to facilitate continued cooperation and collaboration between these two allied higher education sectors.

AAC&U has perhaps the most enduring commitment to developing and advancing assessment practices that deepen, integrate, and demonstrate student learning. For decades, it has led the higher education community in a search for ways to advance assessment practice by advocating learning-centered assessment policies, supporting campus work to develop meaningful assessment approaches, and experimenting with ePortfolios, rubrics, and other collaborative assessment activities (Schneider, 2009). Through its VALUE initiative, the organization worked with faculty members and assessment teams across the country to develop a set of rubrics through which institutions could evaluate students' capacity. Recognition of the VALUE rubrics as a way to achieve direct assessment of student learning has grown exponentially since their release in fall 2010, and hundreds of institutions have explored the rubrics as part of their assessment tool kit (Rhodes & Finley, 2013). Another example is AAC&U's Quality Collaboratives project, an effort by teams from two- and four-year institutions, with the active involvement of the SHEEO organization in nine states (California, Indiana, Kentucky, Massachusetts, North Dakota, Oregon, Utah, Virginia, and Wisconsin), to promote more efficient and effective patterns of transfer by aligning expectations of student learning outcomes across sectors through Lumina Foundation's Degree Qualifications Profile (DQP). This is a good example of a win-win approach with respect to accountability and improvement because, especially within participating two-year institutions, the influence of the state in aligning transfer expectations generates significant campus-level engagement in using the AAC&U VALUE rubrics to assess student learning.

In addition, with support from the Teagle Foundation and the Council for Higher Education Accreditation (CHEA), AAC&U helped create the New Leadership Alliance for Student Learning and Accountability (2008), which promulgated guidelines for institutional assessment and accountability. Indeed, through the sustained national focus reflected in its annual program and a large number of targeted initiatives over an extended period of time, AAC&U has been a pacesetter in seeing the need for gathering and using evidence of what students know and are able to do and in empowering institutions to engage in this work.

Also worthy of special note is the work of the CIC, an association of nonprofit independent colleges and universities that for over 50 years has worked to support and advance the contributions of private institutions. A key part of the CIC agenda focuses on programs designed to help member institutions assess and improve the quality of education on their campuses—making it a leader in the area of learning outcomes assessment. CIC campuses were early participants in NSSE to assess educational quality and in the use of a standardized test—the CLA—as a means to gauge and improve learning. More recently, a significant number of CIC campuses joined together to work with Lumina Foundation's DQP as a framework for assessing and improving student performance.

The Association of Governing Boards (2010) has become increasingly active in issues of academic quality (Ewell, 2012). The only national association serving the interests and needs of academic governing boards and campus CEOs and other senior-level campus administrators on issues related to higher education governance and leadership, AGB has featured learning outcomes assessment at its national meetings and has issued proclamations and policies suggesting standards and best practices for governance. NILOA's 2013 provost survey results indicated that since 2009 the influence of governing boards in student learning outcomes assessment has increased, perhaps reflecting greater awareness of governing boards regarding matters of educational quality (Kuh et al., 2014). In 2011, with funding from the Teagle Foundation, AGB launched a two-year project to develop a set of tools and resources for college and university boards to work more effectively with campus leaders and faculty on monitoring the assessment and improvement of student learning and academic quality (Chaffee, 2014; Ewell, 2014).

No discussion of the assessment of student learning and the impact of higher education associations would be complete without mention of CHEA's role. As the largest institutional membership association in the

United States, with approximately 3,000 degree-granting colleges and universities, it is a national voice for higher education accreditation. Its most central role is the review and recognition of accrediting agencies. While CHEA recognition does not supplant recognition by the federal government (which carries out its own independent recognition process, described in Chapter 7), CHEA examines emerging issues in accreditation and quality assurance—and does this more directly with the oversight and coordination of the institution and program accreditors that interface with U.S. higher education institutions. CHEA also provides resources and convenes campuses to focus on issues of educational quality and to explore approaches for gathering evidence of learning outcomes and institutional effectiveness. Most important, CHEA offers an independent voice for academic self-regulation that is responsible to member academic institutions—not to government.

So far, scholarly societies have not been as actively involved as institutional membership organizations in promoting student learning outcomes assessment work. According to David Glenn (2010), disciplinary associations, for example, in biology, political science, and history have fairly well-established, large-scale programs aimed at assessing and improving the quality of instruction in their fields, and most also publish journals dedicated to teaching and learning. Yet these associations are often ignored in national conversations about assessment and educational quality. Faculty members, who may not invest much in institution-level learning outcomes assessment projects, likely trust their own disciplinary associations. National disciplinary conversations about how to understand and assess student learning, for example, prompted meaningful assessment projects at Villanova's college of engineering and Swarthmore's classics department (2010). Pat Hutchings (2011) noted that the lack of disciplinary association recognition in student learning outcomes assessment can partly be explained by assessment's focus on cross-cutting outcomes like critical thinking, resulting in less assessment attention on students' knowledge and abilities within particular fields. The involvement of disciplinary associations in student learning outcomes assessment may in fact be just the thing to deepen faculty involvement in assessment and to generate greater evidence of student learning.

The Philanthropic Frame

The philanthropic community, often in collaboration with national higher education associations and other partners, has played a major role in advancing the student learning outcomes assessment agenda.

Foundations such as Lumina Foundation, the Teagle Foundation, the Bill and Melinda Gates Foundation, and the Carnegie Corporation of New York have supported projects emanating from higher education associations to enhance assessment at member institutions. For example, Lumina Foundation along with the Gates Foundation has underwritten AAC&U's work in related areas.

Lumina also provided resources to help AASCU and APLU develop the VSA and also sponsored the development and implementation of the DQP. Lumina, along with the Carnegie Corporation and Teagle, provided support to launch NILOA in 2008, and Lumina has also supported NILOA to track and document institutional experiments with the DQP and Tuning USA. The latter initiative, bringing together faculty members from diverse institutions to construct degree profiles around what students in particular fields should be expected to learn, is a good example of how foundations have helped expand conversations about student learning outcomes.

Lumina Foundation was also a major investor in Achieving the Dream (AtD), a multiyear initiative to help community colleges build a culture of evidence by using student records and other data to examine students' performance over time and to identify barriers to academic progress. Participating community colleges developed intervention strategies designed to improve student outcomes, conducted further research on student progress, and brought effective programs to scale. Evaluations of AtD suggest that through their involvement institutions developed more consistent use of data but that real change in student outcomes occurs only when improved programs and services meaningfully touch significant number of students (Rutschow, 2011).

On a more modest scale, although no less effective, have been the resources of the Teagle Foundation in enhancing assessment capacity among liberal arts institutions and facilitating multi-institutional assessment initiatives such as the Wabash National Study, housed at the Center for Inquiry in the Liberal Arts at Wabash College (which has also benefited from significant support from the Lilly Endowment). Teagle's approach to grant making is grounded in knowledge about how college students learn and is designed to increase institutional capacity to bring student engagement and learning to higher levels. Teagle's signature Outcomes and Assessment initiatives have demonstrated the foundation's conviction that nothing has as much potential to affect educational experience as a sustained and systematic assessment of what and how students learn (http://www.asha.org/academic/assessment/#sthash.pM5AciNI.dpuf). Its early significant grant initiatives included the Systematic Improvement of

Student Learning at Liberal Arts Colleges and the Faculty Driven Value Added Assessment collaboratives. These two projects provided hundreds of institutions opportunities to work independently and in collaboration to test approaches for assessing critical thinking and writing skills, creativity, collaborative abilities, and ethical judgment and to build needed capacity to use evidence to improve student learning. For example, Kalamazoo College used Teagle support to test new ways of using NSSE and CLA results to stimulate more vigorous inquiries and to enrich faculty deliberations about how to bring student learning to higher levels.

Committed to sparking meaningful institutional action, the Teagle Foundation funded even more institutions through its Engaging Evidence grants. These projects helped institutions develop policies and programs focused on student learning in ways that tied into the processes by which colleges and universities govern themselves, make decisions, set priorities, allocate resources, reward performance, and use information about student learning. Under this initiative, CIC created a network of more than 40 independent colleges and universities systemically trained to more fully use their assessment data to improve student learning. As a result, participating institutions made significant adjustments in curriculum, pedagogy, and student support. Their work revealed important lessons about engaging faculty and the value of a collaborative approach that includes administrators and faculty leaders and that is grounded in interinstitutional collaboration for institutional change (Council of Independent Colleges, 2014).

Some of the most extensive work supported by higher education foundations has involved collaborations with higher education associations to advance assessment and quality improvement in higher education. The aforementioned AAC&U Quality Collaboratives project nicely illustrates this point. Launched with support from Lumina Foundation and the William and Flora Hewlett Foundation as part of AAC&U's ongoing LEAP initiative, AAC&U engaged teams of education, assessment, and policy leaders in nine states involving two- and four-year institutions to work on issues of learning outcomes, transfer competencies, curricular change, high-impact practices, and assessment practice. Specific to the assessment of student learning outcomes, the institutions developed approaches to track and demonstrate student DQP competencies across levels of learning. This project exemplifies the value of partnerships among foundations, associations, the states, and institutions—and, most important, the value of promoting work inspired and developed within and across colleges and universities. Eduardo Ochoa (2012) pointed to these and related efforts as key to establishing well-articulated, measurable education outcomes associated with all academic programs in colleges and universities.

Implications

What can colleges and universities do to more effectively manage the influences, opportunities, and demands of external entities as these relate to evidence of student learning? How might proactive institutional leadership create a more strategic approach to gathering and using evidence of learning that would be of genuine value to students and the institution? In short, understanding the reality of these external pressures to assess student learning, how can institutions respond to them in ways that more powerfully and productively benefit students and strengthen institutions?

Expectations and demands expressed over decades through federal and state policies, national higher education associations, and philanthropic organizations have stimulated assessment work on college and university campuses. Indeed, it is hard to imagine that institutions of higher education would be nearly as active in assessing student learning absent pressure as well as support from the outside. The interests of external groups reflect society's imperative to build the knowledge and skills for its contemporary and future needs. Our quality of individual and community life, our standing in the global economy, the health of our democracy, and the capacity of our country to innovate, create, and compete all rest on high-level education outcomes among our citizens and institutions.

These external forces—the interest of governments, the activity of associations, and the engagement of foundations—will not likely dissipate in the years ahead. What needs to change, however, is the higher education community's response. Step by incremental step, year by year, colleges and universities have struggled to adapt and respond first to one and then to another outside demand. While this reactive posture is understandable, the unfortunate consequence is that many if not most institutions are saddled with a counterproductive *culture of compliance* that is severely limiting the usefulness of assessment to the very campuses and students it is intended serve.

To be meaningful and actionable, systems of quality assurance in higher education—gathering and using evidence of student learning to improve results—must be designed and implemented by faculty members, student affairs professionals, deans, provosts, and presidents, in concert with faculty senates and governing boards. The primary focus needs to be on campus needs and priorities. *The ultimate value of assessment must be measured by the contribution it makes to student success and the impact it has on improved institutional performance.* If this aim can be achieved, accountability will largely take care of itself. Yet, as the examples cited in this chapter suggest, this work can also be accomplished in partnership with colleges and universities. Even more valuable, bringing related initiatives together can help ward off initiative fatigue, which easily sets in under the stress of multiple projects and competing forces. External needs for evidence of student learning will not diminish, but they can be met more rationally and efficiently by focusing first on the needs of students and the campus itself.

At a minimum, this requires creation of electronic databases of assessment findings integrated with the institution's record-keeping systems that are capable of efficiently generating reports in response to shifting needs and demands. It also means developing frameworks for using assessment results to improve student success and in program review in response to changing conditions. Finally, it means establishing a robust process for periodically assessing assessment to confirm that evidence of student learning is having an impact, that assessment evidence is being harnessed productively, and that the assessment program has the capacity to adapt and respond to changing requirements from within and beyond the campus.

In sum, over the past three decades, much of the impetus for the assessment movement in American higher education has come from the outside. While external entities have a genuine interest in the effectiveness of higher education and evidence of academic quality, the locus for harnessing evidence of student learning to empower change is within the academy, on campus. We shall return to this major task in the last chapter.

PART THREE

WHAT NOW?
FOCUSING
ASSESSMENT ON
LEARNING

9

ASSESSMENT AND INITIATIVE FATIGUE

KEEPING THE FOCUS ON LEARNING

George D. Kuh and Pat Hutchings

Oh, great! Another good idea for us to try to incorporate here, on top of the five or six other new potentially transformative things we've been asked to do in the past few years. And we're supposed to do all this on top of our day jobs?

—Overheard at a faculty development workshop

AT CONVENINGS ABOUT IMPROVING TEACHING and learning, faculty and staff frequently report being overwhelmed by the number of initiatives they have been asked to implement in recent years. Just as one institutional effort is getting traction, it seems, the provost, a dean, or a faculty task force comes forward with yet another compelling improvement project the campus simply cannot afford to ignore. The exasperated sarcasm in the opening quote suggests that managing these multiple new so-called good ideas—deciding which to take on, which to bypass, and how to allocate scarce time and institutional resources for them—can be confusing and exhausting.

This syndrome is now so common that it has acquired a name—*initiative fatigue*—and is so widespread that many faculty and staff who have been around a while have become jaded toward new initiatives. As one person described the situation to us, her campus was plagued by a case of CAVE: Colleagues Against Virtually Everything.

With expectations of higher education having escalated on just about every front (Finkelstein, 2010; Gappa, Austin, & Trice, 2007; Schuster & Finkelstein, 2006), seeing little interest in and low enthusiasm for yet one more special project or initiative is hardly surprising. Administrators and faculty cannot be blamed for cynically predicting that the new idea will not stick or that yet another new idea will replace it—perhaps when the current dean or provost moves on.

Almost always, the new initiative includes an assessment component. Even though assessment has been around for almost three decades, its reception is typically like that for just another new idea. The comment of a National Institute for Learning Outcomes Assessment (NILOA) survey respondent from a two-year college captures this: "Many faculty members see an 'assessment push' as another in a long line of academic change initiatives. If they just hold out long enough, the initiative will go away. . . ."

What Is Initiative Fatigue?

To be clear, as we use the term in this chapter, initiative fatigue is not simply recalcitrance on the part of particularly grumpy personnel. Rather, it should be understood as a genuine heightened psychological and physiological state in which faculty and staff members feel overwhelmed by and sometimes conflicted about the number of improvement efforts to which institutional leaders and external authorities are asking them to devote time and effort—all of this on top of the fact that administrators, faculty, and staff on nearly every campus are doing more with less (http://www.acenet.edu/the-presidency/columns-and-features/Pages/The-New-Frontier-in-Higher-Education.aspx). Individuals already reeling from budget cuts in the wake of the Great Recession who are asked to incorporate a string of new approaches in rapid succession will often exhibit low energy and indecisiveness—not just in relation to the most recent initiative but also in their other work. They also may not see the possible connections and potential synergies between the new initiatives and their other work.

Fortunately, not everyone is equally at risk of initiative fatigue. Every campus has a small group of faculty and staff with a seemingly endless supply of energy to devote to multiple initiatives. But the point remains, and it is serious: campuses risk succumbing to initiative fatigue if asked to take on too many new assignments in an environment already rife with disruption. This risk confronts many institutions contending with metachallenges such the Obama administration's Big Goal of 60% of adults with postsecondary credentials by 2025, reductions in state support for public institutions, technology-infused innovations like massive open online courses (MOOCs), and tighter accreditation standards for evidence of student accomplishment. As a provost at a baccalaureate college put it, "Initiative overload is a very real problem. Shrinking state funding compounds this by reducing staff and increasing administrative requirements at the same time" (Kuh, Jankowski, Ikenberry, & Kinzie, 2014, p. 32).

The value that the initiative's work may have is not the issue. While there have been some nonstarters over the years—improvement fads like management by objectives, zero-base budgeting, total quality management, and business process reengineering that never did much to make things better (Birnbaum, 2000)—many of the new initiatives introduced during the past decade hold real promise. Engaging pedagogical practices like problem-based learning, crafting rubrics to assess specific proficiencies, and using ePortfolios to document and communicate student growth and development all can add value to the student experience and enhance institutional effectiveness. But when good ideas come too fast, or do not seem to be functionally connected with one another or larger institutional goals, the result can be pessimism and underlying anxiety. Taken together, these symptoms are not just unpleasant. Indeed, they interfere with individual and group performance, leading to a loss of confidence and enthusiasm for taking on additional tasks, a lack of direction and focus, and, in the worse cases, a sense of fragmentation and incoherence that can undermine the capacity of higher education to make needed improvements.

Factors That Contribute to Assessment Fatigue

Most new initiatives on the higher education landscape today come with assessment expectations. A campus has just redesigned its general education core or has put in place a new problem-based learning model in science, technology, engineering, and math (STEM) fields or has established a wonderful new first-year seminar. Each innovation raises questions about student learning and requires an assessment plan. These requirements clearly pose burdens for faculty and student affairs staff who must figure out how to meet them, often within a challenging timeframe. The requirements can also affect students, who are peppered with requests to complete yet another survey or course or program evaluation activity.

Concern about the number of surveys that students are asked to complete—whether for institutional assessment, by companies and organizations external to the institution, or as part of an institutional research request—has led many campuses to create survey permission policies, establish and publicize annual survey schedules, or implement survey coordination policies (Porter, 2005). These policies aim to support high-quality data collection while minimizing competing survey requests, but they also illustrate the level of institutional concern about the assessment burden on students.

Thus, assessment often figures prominently in cases of initiative fatigue that affect a broad swath of the academic community. The dynamics of such cases tend to take one of two patterns. The first occurs when an institution pursues multiple initiatives intended to improve different aspects of institutional or student performance (a perfectly reasonable thing to do, of course). The second occurs when an institution is presented with opportunities that seem similar in purpose and substance on the surface but, in fact, differ in important ways.

Multiple Initiatives with Different Purposes

The first pattern in the dynamics of initiative fatigue is aptly illustrated by a comment we heard in a session at a recent national meeting from a faculty member representing his institution's assessment steering committee. Clearly exasperated, he noted that within the previous 18 months members of the campus assessment committee were individually assigned to the following recently constituted institutional working groups: (1) reviewing and possibly revising the institution's general education program to align it with the Common Core standards; (2) responding to a request for proposal (RFP) to use the Degree Qualifications Profile (DQP) or some other framework to evaluate the preparation of transfer students from local feeder community colleges; (3) scaling up the use of electronic portfolios to document individual students' learning outcomes; and (4) making it possible for all first-year students to participate in a high-impact practice (Kuh, 2008).

"How," he asked, "do you suggest we prioritize these requests, keeping in mind we all have full teaching loads along with other commitments?" The question is a good one. Each of these initiatives has the potential to improve some aspect of the student experience, and each calls on the institution to find out whether that potential is being fulfilled, how fully, and how the innovation might be improved. The difficulty comes when each is seen as independent of the others and each has its own assessment approach and plan.

A similar example emerged in the Higher Learning Commission DQP consortium, funded by the Lumina Foundation for Education. Administrators and faculty at the 23 colleges and universities participating in that project were doing quite different things with the DQP as they worked to apply that framework in their own local circumstances. Participants acknowledged that good things were accomplished and interesting developments emerged. But what also emerged was a general sense of initiative fatigue as participants at campus after campus felt overwhelmed with the number of very different initiatives underway and struggled to figure out how the DQP fit into institutional priorities. As one insider in that work told us, "There are institutions trying to integrate assessment of student learning, competency-based education, high-impact practices, unique and sequential assessments, and common student assignments across courses and degree programs." Admittedly, this was a special project in which campuses were asked to engage with yet another new thing, the DQP, but our sense is that the centrifugal effect of multiple and, at least apparently, disconnected initiatives is all too common. As our informant put it, the effect was that participants were "about to hit a wall."

Multiple Initiatives with Seemingly Similar Purposes

As evidenced in the second pattern in the dynamics of initiative fatigue, a high degree of alignment and integration, ironically, can also be a source of confusion and fatigue. One of the more bedeviling challenges we have seen in the past several years has emerged around two very similar frameworks for assessment: the Essential Learning Outcomes (ELOs), from the Association of American Colleges and Universities (AAC&U), and the DQP (Figure 9.1). The developers of these frameworks have explained the considerable overlap between the two frameworks (see http://www.aacu.org/qc/dqp.cfm), but the ELOs, which are foundational to AAC&U's multiyear LEAP campaign, were released in 2007—several years prior to the 2011 launch of the DQP. As a result, before the DQP was available, many institutions had already adopted or adapted the ELOs to revise their learning goals, to guide curriculum revisions, and—especially relevant to the purposes of this book—to shape assessment approaches designed to measure their learning outcomes. Consequently, many faculty and staff members at institutions where the DQP has been introduced are understandably confused by working with two frameworks that look so similar.

Figure 9.1: Comparison of AAC&U Essential Learning Outcomes and Degree Qualifications Profile Proficiencies. (From http://leap.aacu.org/toolkit/wp-content/uploads/2012/02/DQP_ELOs_onepage.pdf)

The Essential Learning Outcomes

★ ★ ★ ★ ★ ★ ★ ★ ★ ★ ★ ★ ★

Beginning in school, and continuing at successively higher levels across their college studies, students should prepare for twenty-first-century challenges by gaining:

★ **Knowledge of Human Cultures and the Physical and Natural World**

- Through study in the sciences and mathematics, social sciences, humanities, histories, languages, and the arts

Focused by engagement with big questions, both contemporary and enduring

★ **Intellectual and Practical Skills, including**

- Inquiry and analysis
- Critical and creative thinking
- Written and oral communication
- Quantitative literacy
- Information literacy
- Teamwork and problem solving

Practiced extensively across the curriculum, in the context of progressively more challenging problems, projects, and standards for performance

★ **Personal and Social Responsibility, including**

- Civic knowledge and engagement—local and global
- Intercultural knowledge and competence
- Ethical reasoning and action
- Foundations and skills for lifelong learning

Anchored through active involvement with diverse communities and real-world challenges

★ **Integrative and Applied Learning, including**

- Synthesis and advanced accomplishment across general and specialized studies

Demonstrated through the application of knowledge, skills, and responsibilities to new settings and complex problems

Note: This listing was developed through a multiyear dialogue with hundreds of colleges and universities about needed goals for student learning; analysis of a long series of recommendations and reports from the business community; and analysis of the accreditation requirements for engineering, business, nursing, and teacher education. The findings are documented in previous publications of the Association of American Colleges and Universities: *Greater Expectations: A New Vision for Learning as a Nation Goes to College* (2002), *Taking Responsibility for the Quality of the Baccalaureate Degree* (2004), and *College Learning for the New Global Century* (2007). For further information, see www.aacu.org/leap.

LEAP

Degree Qualifications Profile

"A template of competencies required for the award of college degrees at the associate, bachelor's, and master's levels

Knowledge

At each degree level, every college student should demonstrate competence in using both specialized knowledge from at least one field **and broad**, integrative knowledge from arts and sciences fields. **Both kinds of knowledge** should be pursued from first to final year, providing opportunities for **integration across fields and application to complex problems**—in the student's area of emphasis, in out-of-school settings, and in civil society.

Broad/Integrative Knowledge

Key areas include the sciences, social sciences, humanities, arts, and global, intercultural and democratic learning.

In **each area**, students:
- Learn key concepts and methods of inquiry
- Examine significant debates and questions
- Make evidence-base arguments

In **addition**, at each degree level, students:
- Produce work that integrates concepts and methods from at least two fields

Specialized Knowledge

Students demonstrate depth of knowledge in a field and produce field-appropriate applications drawing on both major field and, at the B.A. level and beyond, other fields. Students learn:
- Discipline and field-specific knowledge
- Purposes, methods, and limitations of field
- Applied skills in field
- Integrative skills and methods drawing from multiple fields and disciplines.

Intellectual Skills

Students **hone and integrate intellectual skills across the curriculum**, applying those skills both to complex challenges within major fields and to broad, integrative problem-solving challenges. Skills include:

- Analytic inquiry
- Information literacy
- Engaging diverse perspectives
- Quantitative fluency
- Communication fluency

Civic Learning

Students acquire knowledge required for responsible citizenship both from their formal studies (see knowledge and skills, above) and from community-based learning, and **demonstrate their ability to integrate both forms of learning in analyzing and addressing significant public problems and questions.** Civic learning may be demonstrated through: research, collaborative projects and/or field-based assignments.

Applied Learning

Students demonstrate their ability to **integrate and apply their learning** (see knowledge and skills, above) in complex projects and assignments that may include: research, projects, practicums, internships, work assignments, performances, and creative tasks.

*"The Degree Qualifications Profile was commissioned by the Lumina Foundation following a series of national discussions about learning outcomes frameworks. It was released by the foundation as a **beta version** in January 2011 and is being tested in a number of grant-funded national experiments.*

Point Loma Nazarene University, for example, introduced the DQP as a way to enhance its already well-established work on assessment, which included the use of the NILOA Transparency Framework (discussed more fully in Chapter 10), a graphically enhanced representation of the assessment cycle for continuous improvement, and the AAC&U VALUE Rubrics for assessing undergraduate core competencies and general education. When the DQP was then added to the picture, one Point Loma department chair told us, some faculty were put off by the prospect of one more thing in the growing litany of demands and expectations that characterize academic life today. Then, as the substance of the DQP became better understood, there were more specific questions and concerns as well: How did the DQP relate to the newly adopted AAC&U Rubrics, and to AAC&U's Essential Learning Outcomes? How did any and all of these relate to Point Loma's *own* institutional outcomes, general education outcomes, program-level outcomes, WASC core competencies, and outcomes specified by professional accreditation? In short, faculty were understandably confused about how these multiple student learning outcomes fit together and complemented each other. Like many institutions engaging with the DQP, Point Loma had to overcome issues of overload and initiative fatigue as it worked to develop a set of promising new capstone assessments based on the DQP (Hutchings, 2014b).

Institutions in the state of Oregon provide other examples in which several seemingly related initiatives didn't quite come together. These included the Western Interstate Commission for Higher Education (WICHE) Passport Project, designed to further streamline transfer articulation, and work on LEAP sponsored by the state four-year system, which included the adoption of the LEAP Essential Learning Outcomes (ELOs) and VALUE Rubrics as well as encouraging campuses to feature high-impact practices (Kuh, 2008), all with implications for assessment. Additionally, Oregon institutions were becoming involved in the Multistate Collaborative Assessment Initiative, described in Chapter 8.

With these projects at different points in play (the Passport project coming to a conclusion, LEAP work continuing, and the Multistate Initiative just beginning), Oregon received a Lumina grant to experiment with the DQP, which as noted already focuses on proficiencies perceived to overlap significantly with the outcomes described in LEAP. Although previous work on aligning outcomes for transfer through the Passport project should, in theory, have laid the ground work for meaningful discussions about the DQP, in actuality, the Lumina project began to seem redundant and caused confusion and initiative fatigue.

These initiatives do not have to be seen or implemented as discrete, separate, or conflicting. Taken together, they have the potential to address multiple issues at once. To realize this synergy, however, programs, policies, and practices must be aligned to produce learning outcomes that are similar but not exactly the same. These tasks are especially demanding because—as with other situations that involve multiple bundled initiatives—the same people on the participating campuses are doing much of the work in each initiative. Thus, what should, in theory, be synergistic and reinforcing turns out to be enervating and confusing.

This problem is not unique to higher education, certainly. School reform scholar Thomas Hatch (2002), examining the proliferation of improvement initiatives in K–12 schools, found that projects that on the surface look similar and at first blush appear to be addressing the same challenges often in practice work at cross purposes, operating in different ways and based on assumptions about change that actually conflict. The result is that when schools take on too many such projects at once—which they often do—reform efforts end up competing with one another, with more losses than gains. What's missing, it seems, is a larger vision of the learning that is being sought, which could, in turn, drive a more integrated approach to improving the undergraduate experience and perhaps a simpler, less fragmented approach to assessment as well.

Assessment as One More Thing

Beyond the previously described broad patterns, assessment presents a particular hazard in respect to initiative fatigue in that it has historically been framed as an add on and is still seen by many faculty as an extra set of tasks that are independent of what they do regularly in the process of evaluating student performance on class assignments and giving grades. Student affairs staff are also at risk of assessment fatigue when they are asked to produce evidence of the impact of students' out-of-class experiences on valued learning outcomes (Schuh & Gansamer-Topf, 2010). As such, assessment is made to order to feel like one more thing.

Thinking about and approaching assessment as separate from one's core instructional functions dates back to the earliest days of the movement in the mid-1980s, as described in Chapter 5, when assessment proponents went out of their way to distinguish outcomes assessment from the common practice of assigning grades. To be sure, grading and assessing student learning are not synonymous, but they are not and should not be mutually exclusive. That is, formative assessments of student performance in the form of well-designed assignments should be the basis for determining the summative judgment reflected in a final grade. Even so, the early efforts to articulate the purposes and methods of student learning outcomes assessment by conceptually separating the two activities—assessment and grades—contributed to what became a widely held, counterproductive view that assessment was a new, additional (and fatiguing) function required of faculty.

Also contributing to faculty skepticism about assessment as originally introduced is the difference between evaluating student performance as a course- or program-focused responsibility, as contrasted with an institution-level estimate of aggregated student accomplishment. Many tools for institutions now exist that address the latter purpose. While, by one estimate, only a couple dozen assessment tools and approaches were available for institutional use at the turn of this century, this number ballooned to more than 200 just a few years later (Borden & Kernel, 2013).

The prospect of judging the quality of student performance with a tool developed by an external entity unfamiliar with a given course's content and learning objectives is perplexing to many faculty—and, to some, intellectually offensive. That the majority of these tools were created and marketed by for-profit vendors adds insult to injury and may be viewed as further evidence of the corporatization of the academy. Meanwhile, however, many more homegrown approaches to assessment have now emerged, and in NILOA's most recent survey of provosts those approaches were among the most highly valued for institutional improvement (Kuh et al., 2014).

Here's the catch: while the explosion of assessment resources offers more options and potentially greater coverage of different desired collegiate outcomes, having so many options makes it more challenging for faculty members who cannot possibly keep up with these developments as well as those in their own discipline. Even assessment and institutional research professionals responsible for conducting institution-level assessment activities have difficulty staying abreast of the advances in the field. In short, the prospects for fatigue are widespread. Yet we believe assessment can be part of the solution.

Strategies for Dealing with Initiative Fatigue

As with any organizational intervention, there is no single blueprint for ameliorating or avoiding initiative fatigue. Campus leaders must adapt their efforts and approaches to local circumstances. Even so, a handful of strategies can help.

Sell the Merits of the Initiative

The thesis of Daniel Pink's (2014) book, *To Sell Is Human: The Surprising Truth About Moving Others*, is that virtually everyone is in sales, whether selling shoes or real estate or trying to persuade one's child to eat her vegetables. Colleges and universities are highly professionalized, consultative, voluntaristic, and self-governing organizations in which most employees enjoy considerable autonomy (Trow, 1988). Thus, persuasion is one of the few effective tactics available. When it comes to institutional change, a first-order step is to *convince key actors* (opinion leaders among the faculty, for instance, and department chairs) that the idea has the potential to affect student and institutional performance in a positive way. Of course, there are no guarantees that a program or policy successfully implemented at another institution or in even another unit on a campus will have comparable effects when tried elsewhere. But at the least, there should be a strong, persuasive rationale presented—buttressed whenever possible with persuasive, high-quality assessment evidence—before attempting to mobilize human and other resources to launch another set of activities. Of course, there are occasions when it does not make sense to wait for others to try something first. With so many ineffective or failed efforts littering most campuses, however, it seems wise to mitigate the desultory effects of initiative fatigue by waiting at least one implementation cycle before asking faculty and staff to take on another innovation. Also important is having in place a set of decision rules or guidelines to help determine when a program or assessment practice is no longer worth continuing.

Hold Large-Scale Events

One approach to generating enthusiasm for and commitment to participate in the new venture is to convene large groups to introduce many more people to the innovation and the rationale for its importance (Brigham, 1996). Such events can be used to illustrate overlaps and complementarity with existing work, to describe how students and the institution will benefit, and to explain to faculty how the innovation will advance the work they care about. One of the five criteria used to evaluate the feasibility of an institution's Quality Enhancement Plan (QEP) to achieve accreditation by the Southern Association of Colleges and Schools is demonstrated evidence of broad-based involvement by institutional constituents in the development and proposed implementation of the plan. A weak plan would involve a small group of individuals not representative of key constituents, while an exceptional one would entail input from all relevant constituencies. Events that bring broad-based, relevant institutional constituents together facilitate shared understanding of new ventures and set the stage for successful implementation by underscoring the opportunities promised by the new effort and sustaining momentum. Another benefit of such gatherings is the opportunity to clarify the language used to represent the new work. What, after all, is a portfolio? What is a *capstone* or *culminating experience*? What is meant by the term *proficiency*? These are matters that must be fleshed out and agreed upon over time, and a public event is a good place to begin.

Conduct Short-Cycle Assessments

Many initiatives and their accompanying assessment projects appear daunting and, perhaps, not worth the trouble because of the substantial amount of lag time between generating the questions of interest about student learning and getting the results. In the face of feeling overwhelmed with one more time-consuming task, an understandable response is to do nothing. One counterpoint to this dilemma is to fashion one or more short-cycle projects in which a question is asked, data collected, and improvements made, sometimes within a few days. Short-cycle assessments are more common in K–12 settings than in higher education. Even so, there are some noteworthy examples, such as Carol Twigg's National Center for Academic Transformation, which devised a way to determine the learning effects of technology-enriched first-year courses with results apparent almost immediately, making it possible to change the instructional approach without having to wait a year or more (http://www.thencat.org/Mathematics/CTE/CTE_Lessons.html).

This type of assessment is analogous to what Karl Weick (1984) called small wins. That is, completing a series of short-term studies that produce immediate results of moderate importance to one or more groups can help ameliorate some of the fatigue challenges associated with student learning outcomes assessment. One small-scale assessment project may seem unimportant by itself, but a series of completed assessments over time can gain the attention of others and alter perceptions about the utility of the work. Moreover, short cycle, small-win assessments not only generate results about student performance in short order but also facilitate organizational learning about how to efficaciously conduct assessment in other areas.

Calculate the Return on Investment

Even when there are good reasons and enthusiasm to take on a new initiative (and good assessment evidence that doing so will likely bear fruit), there are questions of cost and return on investment that leaders must weigh. These include both the institutional and individual costs of taking on the additional tasks needed to reap the rewards, even if funds are available to help establish the program. Indeed, funding—especially external funding—is a double-edged sword. On one hand, most campuses are eager to supplement their own typically thin discretionary resource pool with external funds to support meaningful improvement efforts. If a campus wants to attract additional resources from external entities, however, it has to do something new or different to merit funding. On the other hand, the advance work required to plan and develop proposals is nontrivial. Should one or more proposals be successful, more effort from some group is required on top of what the faculty member quoted in this chapter's epigraph called a full-time day job, since it is uncommon for existing duties to be substantially reduced on the heels of an external award. Thus, securing a grant to do something because the grant is a sure thing can spread human resources too thin to take advantage of an as-yet-unknown opportunity around the corner. So, as odd as it sounds, strategic refusal—the capacity to say no at the right time—is the first defense against initiative fatigue.

Clarify and Connect the Dots

Most important, perhaps, campus leaders can mitigate initiative fatigue by making clear and explicit the connections among various projects and institutional agendas. One step in this direction is to inventory the range of initiatives already underway across the campus—general education reform, program reviews, accreditation and other self-studies, retention efforts, diversity work, and so forth—a process that may reveal overlaps in the initiatives' educational purposes. That overlaps exist, of course, is not a problem. If these efforts do not overlap somewhat, in fact, something is amiss. The connections must be identified, though, and people working on efforts with similar purposes should be reassured of the value of these connections. In short, the point of the inventory is to bring people together to realize the potential synergies from their respective efforts and to illustrate concretely the connections between existing programs and practices. Utah State University, for example, illustrated how five of their current projects—AAC&U's Liberal Education and America's

Promise, Essential Learning Outcomes, the VALUE Rubrics, the Tuning project, and the DQP—work together to answer multiple questions about intended learning outcomes, the quality of degrees, the intentionality of academic programs, and the clarity with which this information is communicated (http://www.aacu.org/meetings/annualmeeting/AM13/documents/ReformsinPostsecondaryEducation.pdf).

The bottom line is this: no initiative—funded or unfunded—should be launched without clear connections to the whole. This means that the president or provost must persuasively explain on multiple occasions how the new initiative or project addresses one or more aspirations outlined in the institution's strategic plan and goals for students learning. This brings us to the special role assessment can play in mitigating initiative fatigue—through its connection to learning.

It's About the Learning

As we travel around the country, visit campuses, attend conferences, and participate in working meetings, we hear more stories than we can count about initiative fatigue. True enough, we do not always hear the words *initiative fatigue*, but the sense that people are at a breaking point, that something's got to give, is palpable. And yes, many people see assessment as exacerbating the overload problem.

In this sense, one of the most important steps campus leaders can take toward making assessment part of the solution is to heed the advice offered by the CEO of a major corporation during a Q&A session with Harvard Graduate School of Education professor Richard Chait about university governance and management (Doyle, 2009): "The main thing is to make sure the main thing *is* the main thing." As emphasized in Chapter 6, it is incumbent on institutional leaders at various levels—campus senior academic officers, deans, department and program heads—to make sure *the main thing is student learning*. The common learning outcomes associated with improvement initiatives—existing or new—will not necessarily be evident, even to those directly involved in or responsible for them. This means that campus leaders and people on the assessment committee must develop and persuasively and consistently communicate a coherent framework to guide decisions about the educational work (including assessment) that is and is not worth doing, to connect the various efforts underway on campus, and to take advantage of synergies, especially with what has already been learned and what a new initiative can offer to ongoing efforts. It also means incentivizing, recognizing, and appropriately rewarding people who contribute to the larger goals that connect those efforts and, also, making available professional development opportunities for faculty and staff to increase the number of people prepared to do this work.

Keeping learning outcomes in view means keeping evidence about student performance in view as well, and here, too, is where assessment can be helpful in mitigating initiative fatigue. Higher education, thankfully, is not short on interesting innovations, as anyone attending a meeting of the Association of American Colleges and Universities, for example, can attest. How do we choose, though, which to take to scale and which to sunset? One answer: Look at the evidence. Does the campus have goals for student learning that are not being met at a satisfactory level? Or that certain groups of students are finding difficult?

The experiences of a number of institutions participating in NSSE provide examples. After NSSE results revealed its computer science students were underperforming on presentation skills, Wofford College's computer science department organized workshops and guest lectures on public speaking. Auburn University triangulated Collegiate Learning Assessment (CLA) and NSSE results to help departments improve the quality of student writing, with the key intervention being department-specific workshops focused on identifying competencies expected of graduates, using rubrics to evaluate writing in the respective discipline, and developing an assessment plan. As a result, Auburn's civil engineering program described seven different kinds of writing, five different purposes of writing, and four forms of feedback students should receive on their written work. The Kansas City Kansas Community College's nursing program saw results from the campus's new DQP-based data management system (which draws on the results of regular coursework) indicating that students were not achieving outcomes in the area of civic learning; to respond, the program added opportunities for community-based experiences.

Keeping goals for (and evidence of) student learning clearly in view can be helpful at multiple levels, as well—not only at the institutional level (where decisions about campus-wide initiatives are made) but also at the program and course levels, which can suffer from their own kind of fatigue. For his introductory course in American literature, Randy Bass (1999), professor of English at Georgetown University, undertook a process of "reflection and redesign" to determine which classroom activities were most valuable and worth keeping, (para. 6), and he discovered that he "had the process upside down" (para. 14), and that the learning goal most important to him was the one on which he was spending the *least* amount of class time. Thus, in his redesign, he says, he was able to create a more efficient and effective approach to "teaching more directly the student learning goals I value most." Bass's story illustrates how a sharp focus on student learning can streamline the teaching and learning process and reduce what might be called "course fatigue." After all, like institutions tempted to take on too many initiatives, faculty in their individual courses often have a tendency to try to do too much. In this sense, the process Bass went through is an example, at the course level, of a process of curriculum mapping and assessment that many campuses are finding valuable at the program level. It is not simple or quick, but it is one that pays dividends in rendering smart choices, and smart choices are key to reducing fatigue.

Finally, a focus on student learning can help create synergies between functions and roles that often operate independently of one another, a condition that exacerbates initiative fatigue. Most important among these is connecting assessment to the work of faculty in their own classrooms. As noted earlier, assessment was originally framed in ways that distanced it from teaching and learning, positioning assessment as an exoskeletal phenomenon, as something added on and external to the interactions between teachers and students (Ewell, 2013a). In this scenario, assessment has often and understandably been a point of faculty resistance, cynicism, and disengagement.

A tipping point in this situation seems to be approaching. Provosts (Kuh et al., 2014) and program heads (Ewell, Paulson, & Kinzie, 2011) both have reported more widespread use of assessment approaches that draw on students' work in the classroom: portfolios, rubrics, capstone projects and performances, and the like. On one hand, this development underscores the need to support faculty members in becoming more thoughtful about assignment design, crafting tasks that "unavoidably elicit a demonstration of the competency" they seek to foster and evaluate (Ewell, 2013a, p. 8). On the other hand, such well-designed assignments—the goal of NILOA's assignment library work—can be an antidote to the fatigue often engendered by the assessment juggernaut (www.assignmentlibrary.org). The design and evaluation of assignments, after all, is at the very core of the faculty's intellectual work as teachers, and demonstrations of learning through assignments are likely to be energizing rather than distracting or a drain on competence and focus. In this sense, assessment is fundamentally a faculty development activity, one that requires partnerships between academic units, department chairs, and the teaching excellence center or its counterpart—all focused on enhancing student learning.

Thinking about assessment in this way also opens the door to other kinds of synergies and productive connections. In its early days, assessment was something that teaching centers, for example, worked to keep at arm's length, wary of mixing their (almost completely voluntary) services with an enterprise associated with mandates and evaluation. This has begun to change as assessment has taken firmer root in the work of faculty and as teaching centers have sought ways to be more engaged with institutional agendas. Nancy Chism, a national leader in the faculty development community, argues that teaching improves through "naturally occurring cycles of inquiry" in which faculty plan, act, observe, and reflect. Teaching center staff can support this process, she says, by assisting faculty with data collection and by suggesting instruments and methods for obtaining "good information on the impact of teaching" (2008, p. 6). Bringing faculty together around such evidence, facilitating constructive conversations about its meaning and implications, setting local efforts in the context of a larger body of research—these are important roles that many teaching centers are now taking up, roles that strengthen the growing sense of community around pedagogy and a shared commitment to evidence. As these activities are woven into the life of the institution, they become less a source of stress and fatigue, less one more thing, and more likely to lead to real improvement.

Returning to a central theme in the introduction to this volume, this approach points to the power of assessment that asks authentic questions about student achievement posed by faculty, staff, governing boards, accreditors, and others. Initiative fatigue is much more likely when choices are limited, when the available measures are not sensitive to the animating questions about student performance, when people feel that they must respond to this or that opportunity, when compliance rules the day. Consider, in this regard, the grass-roots growth of the scholarship of teaching and learning movement over the last two decades. Largely thanks to leadership from the Carnegie Foundation for the Advancement of Teaching, faculty from a full range of fields and all institution types are now posing and investigating questions about their students' learning, using what they discover to improve their own classrooms and to contribute to a body of knowledge on which others can build. Such work has become an entrée for those who perhaps would not be drawn to assessment—which often seems top-down, imposed by others—yet feel welcomed by the idea of seeing their teaching and their students' learning as sites for scholarly inquiry, particularly in a community of like-minded educators interested in learning from their findings.

A 2009 Carnegie study indicates that such work, even when involving relatively small numbers of faculty on a given campus, brings energy and openness to institutional assessment activities. Where the scholarship of teaching and learning has taken root, as one campus leader reported, assessment is less likely to be "a four-letter word" (Ciccone, Huber, Hutchings, & Cambridge, 2009, p. 9). Not coincidentally, serious investigations of teaching and learning are increasingly valued and rewarded by institutions, as well, whether as an aspect of faculty's teaching or as a form of scholarship (O'Meara, 2005). Clearly, productive bridge-building possibilities are here, as the scholarship of teaching and learning and assessment share overlapping agendas, practices, and institutional constituencies. Indeed, some campuses are making the link explicit. For instance, in its call for proposals, Gonzaga University's scholarship of teaching and learning initiative, coordinated by the Center for Teaching and Advising, invites projects that advance departmental assessment activities. The idea is to bring together initiatives that might otherwise operate separately, to make them more productive, more connected, more likely to make a difference—being grounded in the work that faculty and all campus educators actually do with students (Beyer, Taylor, & Gillmore, 2013).

We end this section with a suggestion of a different kind, but one consistent with maintaining a laser-like focus on enhancing learning. Institutional leaders can dampen the effects of initiative fatigue by enacting a year-long moratorium on new initiatives, with the proviso that part of the year will be spent deciding what to drop or scale back in order to create some space for worthwhile new ideas and efforts that address pressing, high-priority institutional needs. That is, a moratorium can be a time for *institutional* learning—a time to take stock, talk, and plan. The campus can still maintain improvement momentum during this time by doing a comprehensive inventory of the variety of initiatives recently implemented and their effects, however measured. The goal of such an inventory process is not simply to make a list but to identify those programs and practices that have outlasted their usefulness. Sun-setting existing programs can be difficult, but it is essential to reallocate resources to new, promising initiatives. Key to taking this action is to charge a representative group to develop a set of coherent principles by which to make such decisions. In addition, a moratorium year will create space to allow people to concentrate on core tasks and replenish their energy. Especially on campuses where a small number of faculty and staff routinely are recruited to lead new initiatives, the psychological benefits of a moratorium cannot be overstated.

Conclusion

Initiative fatigue can be both specific to as well as occasionally exacerbated by assessment work. This fatigue is real and all too common. Every campus is subject to its potentially debilitating effects. While it has no known vaccine, tactics exist that institutional leaders at every organizational level can employ to ameliorate its drag on student performance and improvement efforts. Frequent public and private support from leaders at all levels—provosts, deans, department heads—is essential, of course, especially if the campus is working on several improvement efforts simultaneously. Also critical is ensuring that the institutional reward system adequately recognizes such activities.

After all is said and done, the best antidote for assessment-associated initiative fatigue is for faculty to see that good evidence about what helps and does not help their students succeed is also the route to more effective, efficient, and gratifying work as teachers. Understood and enacted in this way, assessment is not just the right thing to do—an essential instructional responsibility that only faculty can adequately perform—but also the smart thing.

10

FROM COMPLIANCE REPORTING TO EFFECTIVE COMMUNICATION

ASSESSMENT AND TRANSPARENCY

Natasha A. Jankowski and Timothy Reese Cain

The two words "information" and "communication" are often used interchangeably, but they signify quite different things. Information is giving out; communication is getting through.

—Sydney J. Harris

FOR EVIDENCE OF STUDENT LEARNING to be meaningful, useful, and consequential, information about it must be available in a comprehensible form. In the current accountability climate, the focus of transparency is often on making results available to external audiences—lawmakers, accreditors, potential students, and the general public (Brown, 2013; Krzykowski & Kinser, 2014). Campuses are pushed to post information on websites, file reports with government agencies, and provide accreditors evidence of learning, all in the name of being transparent and accountable. In this chapter, though, we argue for a more expansive view of transparency, one focused on sharing and using assessment results in consequential ways. To realize the promise that assessment holds for improving student learning and enhancing institutional effectiveness, colleges and universities must do more than make information public. They need to effectively communicate and share information with both external and internal audiences in ways that provide context, answer questions, inform decisions, and respond to audience needs. Additionally, they need to communicate about the processes of assessment, the outcomes of student learning, and the institutional responses to those outcomes.

This chapter explores what it means for institutions to be transparent regarding the assessment of student learning. We begin by defining transparency in terms of effective communication in support of evidence-based arguments around student learning. We consider the implications of transparency as effective communication for external and internal constituents, and we highlight the ways sharing assessment information may be modified to promote effective communication with various audiences. We conclude the chapter with a brief presentation of the National Institute for Learning Outcomes Assessment (NILOA) Transparency Framework and final thoughts on transparency as effective communication.

What Is Transparency?

Too often, transparency is viewed as merely providing *access* to information, leaving it to others to make meaning of the implications. Providing information is only part of the equation, however. Furthermore, decontextualized or too much information can actually work against transparency (Gladwell, 2011). As discussed in Chapter 3, the Wabash National Study of Liberal Arts Education, a large-sale longitudinal investigation of the outcomes associated with liberal arts education and the conditions that foster them, demonstrated that mere access to information does not lead to better comprehension and use of the information by internal decision makers (Blaich & Wise, 2011). Moreover, providing information about student learning to potential students has not led to its increased use in the college choice process (Dill, 2014). Put another way, if transparency is conceived as an act of communication that enhances understanding, it requires more than providing access to as much information as possible—undertaking a data dump—or routinely offering information that paints the institution in a positive light. Transparency calls for relevant context, including information about the needs and characteristics of the students served, the core institutional mission, and the ways the institution attempts to foster student learning and improve success.

Seen as communication and enablement of action, transparency moves from simple compliance and a willingness to make information available to placing information relevant to student learning and success in the hands of the audiences who need and can use it. It is not only about reporting and disseminating data but also about making meaningful evidence-based arguments that address audience needs. Who are these audiences, and what are their specific needs and interests? How can messages be both authentic and tailored to audience needs? How can institutions provide clear and compelling evidence of learning and the processes of acquiring that evidence? Focusing on these important questions is key to making assessment useful and relevant.

Natasha Jankowski and Staci Provezis (2014) argued that, for purposes of accountability, transparency takes different forms where the *process* of assessing student learning is clearly communicated beyond the campus as a mechanism to assure quality, the actual *outcomes* of student learning are clearly communicated and readily available, and the institution wishes to be regarded as trustworthy and uses transparency as a necessary vehicle toward that end. All three aspects share the common trait of communicating information to *external* stakeholders. Yet, as we have argued throughout this book, accountability to external stakeholders is but one element of learning outcomes assessment. More important is the use of evidence of student learning on campus to guide change and improve learning. As such, transparency in student learning outcomes must have a more expansive reach, focusing on communicating about processes of assessment to both internal and external audiences to assure quality, making outcomes readily available for use by both internal and external audiences, and communicating to both internal and external audiences that institutions are operating with integrity and are open about student learning outcomes.

If institutions wish to demonstrate that they are trustworthy, they must clearly communicate—make transparent—information about how student learning is assessed, what constitutes student success, what steps have been taken to improve student learning as a result of the evidence collected, and what the results of those efforts have been. Furthermore, if institutions wish to improve student learning, they must communicate to various audiences the information needed to inform decisions, enhance considerations regarding students served and their learning needs, and subsequently create an environment for use to occur. The creation of such an environment relies on transparency of a different sort than that required for mere compliance reporting. It implies a mindset that views transparency as communication for effectively conveying a variety of information including assessment processes, results, and context.

Internal and External Transparency

Communicating with internal and external audiences may serve different purposes and the audiences may have different needs, but both are important and both require careful attention for transparency to be achieved. That careful attention begins with ensuring that the assessment mechanisms in place capture the myriad approaches to student learning that are being used. It includes tailoring information to meet specific audience needs, educating audiences about the various sources of evidence that might address their questions of interest, and creating opportunities to make sense of evidence. Importantly, it also involves sharing stories of successful assessment processes and practices to both enhance the value of assessment and to convey the learning that is taking place.

External Communication for Transparency

There have been various calls for institutions to share assessment-related information externally in an effort to demonstrate that they are being responsible stewards and assuring quality (Belkin, 2014; Dill & Soo, 2004; Reindl, 2013; Stensaker, 2003). Yet the questions being asked of institutions and what counts as evidence may differ substantially by audience. Travis Reindl and Ryan Reyna (2011), for example, argue that governors and state policymakers need substantive and direct measures of efficiency and outcomes, and they call for state officials to request evidence that improvements in completion rates do not occur at the expense of student learning. Additionally, the Secretary of Education's Commission on the Future of Higher Education (2006), commonly referred to as the Spellings Commission, argued that prospective students and their families should have access to comparable information on a variety of educational outcomes to be able to make informed choices about college and university attendance. More recently, President Barack Obama called for a college rating system that would link institutional access to financial aid to comparable measures of access, affordability, and job placement (The White House, Office of the Press Secretary, 2013). These and similar external demands point to two key elements of the general approach to external reporting: disclosure and the comparability of information. Yet neither disclosure on its own nor the disclosure of comparable information necessarily enhances meaningful communication around questions of student learning.

DISCLOSURE "Public disclosure of information about effectiveness is increasingly a fact of life" (Ewell, 2005b, p. 9), grounded in the idea that such disclosure will press institutions to improve out of a fear of negative consequences. It is based on the assumption that institutions are not interested in, and are not able to provide, internal incentives to improve student learning (Jankowski & Provezis, 2014). Leaving aside the potential public relations issues for higher education that such framings raise, disclosure of outcomes—as it is often conceived—does not focus on institutions communicating meaningful information regarding student learning. Rather, it asks institutions to simply publicly report data—often large amounts of data. Yet the idea that public disclosure of results of student learning will advance institutional improvement is a policy objective, not an improvement exercise. Moreover, "as experience with the assessment movement has demonstrated repeatedly, [public disclosure] is insufficient for improvement" (Ewell, 2005b, p. 9).

Disclosure of information works better when information is provided to specific audiences in a useful format at a time when it is needed in the decision-making process (Fung, Graham, Weil, & Fagotto, 2005). However, a report by the American Council on Education (2013) stated, "A point seems to have been reached where information for information's sake has become the goal rather than information that is needed or has value for a student" (p. 8). More information is made available to potential students than ever before, but many of them do not view it (Fain, 2013; Jankowski, Ikenberry, Kinzie, Kuh, Shenoy, & Baker, 2012). Those who do view this information do not know how to use it (Supiano, 2014). Moreover, providing more information has not resulted in better-informed consumers (Hillman, 2014; Supiano, 2013). Not only does simple disclosure fail to meet the needs of students considering which institution to attend, but it also does not help students already attending an institution. Disclosing data through compliance reporting without considering institutional context, meaning of results, or opportunities to make sense of the results does little to advance institutional improvement or user understanding. As the 2013 NILOA survey of provosts demonstrated, institutions are adept at disclosing some data about learning outcomes, with 90% doing so on their websites or in publications, but the information is not necessarily complete or contextualized. Most often, institutions share learning outcomes statements or goals, while only 35% share results and only 8% share information on how assessment affected policy or practice (Kuh et al., 2014).

What is needed is not just the disclosure of more information but more targeted, purposeful communication of *relevant* evidence of student learning to specific audiences that need and can use it. By focusing on sharing evidence-based stories of institutional improvement, for example, institutions are able to both meet external accountability demands and show how they are assuring quality through improving results. This can also address a challenge identified by a NILOA survey respondent who indicated that being transparent necessitates you to "look at your failures and discuss them openly" in self-examination, which external audiences may misinterpret and misuse. Communicating through evidence-based stories mitigates this possibility, as it provides the opportunity to address why these results may have occurred and what institutions are doing to improve them. As of yet, though, the promises of this approach remain largely unfulfilled.

COMPARABILITY Comparing information about the performance of colleges and universities has been an important issue in the twenty-first century, as evidenced by the numerous online tools aimed at providing information for student choice and consumer protection purposes. Sites such as College Navigator (http://nces.ed.gov/collegenavigator/), College Scorecard (http://www.whitehouse.gov/issues/education/higher-education/college-score-card), Shopping Sheet (http://www.ifap.ed.gov/dpcletters/attachments/ShoppingSheetTemplateGEN1326.pdf), College Measures (http://collegemeasures.org), and College Reality Check (https://collegerealitycheck.com/en/) are intended to make it possible for students and others to compare key indicators across institutions. In addition, after the Spellings Commission report, several higher education organizations developed templates such as the Voluntary System of Accountability (VSA), Voluntary Framework of Accountability (VFA), University and College Accountability Network (U-CAN), and Transparency by Design to attend to accountability demands. While not all of these efforts include information on student learning—and not all remain in existence—all were created with the assumption that as part of their college choice process students needed to be able to access and compare information (Gillen, Selingo, & Zatynsi, 2013). These tools, according to their advocates, were intended to facilitate access to corresponding information about multiple institutions in an effort to foster market forces that provide incentive for educational improvement (Dill, 2014; Howard, 2013; McCormick, 2010).

Yet the emergence of these tools has not successfully prompted potential students to give much consideration to learning outcomes as they compare institutions. Students, including adult students, rarely look to online comparability tools for information beyond price, perhaps because they rarely act as rational actors with the freedom to attend any institution they choose. In their examination of the VSA pilot, Jankowski and colleagues (2012) found that visits to the sites' student learning page accounted for less than 1% of the views. In a study of prospective adult students' college choice information sources, Carolin Hagelskamp, David Schleifer, and Christopher DiStasi (2013) discovered that only 18% used a national transparency initiative website such as the College Scorecard to inform their decisions. They discovered that the most common sources of information were friends, family, and specific institutional websites, not tools that allowed for comparison. As such, the authors argued both for more meaningful presentations of data, specifically for adult populations, and for better communication about why such information should inform enrollment decisions.

Despite these and other somewhat discouraging findings regarding use, comparability tools and disclosure websites do have the potential to provide value both for institutions and for the students they might serve. Jankowski and Provezis (2011), for example, found that participating in a national transparency initiative (such as the VSA) was positively correlated with providing information on student learning on institutional websites. That value, though, can be enhanced through a shift from the emphasis on simple comparability to one that pursues transparency in terms of context and communication. Fortunately, while the first generation of national transparency initiatives focused on comparability of information in a manner that decontextualized the information (Stassen, 2012), there are indications that the situation is changing. The VSA, for example, is creating tools to help member institutions communicate their institutions' stories regarding student learning in more meaningful ways and is making a place for approaches such as rubrics that have the potential to provide more holistic pictures of student learning. This is a shift toward complexity and more effective communication and away from simple metrics devoid of needed context. It emphasizes both student learning and how institutions are working to improve it.

Other examples exist as well including the State Higher Education Executive Officers Association (SHEEO) project mentioned in Chapter 2. This project is a multistate collaborative with nine participating states working to balance the need for comparable information to external consumers with the importance of locally meaningful information from classroom assignments and projects. The idea is to create alternative measures that provide cross-institutional benchmarking for external reporting and accountability while at the same time providing useful evidence of student learning to institutions for making internal improvements (Crosson & Orcutt, 2014). Further, institutions are responding with their own institutionally focused accountability pages on institution websites such as Juniata's College page on "Just the Facts," which presents a variety of information on students tailored to external audiences (http://www.juniata.edu/justthefacts/) or Slippery Rock University's "Accountability" page, available directly off its institution homepage (http://administration.sru.edu/publicrelations/accountability/accountabilityreport.htm). Efforts such as these augur well for moving toward transparency as communication as opposed to compliance reporting.

Internal Communication

The challenges of external transparency are important, but those involving internal transparency might be even more so. For assessment to meet its potential to improve student learning, institutions must devote more attention to effectively communicating with a variety of internal constituents including faculty members, student and academic administrators, members of governing boards, and others throughout the campus community. However, such communication is a challenging and too often neglected task in complex organizations (Azziz, 2014), including colleges and universities where assessment is happening at numerous levels and various places—course, program, general education, and institution. Any number of factors impedes the sharing of assessment information internally, including organizational silos and a lack of buy-in or training among administrators around transparent communication, faculty cultures that might dissuade from engagement in assessment work due to skepticism or distrust, and the highly decentralized nature of many colleges and universities. In the specific realm of assessment, another concern is apparent as revealed by the 2013 NILOA survey: when faculty do engage, their needs for high-quality data can be significant. Still, effective internal communication can help develop shared understandings of the value and purpose of assessment, allow those within the institution to work collectively to make sense of the results of assessment, and ultimately enact changes to improve student learning.

Institutions have used various means to enhance internal data sharing. For the most part, though, the primary focus has been on gathering, disseminating, or providing access to information as opposed to communicating effectively. Institutions tend to utilize multiple internal mechanisms to share assessment results, the most effective of which, according to the NILOA survey, were via faculty meetings or retreats, assessment committees, and deans' council meetings (Kuh et al., 2014). In his discussion of internal communication during a period of significant change at Georgia Regents University, President Ricardo Azziz (2014) noted that the institution shared information through blogs, articles, email messages, intranet site, town hall and department meetings, and staff retreats. To make communication more effective, the institution surveyed internal audiences asking for preferred information-sharing mediums, the results of which were used to develop a variety of approaches and preferred meeting times so that the widest group of participants could be reached. Other institutions similarly adopt multiple approaches to internal communication of assessment practices and results. The University of Kentucky, for example, employs a newsletter with information on "What's Hot in Assessment," called the *Sizzle* (http://www.uky. edu/ie/content/sizzle-whats-hot-assessment) while also providing department-specific workshops and individual faculty consultations. Miami University promotes assessment through short faculty-authored success stories (http://www.units.miamioh.edu/celt/assessment/Successstories/stories.php) in addition to short assessment briefs that communicate various activities (http://www.units.miamioh.edu/celt/assessment/briefs/).

An increasingly popular approach to organizing and making information accessible is utilizing assessment management software. Such systems store reports of assessment activities and the subsequent results from a variety of levels of assessment, and allow for access to shared information from multiple points of entry. Yet while they provide an archival storage mechanism for assessment-related information, they may do little on their own to further enhance internal communication. If there are no opportunities for internal conversations to make sense of or review and weigh the information provided in the assessment management system, it is quickly reduced to a reporting tool for compliance. Further, if the reporting templates do not accurately capture assessment-related activities across the campus, they may potentially hinder effective transparent communication and serve to disengage the very people who most need to be engaged. Regularly reviewing the reporting mechanisms and processes, as well as gathering feedback on their use and accuracy, may serve to signal to those responsible for assessing student learning that the act of sharing assessment-related information is one undertaken for more than mere external accountability reporting.

To facilitate the exchange of assessment information internally, institutions should begin by examining the processes through which assessment data are captured and reported. Keston Fulcher, Matthew Swain, and Chris Orem (2012) outlined a process of examining current reporting structures through the use of meta-assessment rubrics based on the understanding that reports are the "best, or at least most official, vehicle for conveying information about student learning and the program experiences that contribute to such learning" (p. 1). Ensuring that the assessment-reporting structure in place allows for the multiple ways faculty are assessing student learning is important, they say, because "assessment reports typically underrepresent both the strength of assessment within programs and the thoughtfulness of faculty in identifying and resolving problems related to student learning" (p. 1). Crafting reporting structures that adequately capture the use of assessment results, as well as the processes that enable faculty to put results to work, will enhance engagement and provide stories of good assessment to share across the institution, like what occurred at Point Loma Nazarene University. The implementation of the NILOA Transparency Framework's Assessment Wheel at the academic unit level at Point Loma has, according to vice provost for program development and accreditation Maggie Bailey, "increased faculty ownership when telling the assessment story that is unique to the departments, promoted the exchange of best practices among faculty, increased accountability, and engaged students" (personal communication, October 3, 2012).

Transparency requires providing mechanisms to facilitate communication throughout the campus community and locations where assessment is occurring. Moreover, if assessment activities are occurring at multiple levels within an institution, which is almost always the case, facilitating cross-level dialogue and reflection on what the collective picture of student learning might mean for students will minimize fragmentation of assessment efforts and help to encourage dialogue on the meaning of assessment information across the various levels. Program review involving cross-campus committees provides such an opportunity as does institutional work to roll up assessment efforts from course-based assessments to institutional views of overall effectiveness (Richman & Ariovich, 2013). A program review process that does not include meaningful feedback or cross-program communication may not be taking full advantage of the potential available. Accreditation self-study processes might likewise prove to be useful mechanisms to minimize fragmentation and duplication of assessment efforts and connect various levels of assessment activities, but they are generally undertaken by a limited subsection of the institution and sporadically rather than continuously. Thus, relying solely on accreditation processes will not by itself ensure adequate internal communication either (Krzykowski, 2012).

Of course, not all faculty and academic staff will be involved in program review or accreditation efforts, and certainly not all will do so on a yearly basis. As such, opportunities to promote conversations more broadly are needed. As is noted in Chapter 5, some of these can be and are done through the creation of teaching commons, which allow for in-depth dialogue about student learning. The provosts who responded to the 2013 NILOA survey indicated that the single most useful means of communicating internally was through larger faculty retreats and faculty development opportunities. Many institutions, such as James Madison University, Montclair State University, Marshall University, and Huntingdon College, schedule assessment days where faculty and staff can gather to make sense of assessment results and share promising practices. Sharing stories of effective assessment practices internally can help to counter narratives based on misunderstanding of the value and purpose of assessment and to create a shared culture of using evidence to improve student learning. As Karen Handley, Birgit den Outer, and Margaret Price (2013) emphasize, sharing institutional exemplars is important for all actors but might be especially important for helping new faculty and staff understand local assessment practices and processes.

While many of these approaches are used in efforts to meet the needs of faculty, student affairs professionals, and academic administrators, another internal constituency must be considered and included as well. As discussed in Chapter 5, students play important roles in learning outcomes assessment, and institutions must be transparent with them. Moreover, including them in the assessment process might help overall institutional transparency (Krzykowski & Kinser, 2014). Being transparent with students may include communicating expectations and outcomes, alerting students to the intent of the curriculum or general education courses, explaining what is done with the information gathered, and helping students understand the outcomes of a degree so they can effectively convey their learning internally and externally. Tunxis Community College, for example, presents a video of faculty describing the outcomes students should expect from their education (http://www.tunxis.edu/ability-based-education/), while Salt Lake Community College offers short videos of faculty talking about the changes they have made to courses and programs based on assessment results to enhance student learning (http://www.slcc.edu/assessment/examples-of-excellence.aspx).

As with other constituents, communicating with students can and should be done in multiple ways. It may include communicating to students the value of general education by combining responses from alumni surveys, employer surveys, and student assessments to the various areas of general education, as with St. Olaf College's "Don't Just Check Off the Requirements" flyer (http://wp.stolaf.edu/ir-e/files/2014/05/DJCOTR.pdf). Or it may include describing the changes made as a result of student participation in assessment activities through posters placed in residence halls or through websites such as University of Georgia's "Your Voice Has Been Heard" (http://studentaffairs.uga.edu/assess/yourvoice/index.htm). These efforts may be more complicated, including, for example, engaging various student organizations or student governance structures in conversations centered on making sense of assessment results and engaging them in dialogue around evidence of their own learning, or, if the approach suggested in Chapter 5 is taken seriously, integrating these communications into classroom-based experiences.

From Reporting to Transparent Communication

Identifying and sharing audience-specific transparent information is important, whether internally or externally focused, and there are challenges to doing it well. Fortunately, much has been written about effective, transparent communication, and there are principles that can help guide practice. When communicating evidence of student learning and institutional quality assurance, key ideas include framing arguments around audience-specific needs, ensuring that the appropriate context is provided, and sharing evidence in multiple forums and ways. Implementing these ideas can help shift from a reporting paradigm to a transparent communication paradigm.

Meet Audience-Specific Needs

George Kuh (2013b) stressed that different audiences are interested in different kinds of information and, further, that such information must be communicated in "clear and meaningful" ways. This is often not done, though, even in the lengthy reports that remain a common format for providing assessment-related information. In their study of institutional websites, Jankowski and Provezis (2011) found that assessment information was most often presented through written documents containing little contextual information to facilitate understanding and with no clear audience identified. April Zenisky and Jerold Laguilles (2012) offer a framework that might address this shortcoming and facilitate the creation of written reports that meet audience needs. They recommend defining the purposes of the report, identifying likely audiences, drafting the report in light of literature and examples of effective reporting, securing feedback on the report and revising it, and then performing ongoing review and maintenance of the report. If institutions tailor transparent communication to specific audiences, presentation of information and the language used will change in ways that allow those familiar as well as those less familiar with the topic to better understand the evidence presented (Danielewicz & Jack, 2009). Indeed, Oklahoma State University's assessment site allows viewers to self-identify as faculty, students, or members of the public and then tailors information accordingly (https:// uat.okstate.edu). Such an approach will address the areas of need raised by those external to higher education and demonstrate that institutions are not trying to shun public scrutiny (Wyden & Rubio, 2014) but are instead assuring quality through determining what works for their students and subsequently modifying practices to enhance learning.

Provide Appropriate Context

As in many things, context is crucial in assessment. Context allows evidence to be robustly understood, mitigates its misuse, and provides a basis for use. Data alone do not present meaningful information. Only in the context of the specific institution, mission, students served, assessment processes, and subsequent action taken are various audiences in a position to understand the information communicated. Sharing more fully the context surrounding assessment information serves to further reinforce that assessment is undertaken for purposes of improvement, that results are open to discussion, and that institutions are worthy of public trust by their engagement in ongoing reflection on internal practices and outcomes.

Using the aforementioned techniques to display the appropriate data is one way of moving beyond simplistic metrics that serve a reporting compliance need toward transparent communication. Another is evidence-based storytelling, or "using evidence of student learning in support of claims or arguments about improvement and accountability told through stories to persuade a specific audience" (Jankowski, 2012b, p. 24). In their case studies of assessment practices, Gianina Baker, Jankowski, Provezis, and Jillian Kinzie (2012) found such storytelling to be an effective mechanism for conveying the use of evidence to make meaningful changes for student learning as well as for outlining what the results of assessment meant for students and subsequent learning. Sharing these stories internally allowed others to understand the value of this work for the institution and its students while also providing the context necessary to understand the information presented. Kalamazoo College's sharing of stories about how evidence of student learning was used to work toward greater diversity and inclusiveness, as well as toward becoming a more supportive campus environment, is an example of such an approach (https://reason.kzoo.edu/eqa/ue/).

Share Evidence in Multiple Formats and Forums

As discussed already, institutions should avail themselves of multiple forums to share assessment information in meaningful ways. These include the formal and informal spaces for dialogue and conversation crucial for promoting internal change, the reports that institutions must submit to governing bodies and accreditors, and various online means offered by the Internet, which has created conditions fostering new accountability and data-sharing expectations (Wells, Silk, & Torres, 1999) and has provided avenues to address them. Institutions have attempted to communicate understandings of how and what students learn through email, intranet sites, and assessment management software systems, public websites, and comparability systems. According to Provezis and Jankowski (2012), being transparent online is providing "information about student learning outcomes assessment and institutional performance that is meaningful, understandable, and readily available to internal and external audiences" (p. 604). Yet NILOA's studies of institutional transparency found that institutions post much less information online than they collect and that this information is primarily targeted to internal constituents (Jankowski & Makela, 2010). The point is not simply to provide more information, however. Rather, these NILOA studies highlight the usefulness of linking information in multiple places across institutional websites, providing examples and descriptions targeting various audiences, minimizing password protection without external explanation, and considering whether accessibility guidelines for the American Disabilities Act had been met.

Whether via the Internet or in other forums, Kuh's (2013b) challenge to communicate in clear and meaningful ways further suggests that institutions should consider taking advantage of the various knowledge bases around effective data presentation as an act of communication (e.g., Azzam & Evergreen, 2013a, 2013b; Lefever, 2013; Tufte, 1990, 1997, 2001). Stephanie Evergreen (2014) described visual displays as mechanisms by which we outline and draw a reader's eye to the story being told. This does not mean that information is hidden. Instead, information is presented in a format that highlights the key points and respects the time and energy of the audience with the idea that "effective data presentation creates a shortcut to audience comprehension" (2014, p. 9). Evergreen and Chris Metzner (2013) argued that there is a tendency in reporting to make too much information available for the viewer, and that viewers will abandon overly complex graphs rather than try to discern relevant or key information (Chen & Yu, 2000; Shah, Mayer, & Hegarty, 1999).

Several innovative approaches to understanding and communicating evidence are available to colleges and universities. Importantly, the approaches can also promote new understandings that facilitate use. For example, institutions can take advantage of geographic information systems, or GIS, which highlights relationships between data elements, thus allowing for various points of conversation around what the results might mean (Azzam, 2013). Institutions can map their campus communication networks to examine pockets where information on assessment was not being heard and should be included in conversations. Mapping assessment activities across a campus may also serve as a mechanism to find where good work is happening on campus and connect departments internally to enhance local assessment efforts. In each of the instances of using GIS mapping, the visual representation of the data helps make it actionable. Other institutions have focused on connecting institution-level assessment data in more meaningful ways for programs and departments by modifying reporting structures and outputs. St. Olaf College, for example, realized that its practice of providing assessment reports by type of measure (such as the results of a single survey) could be improved and thus supplemented them with reports on specific shared institution outcomes, pulling from a variety of evidence sources speaking to that outcome   (http://wp.stolaf.edu/ir-e/institutional-reports-by-outcome-or-topic/). Presenting information in different ways, St. Olaf enhanced its transparency and use of student learning information.

Capella University tried something different—designating a website entirely devoted to communicating about student learning (http://capellaresults.com/index.asp). Since 2009, it has been providing a wide range of information internally and externally on assessment in the belief that transparency is a powerful tool. As Michael Offerman, Capella's president emeritus, indicated, "It makes the intended outcomes and experiences very transparent to the learner. . . . They can see what our plan is in terms of what they have to do to start, proceed through, and conclude their programs" (Jankowski, 2011a, p. 5). The various means to communicate information on Capella Results include video explanations of reports, detailed information on how to navigate and understand interactive graphs, and results for individual programs on learning and career outcomes.

NILOA Transparency Framework

As the institutional examples presented in this chapter suggest, websites can be a vehicle for institutional transparency if utilized to bring together modified reporting, considerations of internal and external communication, and sharing of evidence-based stories with multiple audiences. As colleges and universities have grappled with competing demands of transparency and institutional improvement, questions have arisen about what to share, with whom, when, and how. To aid in this important effort, NILOA developed the Transparency Framework (NILOA, 2011) based on a review of more than 2,000 institution websites, in-depth case analysis from institutional websites, expert review, and survey research.

The Transparency Framework serves as a resource and guide for supporting institutions in sharing evidence of student learning on and off campus. The development of the framework was based on the types of information institutions already share regarding assessment of student learning and represents an ideal, comprehensive outline for thinking about communicating information on student learning. The framework is by no means a checklist or rating scale but instead serves as a guide for institutions to enhance their transparent communication of information on student learning. The six components of the framework are shown in Figure 10.1 and outlined as follows. Additional information on the framework, subcomponents, and institutional examples may be found on the NILOA website (http://learningoutcomesassessment.org/TransparencyFramework.htm).

o *Student learning outcomes statements* clearly express the knowledge, skills, attitudes, competencies, and habits of mind that students are expected to acquire at an institution of higher education upon completion of a degree or certificate.

o *Assessment plans* for gathering evidence of student learning outline institution-wide or program-specific approaches on how student learning will be assessed; the data collection tools and measures that will be used; the process for analysis, reflection, and use of the gathered data; and the timeline for implementation.

o *Assessment resources* encompass information or training provided to faculty, staff, students, or administrators to help them understand, develop assessments, implement assessment plans, communicate, engage with, and use evidence of student learning.

o *Current assessment activities* present information on a range of projects and activities currently underway or recently completed to gauge student learning, make improvements, or respond to accountability interests.

o *Evidence of student learning* provides results of assessment activities. Evidence of student learning may be indirect (e.g.,

Figure 10.1: NILOA Transparency Framework.

surveys) or direct (e.g., portfolios) or may include performance indicators (e.g., licensure pass rates).

○ *Use of student learning evidence* represents the extent to which evidence of student learning is used to identify areas in which changes in policies and practices may lead to improvement by informing institutional decision making, problem identification, planning, goal setting, faculty development, course revision, program review, and accountability or accreditation self-study.

While not all institutions will or should have all six components, and some may have additional components based on their mission, vision, and focus, the components serve as elements to include in stories of student learning and assurance of quality.

Institutional Uses of the Framework

Institutions have employed the Transparency Framework to build their websites or to examine whether evidence of student accomplishment is readily accessible and potentially useful to intended audiences. Other uses have also emerged. The framework has aided colleges and universities in organizing and storing assessment information on their websites. Some institutions indicated that their Web pages already had assessment information but that, through the framework, they were able to focus their efforts on connecting that information in more meaningful ways. Adopting the framework as an organizing or sorting mechanism for assessment-related information might be useful, but doing so without also engaging with the principles of transparency within each component might lead to well-organized yet still-not-transparent assessment information. Other institutions have engaged with the framework as a mechanism to conduct a data audit of assessment-related information. A data audit helps institutions understand where assessment-related data comes from, where it goes, and how the institution manages or sorts the flow of information.

Even with the various ways institutions have engaged with the framework, gaps still exist in effectively communicating information on student learning. Principal remaining concerns include a lack of focus on the audience to whom the information is presented, the way information is shared, and the institutional context of the posted information. As institutions attempt to communicate more effectively the information that diverse audiences want and need about student learning, the key seems to be to shift from simply posting a variety of information in an organized framework to presenting contextualized evidence-based arguments in the language of which the specific audience is familiar.

Final Thoughts

In the 2013 NILOA national survey, 80 campus responses to open-ended questions related to transparency. Provosts shared hopes, worries, and areas of need. They hoped that being more transparent would help to explain to students and parents the value of higher education, spark internal discussions, generate a shared vocabulary and outlook within the institution, and provide information on what does and does not work for students. On the other hand, provosts were concerned about the accuracy of their systems in documenting assessment practices across the institution, the usefulness of their assessment reports, and, significantly, the possibility that their shared data might be used against the institution.

These fears of sharing assessment details are tied to a view of transparency as simply making data available. Embracing transparency as a means of effective communication to improve student success and strengthen the effectiveness of the institution, however, puts transparency in a new light.

Effectively communicating information about student learning requires making sense of the data, determining what if anything needs to be done, and then providing context and interpreting the information to specific audiences. Raw data on their own are neither good nor bad; data do not speak for themselves. Data need to be interpreted to become evidence in support of institutional improvement or in explication of how institutions are being accountable through assuring student learning and quality processes. To be transparent about student learning outcomes, therefore, institutions need to consider how best to tell the story, to present relevant contextual information, and to help the target audiences grasp the implications.

To tell their stories well to both internal and external audiences, colleges and universities need to ensure that their reporting mechanisms accurately describe assessment processes as well as the use of assessment data. Internal reporting mechanisms need to include space and time for those within the institution to digest the results and determine the options and changes available to improve student learning. They also need to be multifaceted, as different audiences have different questions and different needs for evidence. Perhaps most important, in stark contrast to the compliance mentality, the focus should be on how best to communicate to a specific audience a meaningful, evidence-based argument about student learning. In sum, as opposed to simply responding to transitory demands for compliance reporting, institutions must communicate coherent evidence-based and audience-specific arguments regarding their effectiveness, their processes for enhancing student learning, and the means by which they are assessing student learning.

II

MAKING ASSESSMENT MATTER

*George D. Kuh, Stanley O. Ikenberry, Natasha A. Jankowski,
Timothy Reese Cain, Peter T. Ewell, Pat Hutchings,
and Jillian Kinzie*

When you come to a fork in the road, take it.

—Yogi Berra

THIS VOLUME IS ORGANIZED around a fairly straightforward premise: the
value of student learning outcomes assessment lies not in the data-gathering
process but in the uses to which evidence is put and the positive changes
that result for both students and institutions. Effective assessment work
is focused on educational issues and questions that matter to the campus
and to the learners it serves. Far too often, that basic test is not met.
Instead, the increase in assessment activity on college and university campuses, while significant and laudable, has been driven from the outside,
in response to the demands and expectations of governments, accreditors,
and others. Yes, the need for accountability is genuine. But for evidence
of what students know and can do to have the desired impact, assessment
must be driven by the needs and priorities of the institution and used by
the institution itself.

Against this backdrop, from perspectives internal and external to the
academy, we probed one central question: *What can be done to help*

*colleges and universities supplant the compliance culture that has damp-
ened the productive use of assessment results?* Said another way, what
is needed to make assessment more consequential so that its results are
used in ways that boost student and institutional performance? In this
concluding chapter we offer some ideas for how to address this challenge.

First, we look at the current state of student learning outcomes assessment in the United States, with an emphasis on the three overarching
themes emphasized throughout the book: moving assessment from a
compliance exercise to an improvement strategy owned by the institution
that is centered on answering important questions about student learning;
shifting the focus of assessment to questions of interest to key partners
and end users; and using evidence of student learning to inform improvements in teaching, learning, and the coherence of the student experience.

We then take a peek around the proverbial corner in an effort to anticipate the assessment implications of some of the major trends and forces
that are likely to shape the higher education enterprise in the years ahead.
Finally, we take up a very practical tactical question: What can colleges
and universities do to gain control and take ownership of assessment
and focus it more strategically on collecting and using data that enhance
student and institutional performance?

The Current Context

Our analysis of the substantial assessment activity underway in all postsecondary sectors points to three overarching observations about making
assessment consequential.

First, for results of assessment to be actionable, they must address the
priorities and questions of key end users and be presented in language
those end users and stakeholders understand. Compared with just a few
years ago, more institutions are using a wider array of tools to collect
more information about the student experience. The consequential aspect
of assessment, however, is not a function of the amount or types of information gathered but of the information's relevance and usefulness to
end users—those on campus who can harness the data to make changes
in curriculum and teaching and learning approaches. Yes, some of this
information may also be of interest to prospective students and their parents who may want to get a sense of the returns on their investment and
to external stakeholders who want assurance that the quality of student
learning is acceptable and scarce resources are being used wisely. Still,
the venues where assessment can make a difference are almost always
on campus. Whether assessment findings can be converted into useful

evidence depends on whether the data are credible, trustworthy, and actionable. For this, the technical qualities of the assessment approaches must be adequate. In addition, the results must speak to the interests and dispositions of partners and end users and suggest changes in policies and practices that can strengthen student accomplishment.

Often the best evidence—compelling and actionable—comes from the regular work of teaching and learning in the forms of rubrics, classroom assignments, demonstrations, and portfolios. Such evidence tends to be relevant to the classroom or academic program and may also include multiple forms such as surveys, comprehensive evaluations of student performance in internships and field placements, or results from focus groups of students, alumni, and employers. Whatever its sources, evidence of student learning should be relevant to the questions being studied and used to inform changes in policies and pedagogical practices that foster higher levels of student engagement and achievement. In the final analysis, to move from compliance to institutional ownership of assessment requires discovering the kinds of information that different audiences consider to be meaningful and useful—and ultimately making changes that hold some promise of benefiting students and institutions.

Second, consequential assessment tends to be linked with certain institutional conditions. The rich diversity of American higher education makes it impossible for a one-size-fits-all approach to assessment. What will work in large, complex universities with multiple missions may not be desirable in smaller institutions with more focused or specialized educational programs. Institutions that have successfully converted information about student learning into actionable evidence share a handful of conditions that support and sustain an assessment agenda. For example, they organize and design assessment with end users and the desired impact in mind. That is, they address the issue of which groups (partners, end users, others) need answers to questions about student learning in order to improve student and institutional performance and more effectively discharge their responsibilities. Because meaningful change takes time and perseverance, the assessment program needs to be ongoing, of use to multiple audiences, available in different formats and venues, and carried out in ways that build a consensus for action. When carried out in this fashion, assessment can meet the needs and demands of external authorities—including accreditors—while also generating information useful in meeting campus needs and priorities.

Assessment needs to be embedded in the ongoing work of teaching and learning, such as the assignments that faculty design, rather than carried out using externally developed tools or to satisfy demands for comparability. Thus, those at the intersections of the teaching–learning process—faculty, student affairs staff, librarians, and others along with students—must help shape priorities and engage in the work in meaningful ways if they are to find the results illuminating and useful. Students benefit, too, as they create portfolios of their work, deepen their learning by documenting it, reflecting on it in parts and in the whole, talking about it with other students and with faculty, and in some cases developing new strategies for studying it and for asking questions about it.

Active involvement of academic leaders and governing boards is also essential for an assessment program to be consequential. Granted, faculty and staff members are the principal actors in setting learning goals, developing methods for gathering evidence of the extent to which these are achieved, and interpreting this body of evidence to develop implications for action. At the same time, for these efforts to pay dividends, academic leadership and support are crucial. To shift from a campus culture of compliance to one that harnesses evidence in ways that foster higher levels of student achievement requires committed, consistent, and aligned leadership from presidents, governing boards, provosts, and deans in partnership with an engaged faculty and staff.

Our third observation is that external entities—especially accreditors but also federal and state government, philanthropic organizations, and higher education associations—can promote more consequential assessment by emphasizing the use of results and the documentation of the impact of changes in policies and practices on learning outcomes and institutional culture. For example, as noted previously NILOA's national surveys of provosts suggest that assessment would not be as varied and widespread in colleges and universities without regional and specialized accreditation. At the same time, institutions all too often look to accreditors and government to tell them what to do, further reinforcing a compliance mentality. Ensuring a strong system of academic quality assurance requires that institutions and accreditors work together to produce relevant, reliable, actionable data that address student and institutional needs and inform meaningful changes in policies and practices to promote student learning and institutional vitality. NILOA case studies of effective assessment practice show that institutions that conduct assessment with the aim of improvement tend to collect information that can also serve accreditation and other needs. When the primary aim is to comply with some external expectation, too often the evidence is neither relevant nor actionable to consequential improvement.

Pressure from accreditors and other external entities will not likely fade for the foreseeable future. Colleges and universities need to be more proactive in turning the expectations of external groups into opportunities to improve student and institutional performance and effectively communicating relevant information to various stakeholders. Essential to this task is for academic leaders and allies to help shape the quality assurance expectations of external entities by more clearly and persuasively communicating what constitute appropriate and inappropriate indicators of quality and best practices related to teaching, learning, and assessment.

One final word before we look around the corner. Those who engage in the assessment of student learning as well as those who call for or use the evidence should do so with a touch of patience and humility, recognizing both the power of assessment and its limitations. Students come with multiple motivations, proficiencies, and aspirations. Academic programs and faculty members hold sometimes conflicting views as to what learning outcomes are relevant and which are genuinely important. In this context, there are no easy answers. There is no simple test score or institutional ranking that is likely to reveal a great deal about what students actually know and can do—let alone shed light on the changes that need to be made to improve the outcomes. Those who demand accountability must be willing to accept this reality and complexity, and those within the academy must focus on real questions and academic issues with evidence that will prove useful—not just in verifying academic quality but also in making it stronger and better. It is within this broader context that we believe the shift of assessment of student learning from a culture of compliance to one focused on institutional transformation will be so important in the era that lies ahead.

What's Around the Corner?

Predicting the future is always risky, especially at a moment when so many informed observers agree that higher education in the United States may be at a tipping point. Nevertheless, we ponder some of these trends and forces because the environment in which colleges and universities operate is changing in ways that make it even more important for academic institutions to have evidence about what students know and are able to do. Reflecting on the past can help put the current and near-term future in sharper relief. Looking back over the last century, one can now clearly see its defining features:

1. In the twentieth century, *growth* was the dominant characteristic.

2. Institutions became larger, their missions more complex, and their administrative structures more differentiated.

3. Access to college expanded dramatically, and entering students became more diverse in virtually every dimension.

4. The cost of college to students and families escalated dramatically. Much of this was the result of real increases in college costs, although for public institutions especially, costs rose as well because of a gradual diminution in support from state governments.

5. The range of entities offering postsecondary education proliferated—from community colleges to massive state university systems, from for-profit entities to online virtual institutions—and the currency of accomplishment expanded to include badges as well as degrees, certificates of massive open online course (MOOC) completion, and much more.

6. The mystique of college has all but evaporated as more people have had the experience and interested parties external to the academy are dubious of the quality of undergraduate education and express disappointment in graduates' preparation for the workforce.

7. All the while, the *value of higher learning*—the practical significance of what students know and can do—has escalated, not just in this country but around the world.

Whatever the direction of the academic enterprise in the twenty-first century, several trends are established well enough to almost certainly influence assessment work. In this section, we briefly mention five that warrant special attention.

First, the focus on what students know and can do will shift increasingly in the direction of the *individual student*, who will be the prime repository for recording acquired proficiencies and dispositions, rather than remaining with a third party such as a college or university that may or more likely may not have awarded a degree, certificate, transcript, badge, or some other documentation of achievement.

Many of us—authors and readers alike—attended just one institution on the way to earning a baccalaureate degree. Today, most students attend multiple postsecondary institutions and do so over an extended period of time. As a result, it is difficult to hold any given institution accountable for what a graduate knows and can do (Ewell, 2013c). Moreover, coupling student mobility with the increasing interest in competency-based learning makes it imperative that learning outcomes be assessed in ways that are translatable and portable for multiple purposes. Among other things, this means that students must be able to understand their relative level of performance against reasonable common benchmarks and to demonstrate their personal progress toward higher levels of proficiency.

Given the substantial diversity among institutions, programs, and providers, the continued growth in alternative credentialing frameworks (discussed later) will add even more complexity. At the same time, this new world will give students more flexibility and options to learn and grow as they accumulate evidence of competence gained from an ever-broader range of sources. Technology-enhanced ePortfolios, discussed next, are one very promising vehicle to help manage this; other solutions surely will be developed down the line.

Second, technology-enhanced platforms will make it possible, in real time, both to offer new and more flexible venues for learning as well as to more extensively monitor and document student behavior and proficiencies.

Technology-enhanced, classroom-based assessment strategies such as ePortfolios and alternative transcripts that capture learning in and beyond the classroom can be used to document and enhance our understanding of student knowledge acquisition, intellectual proficiencies, and other desired outcomes. Some relevant questions come immediately to mind: What kinds of new assessment approaches can be used to track how well students integrate their learning from different in-class and out-of-class experiences and transfer their learning and acquired proficiencies to different settings? How might technology-enhanced assessment approaches and tools be used to more effectively manage learning? How can teachers interact with their students, and how can students interact with other students to optimize learning outcomes? How do students develop proficiency at integrating, synthesizing, and transferring knowledge to other contexts?

Much remains to be discovered about the power of technology to change and enhance the ways students learn and the ways proficiency is assessed, confirmed, and documented. Especially promising are big data or learning analytics that can help institutions deploy effective early-alert systems and better understand student's academic behaviors. This new world will not diminish the importance of human contact and the role of the faculty and staff, but it is likely to place these in a new, quite different, more flexible and revealing context.

Third, the roles and characteristics of providers and certifiers of learning—be they tenured faculty members, adjuncts, professional staff, interactive software, or some as yet unimaginable other—will continue to expand.

While traditional graduate programs and disciplinary organizations are encouraging the next generation of academics to become familiar with the means and ends of assessing learning, there is much left to do to help them understand and master the various approaches to documenting student learning. This challenge is exacerbated by the dramatic shift in the characteristics of faculty. Compared with three decades ago, the postsecondary faculty today is largely non-tenure-track and many do not hold positions carrying conventional academic titles. In 1969, tenured and tenure-track positions made up approximately three-quarters (78%) of the American faculty (Schuster & Finkelstein, 2006). In fall 2011, only about one-third (32%) were tenured or tenure eligible (National Center for Education Statistics, 2013). Almost half (48%) of non-tenure-track instructors are part-time. According to Adrianna Kezar and Daniel Maxey (2014), almost nothing is known about non-tenure-track faculty members' involvement in outcomes assessment or, indeed, in other traditional faculty oversight roles including institutional governance. Even so, it is a safe bet that substantial numbers of the non-tenure-track faculty who are doing the bulk of undergraduate instruction have little institutional support and minimal connection with or influence on the institutional processes that assess student learning and enact policy and guide changes in educational practice based on the findings. Most institutions have no formal or systemized process for making sure that new faculty hires are adequately prepared by virtue of formal training or experience to assess student learning. Left unattended, this situation is likely to further professionalize and centralize assessment work or outsource the task to technology, thus, distancing assessment from the core classroom-based teaching and learning context we have known in the past. Such forces are especially likely to emerge in large, multi-mission, and organizationally complex institutions.

As suggested earlier, outcomes assessment is most useful when faculty design assignments that require students to demonstrate proficiencies consistent with stated course and programs goals. As straightforward as this approach seems, linking assessment and the actual learning setting is new for many instructors. Too few faculty members have access to the faculty development resources needed to help them gain the requisite expertise and experience to embed effective assessment in their courses. Provosts responding to our NILOA surveys appear to be aware of this, as they pointed to wanting faculty to learn more about assessment approaches as one of their institution's greatest needs (Kuh & Ikenberry, 2009; Kuh, Jankowski, Ikenberry, & Kinzie, 2013).

A significant rethinking of teaching and learning models is needed to accommodate the more robust and focused assessment efforts that will likely emerge on campuses in the future. What constitutes an appropriate role for part-time instructors and others in student learning outcome assessment will need to be addressed, especially as their numbers continue to grow. Sooner rather than later, the enterprise must determine the assessment basics that every part-time and full-time faculty and staff member should know and be able to deploy in their own classes and programs, and how this work is aligned with and contributes to larger institutional efforts to demonstrate student learning and improve educational quality.

Fourth, the emergence of more comprehensive and transparent credentialing frameworks will bring more order, meaning and legitimacy to the escalating numbers of postsecondary credentials—degrees, diplomas, certificates, certifications, licenses, badges, accreditations, and other mechanisms that recognize what students know and can do.

The rapid growth of technology-based educational alternatives, not the least of which are MOOCs, along with the entrepreneurial initiatives emerging from both the for-profit and not-for-profit sectors will almost certainly further increase the number of alternative—and sometimes overlapping and competing—credentials. Little of this is well understood by the fragmented network of educational providers, let alone by prospective and current students, employers, and the public. The common challenge facing this bewildering and expanding array of credentials is assuring the quality of a credential in a manner that serves learners, employers, and others. A new credentialing registry will require at least three key elements (Lumina Foundation for Education, 2014a, p. 2). *Transparency* requires clear, common descriptions of what the credential represents, including the competencies represented, how these were attained, and the assessment approach used to validate the learning outcomes. *Trust* involves confidence that a credential accurately represents the qualities and competencies it purports to represent. And *portability* is the ability to integrate, stack, or otherwise merge the credential with other evidence of learning in ways that enable students to learn and grow from their experiences with multiple providers in the course of a lifetime, employers to understand and accept the value and utility of the credential, and other stakeholders including the general public to comprehend the new reality.

To be functional, any credentialing framework that has these elements needs quality assurance mechanisms that take into account the nature of the experiences that contribute to the credentialed outcome and the value of the proficiency or outcome itself to the credential holder. Also needed is a broader and deeper data infrastructure that will permit efficient and user-friendly analysis and exchange of information. Because colleges and universities will continue to be a major credentialing supplier—offering courses, certifying degrees, and issuing other types of credentials—student learning outcomes assessment processes must be of sufficient quality to play a needed, meaningful role in the framework. External authorities and assessment practitioners must find ways to collaborate in the design and development of assessment frameworks that will be functional in this emerging, quite different, age.

Fifth, a major driver of change in American higher education in the years ahead will be a harsher, less forgiving economic environment that will place a greater premium on evidence of what students know and are able to do.

For more than a decade, most of American higher education has been struggling with the painful realization that the economic model that sustained the academic enterprise in the past—and that enabled it to flourish—is severely strained and may no longer be sustainable. This trajectory, in one form or another, is almost certain to continue for the foreseeable future. The 2013 survey of private, nonprofit, four-year colleges conducted by the National Association of College and University Business Officers (https://m.moodys.com/mt/www.moodys.com/research/Moodys-New-Survey-Finds-Over-40-of-Universities-Face-Falling—PR_287436) revealed yet another year in which discount rates for first-time, full-time entering students reached a record high: 46.4% in 2013, up from 44.8% in 2012. For the bulk of private as well as public colleges, net tuition income adjusted for inflation has not increased in over a decade, while at the same time expenditures have grown in excess of inflation. In addition, the capacity of the government to support higher education has become more limited.

Up until recently, the strength of the economy combined with the demand for higher learning enabled higher education to pass on cost increases to students, families, governments, and donors. This "elasticity" is now severely strained. Some institutions have frozen tuition at existing levels; others have made significant cuts in tuition levels. Whether frozen or cut, many campuses have experienced declining tuition revenue because of enrollment declines. Income from gifts and endowment earnings remains important but often fails to fill the gap.

Meanwhile, as the number of options available to students and the range of providers of postsecondary education multiply, old-fashioned competition becomes more prevalent. In this unforgiving economic environment, evidence of learning outcomes will be crucial to competitiveness. Understanding what students know and are able to do will be essential not just to academic integrity but also to decision making, cost control, and institutional vitality.

Mobilizing for Effective Use of Evidence of Student Learning

What should an institution do to recalibrate its assessment efforts to respond to these new realities? Consistently, throughout these pages, we have attempted to position assessment of student learning outcomes as both a process and an institutional strategy. As a strategy, assessment—the questions it is designed to answer, the institutional priorities it is intended to inform, and the needs and interests of the end users and external stakeholders such as employers—must be shaped by faculty members, student affairs professionals, deans, provosts, and presidents in concert with the academic senates, governing boards and students themselves. *The value of assessment can only be measured by the contribution it makes to student success and the impact it has on improved institutional performance.* That test can be met only if assessment of student learning is driven by those inside the academy who understand and are responsive to stakeholder interests.

How then can the needed transition and culture shift be made?

Embrace Accountability

There is every reason for all external entities, including state and federal governments, employers, legislatures, and the public, to be interested in the quality of academic outcomes. While government's investment in higher education in terms of student aid, institutional support, research funding, and in other ways may be less than optimal, it is substantial. If for no reason beyond a fiduciary role, federal and state governments have a duty to ensure that public funds are spent wisely and prudently. Furthermore, as in other areas of contemporary life such as health care, transportation safety, and environmental protection to name only a few, there is a broad and very fundamental societal interest in the quality of higher education.

A campus that prioritizes gathering evidence to answer important questions about student learning and uses this evidence to improve student success and strengthen institutional performance realizes the double benefit of getting better while also effectively meeting accountability demands. Indeed, accountability becomes a natural by-product of assessment, not the driving force, when the assessment program is informed, endorsed, and valued by faculty and staff members, academic leaders, provosts, presidents, and governing boards.

Think of End Users at the Outset

Effective assessment work is built on strategically focused, comprehensive approaches to collecting and using evidence of student learning to respond to the needs and interests of end users. This means stakeholders and end users must be identified and involved at the outset of an assessment project. To build interest and momentum, faculty, staff, and students need occasions to come together to make sense of evidence and explore its implications. For assessment findings to become actionable, they must be based on what students do and represent what they gain from their experiences inside and outside the classroom. This means moving the focus of assessment closer to the curriculum, program, classroom, and cocurriculum.

Most important, outcomes assessment is most useful when the focus is on the *outcome*—using evidence in ways that will produce something of consequence that has a chance to improve student success and strengthen the institution. Only the academic community has the expertise and capacity to make these judgments and set those directions for assessment. Proactive steps to address genuine campus questions, a track record of using evidence of student learning in productive ways, and documenting actual improvement—these are the best antidotes for a compliance driven assessment agenda where priorities are dictated by constantly changing external demands.

Organize Assessment Work to Respond to High Priority Questions

Too often, the tendency is to release reports highlighting a particular set of data—the results of this survey or that focus group. A more consequential approach is to weave together evidence from different sources that speak to the same guiding questions. For instance, how proficient are students in writing at the end of the first year, midway through their major, and on the eve of graduation? This set of questions might be illuminated by results from samples of student work from writing-intensive courses and from a national student survey that provides information about the number and length of student papers, the amount and timing of feedback they get from faculty, and the extent to which faculty members expect students in their papers to draw on and integrate ideas from different courses or readings representing diverse perspectives. Other data sources may also be pertinent, such as an examination of the quality of papers produced in capstone courses or results from an external performance measure like the Collegiate Learning Assessment. In other words, emphasize the demand side of assessment—do not just supply evidence and hope that it will trickle down to good effect. Ultimate questions may not be answered easily, but focusing assessment closer to the various in-class and out-of-class venues where learning occurs will almost always increase the odds of pointing to changes in policy and practice that can make a positive difference.

Share Widely and Transparently

The point of transparency is to make relevant information available to those who have a legitimate interest and use for it. Too often, responding to the expectations of external bodies, institutions report about student performance on the institutional website and in annual reports and then move on. Approaching transparency from a compliance perspective gives short shrift to the needs of the campus—faculty and staff members, academic leaders, governing board members, and others. It is these campus constituencies who most need a clear, accurate picture of what students know and are able to do and who are in the best positions to interrogate, interpret, and use evidence of student learning to make decisions and act in ways that will benefit students and the institution.

We had an opportunity recently to work with the academic leaders of some of the nation's leading public and private research universities, exploring and sharing the challenge of gathering evidence of student learning in these huge, multi-mission institutions. What were these highly respected institutions doing, we asked, to gain insight into what their students know and can do? We learned a great deal, but our experience revealed how deep and impenetrable are the enumerable academic silos on many campuses. We observed academic units sharing very little with one other. What student affairs staff learned about student life outside the classroom often failed to connect with evidence from the classroom. In some cases, the institution's center had little or no knowledge of what was or was not happening with respect to student learning and experience in its various parts. Sharing evidence of student learning and using it more broadly in consequential ways inevitably requires faculty and staff engagement and collaboration if improved student learning is the aim of the entire enterprise.

Granted, reporting student learning outcomes to interested parties on or off campus can be risky. Uncomfortable questions may arise; the answers may be unknown and potentially embarrassing. Yet broad transparency—sharing results with faculty committees, the academic affairs committee of the governing board, policymakers, the media, business leaders, alumni, and others—can foster a climate of openness and build confidence and trust. In fact, having people at the table with diverse perspectives and experiences to help interpret findings and debate their implications can only better inform the options for improvement. Student voices are especially important for these tasks. Being transparent communicates institutional values and an agenda shaped by the institution itself, rather than one imposed from the outside.

Finally, transparency is one of the key values of scholarship. As academics, we owe it to ourselves, as much as to our colleagues and the wider world, to be open about our methods, to invite dialogue about our findings, and to challenge all to contribute to the ongoing task of continuous evidence-based improvement.

Lead Rather Than Manage

Much has been written about the difference between leading and managing. Managing, as the old saying goes, is about doing things right; leadership, on the other hand, is about doing the right things. In higher education, academic leaders can *lead* by working with higher education associations, accrediting commissions, policymakers, business leaders, philanthropic foundations, and others to help align accountability demands with institutional assessment and quality assurance mechanisms. Institutional and program accreditation is a creature of the academic community—its institutional members. Too few academics and academic leaders, however, are involved in debating and setting accreditation policy and expectations, especially those related to the assessment of student learning outcomes. Too few presidents and provosts are active in national higher education associations that stand at the intersection of government and academia. More college and university presidents need to spend time with state and federal legislators from their district explaining what their campus is doing to gauge student learning, to improve student success, to reduce costs to students and the public, and to improve institutional effectiveness. More active participation—and, quite honestly, *stronger leadership,* which can and must come from every level of institutions—could make a real difference in shaping external pressure in constructive directions.

Look Behind Demands

Often, demands for accountability from external actors are driven less by a need or envisioned use for the information than by nagging doubts about what institutions really know about student and institutional performance and what they are doing to improve. Requests to make information accessible via a website may be a way of signaling that an institution is responsible to its stakeholders and is rationally managed. Understanding the root causes of external demands and expectations will make accommodating and responding to such requests both more efficient and effective in the long term. Whether related to accreditation or public policy, the goal must be to bend external compliance demands to fit well functioning, productive, internally driven programs of assessment and quality assurance. Designing assessment work to meet someone else's expectations or demands will likely lead to a dead end.

Focus but Adapt

The demands on institutions for assessment emanating from government actors and accrediting organizations are constantly evolving and can change quickly. National associations try to keep up with these demands by organizing their members to undertake new initiatives in assessment of student learning. However, external demands are unpredictable; thus, campuses need to build assessment policies and approaches that are focused on institutional needs and priorities and that are at the same time flexible and adaptable. For example, the assessment questions of interest to faculty members in chemistry and English and to student affairs staff may differ as well as the nature of the data they consider meaningful.

The desired assessment model, thus, is akin to methodological pluralism. This suggests that institutions develop assessment databases (frequently centered on electronic record-keeping systems) capable of quickly producing new kinds of reports as internal and external needs and demands shift. It also suggests they develop frameworks for using assessment results to improve student success and in program reviews in response to changing conditions. Finally, it calls for a robust process for periodically assessing assessment to determine whether evidence of student learning is being productively harnessed and for an assessment program with the capacity to adapt and respond to changing requirements from within and beyond the campus.

Some Final Thoughts

There is a palpable sense that higher education is at a fork in the road. We should act on Yogi Berra's advice, but the fork we take in terms of student learning outcomes assessment will matter a great deal. This is because the importance of and need for higher learning has never been more obvious. The quality of life in communities, economic competitiveness, the health of the democracy, and society's capacity to innovate, create, and compete all rest on high quality educational outcomes. Indeed, the strength of the professions such as medicine, engineering, business, law, and a host of others all turn on what college graduates know and are able to do as a result of their college experience. At the same time, the health of our democracy and the quality of life of our citizens in a rapidly emerging knowledge society depends equally on how well all our citizens can evaluate information, reason quantitatively, and communicate and collaborate effectively.

At its core, assessment in higher education has a very practical goal: to gather and use evidence to improve student learning and institutional performance. Over the decades, assessment has served different purposes. In the early years, the movement prompted institutions to examine students' cognitive gains and the net effects of college on students. In the mid-1980s, the purposes of demonstrating accountability and improving effectiveness took hold. Some improvements in the quality of student learning transpired as a result of these initiatives, but far too few and well short of what was needed and might have been possible. The present era is a harsher, more demanding time in which the needs and interests of students are more varied, the economic strain on both students and institutions more apparent, and the stakes are considerably higher for the society as a whole.

Our crystal ball—although clouded—looks like this: As attention shifts toward individual students and what they know and can do; as the capacity to gather, store and add to proficiency credentials grows as a result of technology; as the nature of the faculty and other learning providers continues to diversify and the range of accepted markers of learning expands (e.g., diplomas, badges, licenses, certificates)—all of this occurring in a challenging economic environment—the internal, on-campus demand for evidence of student learning will and should overshadow externally driven demands for assessment.

After all is said and done, it is the actual outcomes of college—cognitive, attitudinal, and behavioral—that will make a difference to students after college. Understanding what students know and can do will also be important to institutional competitiveness, cost containment, expanded opportunity for those who need and deserve it, a healthy economy, a healthy democracy, and a vibrant society. It is essential to address head-on the culture of compliance if students and institutions are to prosper in the years ahead and if the public's confidence in and support for higher education are to be strengthened. This shift—call it a transformation—will not happen in the absence of committed leadership from faculty and staff members, department and unit chairs, deans, provosts, presidents, and governing boards—from those *inside the academy*. Such a transformation is not the stuff of miracles but of collective responsibility. What remains to be seen is whether we have the will to make student learning outcomes assessment consequential.

REFERENCES

AAHE Assessment Forum. (1992). *Principles of good practice for assessing student learning*. Washington, DC: American Association for Higher Education.

Aiken-Wisniewski, S., Campbell, S., Nutt, C., Robbins, R., Kirk-Kuwaye, M., & Higa, L. (2010). *Guide to assessment in academic advising* (2nd Ed.) (NACADA Monograph No. 23). Manhattan, KS: National Academic Advising Association.

Allen, M., Driscoll, A., & Booth, M. (2013). The impact of the first three years of the WASC assessment leadership academy. *Assessment Update, 25*(6), 4–5, 14–15.

American Association for Higher Education. (AAHE). (1992). *Principles of good practice for assessing student learning* (developed under the auspices of the AAHE Assessment Forum). Washington, DC: Author.

American Association for Higher Education. (AAHE). (1997). *Learning through assessment: A resource guide for higher education*. Washington, DC: Author.

American College Personnel Association. (1996). *The student learning imperative: Implications for student affairs*. Washington, DC: Author.

American College Personnel Association. (2006). *ASK standards: Assessment skills and knowledge content standards for student affairs practitioners and scholars*. Washington, DC: Author.

American Council on Education and others. (ACE). (2006, September 21). *Addressing the challenges facing American undergraduate education. A letter to our members: Next steps*. Retrieved from http://aetl.umd.edu/ NASULGC%20Challenges_%20092106.pdf

American Council on Education. (ACE). (2012a). *The American college president 2012*. Washington, DC: Author.

American Council on Education. (ACE). (2012b). *Assuring academic quality in the 21st century: Self-regulation in a new era*. Report of the ACE National Task Force on Institutional Accreditation. Washington, DC: Author.

American Council on Higher Education. (2013, August 2). *Comments on reauthorizing the higher education act*. Washington, DC: Author.

Retrieved from http://www.acenet.edu/news-room/Pages/Comments-on-Reauthorizing-the-Higher-Education-Act.aspx

American Philosophical Association. (2008). Statement on outcomes assessment (prepared by the committee on the teaching of philosophy). *Proceedings and Addresses of the American Philosophical Association, 82*(5), 80, 89.

Angelo, T. A. (1995). Reassessing (and Defining) assessment. *AAHE Bulletin, 48*(3), 7–9.

Angelo, T. A., & Cross, K. P. (1993). *Classroom assessment techniques: A handbook for college teachers.* San Francisco, CA: Jossey-Bass.

Association of American Colleges. (1985). *Integrity in the college curriculum: A report to the academic community.* Washington, DC: Author.

Association of American Colleges and Universities (AAC&U). (2002). *Greater expectations: A new vision for learning as a nation goes to college* (A national panel report). Washington, DC: Author.

Association of American Colleges and Universities (AAC&U) Board of Directors. (2008). *Our students' best work: A Framework for accountability worthy of our mission* (2nd Ed.). Washington, DC: Author.

Association of American Colleges and Universities (AAC&U) and Council for Higher Education Accreditation (CHEA). (2008). *New leadership for student learning and accountability: A statement of principles, commitments to action.* Washington, DC: Authors.

Association of American Colleges and Universities. (2014, March). *Connecting work and learning at the University of Iowa* (AAC&U Feature). Retrieved from http://www.aacu.org/aacu_news/aacunews14/march14/feature.cfm

Association of American Universities (AAU). (2013). *AAU survey on undergraduate student objectives and assessment. Executive Summary.* Washington, DC: Author. Retrieved from http://www.aau.edu/WorkArea/Download Asset.aspx?id=14849

Association of Governing Boards. (2010). *How boards oversee educational quality: A report on a survey on boards and the assessment of student learning.* Washington, DC: Association of Governing Boards of Universities and Colleges.

Athas, C., Oaks, D. J., & Kennedy-Phillips, L. (2013). Student employee development in student affairs. *Research and Practice in Assessment, 8,* 55–68.

Azzam, T. (2013). Mapping data, geographic information systems. In T. Azzam & S. Evergreen (Eds.), *Data visualization, part 2. New Directions for Evaluation, 140* (pp. 69–84).

Azzam, T., & Evergreen, S. (Eds.). (2013a, Fall). Data visualization, Part 1 (Special Issue). *New Directions for Evaluation, 2013*(139), 1–84.

Azzam, T., & Evergreen, S. (Eds.). (2013b, Winter). Data visualization, Part 2 (Special Issue). *New Directions for Evaluation, 2013*(140), 1–84.

Azziz, R. (2014). Like waves in a tar pit: Academia's internal communications problem. *Change, 46*(2), 32–35.

Baker, G. R. (2012a, April). *Texas A&M International University: A Culture of Assessment INTEGRATEd.* Urbana, IL: University of Illinois and Indiana University, National Institute for Learning Outcomes Assessment.

Baker, G. R. (2012b). *North Carolina A&T State University: A culture of inquiry.* Urbana, IL: University of Illinois and Indiana University, National Institute for Learning Outcomes Assessment.

Baker, G. R., Jankowski, N., Provezis, S. & Kinzie, J. (2012). *Using assessment results: Promising practices of institutions that do it well.* Urbana, IL: University of Illinois and Indiana University, National Institute for Learning Outcomes Assessment. Retrieved from http://www .learningoutcomesassessment.org/UsingAssessmentResults.htm

Banta, T. W. (Ed.). (1986). *Performance funding in higher education: A critical analysis of Tennessee's experience.* Boulder, CO: National Center for Higher Education Management Systems.

Banta, T. W. (1991). Editor's notes: With FIPSE support. *Assessment Update, 3*(1), 3, 9.

Banta, T. W. (2001). Assessing competence in higher education. In C. A. Palomba & T. W. Banta (Eds.), *Assessing student competence in accredited disciplines,* (pp. 1–13). Sterling, VA: Stylus Publishing.

Banta, T. W. (Ed.) (2009). *Assessing student learning in the disciplines.* San Francisco, CA: Jossey-Bass.

Banta, T. W., & Associates (1993). *Making a difference: Outcomes of a decade of assessment in higher education.* San Francisco, CA: Jossey-Bass.

Banta, T. W., & Associates. (2002). *Building a scholarship of assessment.* San Francisco, CA: Jossey-Bass.

Banta, T. W., & Blaich, C. (2011). Closing the assessment loop. *Change, 43*(1), 22–27.

Banta, T. W., Griffin, M., Flateby, T. L., & Kahn, S. (2009). *Three promising alternatives for assessing college students' knowledge and skills* (NILOA Occasional Paper No. 2). Urbana, IL: University of Illinois and Indiana University, National Institute for Learning Outcomes Assessment.

Banta, T. W., Jones, E.A., & Black, K. E. (2009). *Designing effective assessment: Principles and profiles of good practice.* San Francisco, CA: Jossey-Bass.

Banta, T. W., Lund, J. P., Black, K. E., & Oblander, F. W. (1996). *Assessment in practice: Putting principles to work on college campuses.* New York, NY: Jossey-Bass.

Banta, T. W., & Palomba, C. (2014). *Assessment essentials* (2nd Ed.). San Francisco, CA: Jossey-Bass.

Banta, T. W., & Pike, G. R. (2007, January–February). Revisiting the blind alley of value added. *Assessment Update, 19*(1), 1–2, 14–15.

Bass, R. (1999). The scholarship of teaching and learning: What's the problem? *Inventio: Creative Thinking About Learning and Teaching, 1*(1), n.p.

Bastedo, M. N. (2012). Organizing higher education: A manifesto. In M. N. Bastedo (Ed.), *The organization of higher education: Managing colleges for a new era* (pp. 3–17). Baltimore, MD: The Johns Hopkins University Press.

Becher, T. (1987). The disciplinary shaping of the profession. In B.R. Clark (Ed.), *The academic profession.* Berkeley, CA: University of California Press.

Beld, J. M. (2010). Engaging departments in assessing student learning: Overcoming common obstacles. *Peer Review, 12*(1), 6–9.

Beld, J. M. (2013, July). We have our assessment results: Now what? Presentation to the Association of American Colleges and Universities Institute on Integrative Learning and the Departments, Portland, OR.

Belkin, D. (2014, February 20). College uses test data to show value. *Wall Street Journal.* Retrieved from http://online.wsj.com/news/articles/SB100014240 52702304899704579391513428597546

Bennett, M., & Brady, J. (2012). A radical critique of the learning outcomes assessment movement. *Radical Teacher, 94*, 34–44.

Bennett, W. J. (1984). *To reclaim a legacy: A report on the humanities in higher education.* Washington, DC: National Endowment for the Humanities.

Bennion, D. H. (2002). When discussing assessment, we need to define our terms. *Assessment Update, 14*(3), 5, 15–16.

Bentrim, E., Sousa-Peoples, K., Kachellek, G., & Powers, W. (2013). Assessing learning outcomes: Student employees in student affairs. *About Campus, 18*(1), 29–32.

Bers, T. H. (2008). The role of institutional assessment in assessing student learning outcomes. *New Directions for Higher Education, 141*, 31–39.

Bess, J. L., & Dee, J. R. (2008a). *Understanding college and university organization: Theories for effective policy and practice, Vol. 1.* Sterling, VA: Stylus.

Bess, J. L., & Dee, J. R. (2008b). *Understanding college and university organization: Theories for effective policy and practice, Vol. 2.* Sterling, VA: Stylus.

Beyer, C. H., Taylor, E., & Gillmore, G. (2013). *Inside the undergraduate teaching experience: The University of Washington Growth in Faculty Teaching Study.* Albany: State University of New York Press.

Birnbaum, R. (2000). *Management fads in higher education: Where they come from, what they do, why they fail.* New York, NY: Wiley.

Blaich, C. F., & Wise, K. S. (2011). From gathering to using assessment results: Lessons from the Wabash National Study (NILOA Occasional

Paper No. 8). Urbana, IL: University of Illinois and Indiana University, National Institute for Learning Outcomes Assessment.

Blom, R., Davenport, L. D., & Bowe, B. J. (2012). Reputation cycles: The value of accreditation for undergraduate journalism programs. *Journalism and Mass Communication Educator, 67*(4), 392–406.

Bok, D. (1986). *Higher learning.* Cambridge, MA: Harvard University Press.

Bok, D. (2013). *Higher education in America.* Princeton, NJ: Princeton University Press.

Boose, D., & Hutchings, P. (2014). The scholarship of teaching and learning as a subversive activity. Manuscript submitted for publication.

Borden, V.M.H., & Kernel, B. (2013). *Measuring quality in higher education: An inventory of instruments, tools and resources.* Retrieved from http://apps.airweb.org/surveys/Default.aspx

Boyer, E. L. (1987). *College: The undergraduate experience in America.* New York, NY: Harper and Row.

Boyer, E. L. (1990). *Scholarship reconsidered: Priorities of the professoriate.* San Francisco, CA: Jossey-Bass.

Braskamp, L. A., & Engberg, M. E. (2014, February). *Guidelines to consider in being strategic about assessment.* Urbana, IL: University of Illinois and Indiana University, National Institute for Learning Outcomes Assessment. Retrieved from http://illinois.edu/blog/view/915/109546

Bresciani, M. J. (2007). *Assessing student learning in general education: Good practice case studies.* Boston, MA: Anker Publishing.

Bresciani, M. J., Moore Gardner, M., & Hickmott, J. (2009). *Demonstrating student success: A practical guide to outcomes-based assessment of learning and development in student affairs.* Sterling, VA: Stylus.

Brigham, S. E. (1996, November–December). Large scale events: New ways of working across the organization. *Change,* 28–37.

Brittingham, B., O'Brien, P. M., & Alig, J. L. (2008). Accreditation and institutional research; The traditional role and new dimensions. *New Directions for Higher Education, 141,* 69–76.

Brown, H. (2013, September). *Protecting students and taxpayers: The federal government's failed regulatory approach and steps for reform.* Washington, DC: American Enterprise Institute, Center on Higher Education Reform.

Brown, J. S., & Duguid, P. (2000). *The social life of information.* Boston, MA: Harvard Business School Press.

Cain, T. R., & Jankowski, N. (2013, November). Mapping the landscape of learning outcomes assessment: An update from the field. Paper presented at the annual meeting of the Association for the Study of Higher Education, St. Louis, MO.

Campbell, P., DeBlois, P. B., & Oblinger, D. G. (2007). Academic analytics: A new tool for a new era. *EDUCAUSE Review*, 41–57. Retrieved from http://net.educause.edu/ir/library/pdf/ERM0742.pdf

Carless, D. (2009). Trust, distrust, and their impact on assessment reform. *Assessment & Evaluation in Higher Education, 34*(1), 79–89.

Cavanaugh, J. C., & Garland, P. (2012). Performance funding in Pennsylvania. *Change, 44*(3), 34–39.

Center for Research on Teaching Excellence. (2011, August). Involving undergraduates in the assessment of learning. *CRTE Newsletter*, 1–6.

Chaffee, E. (2014). Learning metrics: How can we know that students know what they are supposed to know? *Trusteeship, 1*(22), 15–21.

Champagne, J. (2011). Teaching in the corporate university: Assessment as a labor issue. *AAUP Journal of Academic Freedom, 2*. Retrieved from http://www.aaup.org/sites/default/files/files/JAF/2011%20JAF/Champagne.pdf

Chen, C., & Yu, Y. (2000). Empirical studies of information visualization: A meta-analysis. *International Journal of Human-Computer Studies, 53*(5), 851–866.

Chism, N. (2008, April). *The scholarship of teaching and learning: Implications for professional development*. Keynote presentation at the Thai Professional and Organizational Development (POD) Network 2-Day Workshop, Bangkok, Thailand. Retrieved from http://www.thailandpod.net/resources.html

Chu, E., & Renberg, K. (2014). Assessing teaching practices in predominantly freshman courses: "What helps learning in this class?" Poster presentation at Assessment as Research Symposium, University of California Merced, March 12.

Ciccone, A., Huber, M. T., Hutchings, P., & Cambridge, B. (2009). *Exploring impact: A survey of participants in the CASTL Institutional Leadership and Affiliates Program*. Stanford, CA: Carnegie Foundation for the Advancement of Teaching.

Clark, B. R. (1997). Small worlds, different worlds: The uniqueness and troubles of American academic professions. *Daedalus, 126*(4), 21–42.

Clark, B. R. (2008). *On higher education: Selected writings, 1956–2006*. Baltimore, MD: The Johns Hopkins University Press.

Clark, J. E., & Eynon, B. (2011/2012). Measuring student progress with e-portfolios. *Peer Review, 13*(4)/14(1), 6–8.

Clyburn, G. M. (2013). Improving on the American dream: Mathematics pathways to student success. *Change, 45*(5), 15–23.

Collins, K. M., & Roberts, D. M. (Eds.). (2012). *Learning is not a sprint: assessing and documenting student leader learning in cocurricular involvement*. Washington, DC: National Association of Student Personnel Administrators.

Commission on the Future of Higher Education, Secretary of Education, U.S. Department of Education. (2006). *A test of leadership: Charting the future of U.S. higher education* (A Report of the Commission Appointed by Secretary of Education Margaret Spellings). Washington, DC: U.S. Department of Education. Retrieved from http://www.ed.gov/about/bdscomm/list/hiedfuture/index.html

Cook-Sather, A., Bovill, C., & Felten, P. (2014). *Engaging students as partners in learning and teaching: A guide for faculty.* San Francisco, CA: Jossey-Bass.

Cooper, T., & Terrell, T. (2013, August). What are institutions spending on assessment? Is it worth the cost? (Occasional Paper No. 18). Urbana, IL: University of Illinois and Indiana University, National Institute for Learning Outcomes Assessment.

Cottrell, R. R., Lysoby, L., Rasar King, L., Airhihenbuwa, C. O., Roe, K. M., & Allegrante, J. P. (2009). Current developments in accreditation and certification for health promotion and health education: A perspective on systems of quality assurance in the United States. *Health Education and Behavior, 36*(3), 451–463.

Council of Independent Colleges. (2014). *Engaging evidence: How independent colleges and universities use data to improve student learning.* Retrieved from http://www.cic.edu/Programs-and-Services/Programs/Documents/CIC-Engaging-Evidence-Report.pdf

Council of Regional Accrediting Commissions. (CRAC). (2003). *Regional accreditation and student learning: Principles for good practices.* Retrieved from https://www.msche.org/publications/Regnlsl050208135331.pdf

Council of Regional Accrediting Commissions. (CRAC). (2004a). *A guide for institutions and evaluators.* Retrieved from https://www.anokaramsey.edu/resources/pdf/assessment/assessmentguidecrac.pdf

Council of Regional Accrediting Commissions. (CRAC). (2004b). *Improving institutional practice.* Retrieved from http://www.sacscoc.org/pdf/handbooks/ImprovingPractice.pdf

Council of Regional Accrediting Commissions. (CRAC). (2004c). *Preparing teams for effective deliberation.* Retrieved from http://www.sacscoc.org/pdf/handbooks/PreparingTeams(blue).pdf

Crosson, P., & Orcutt, B. (2014). A Massachusetts and multi-state approach to statewide assessment of student learning. *Change, 46*(3), 24–33.

Danielewicz, J. M., & Jack, J. (2009, February). Writing in the disciplines. Two-day workshop for faculty. Roanoke College, Roanoke, VA.

Deardorff, M. D., Hamann, K., & Ishiyama, J. (2009). *Assessment in political science.* Washington, DC: American Political Science Association.

Deffenbacher, K. (2011). Faculty forum: Assessment metaphors we live by. *Academe.* Retrieved from http://www.aaup.org/article/faculty-forum-assessment-metaphors-we-live#.U3Trdi_fPx4

Dill, D. (2014). Ensuring academic standards in US higher education. *Change*, *46*(3), 53–59.

Dill, D. D., & Soo, M. (2004). *Transparency and quality in higher education markets.* Retrieved from http://www.unc.edu/ppaq/docs/Douro2.pdf

Doyle, J. (2009). *The elements of effective board governance.* Washington, DC: American Association of Community Colleges.

Dundes, L., & Marx, J. (2006). Balancing work and academics in college: Why do students working 10–19 hours per week excel? *Journal of College Student Retention, 8*(1), 107–120.

Eggleston, T. (2013). McKendree University assessment 2.0: A systematic, comprehensive and sustainable model combining assessment and faculty development. *DQP in Practice,* Retrieved from http://illinois.edu/blog/view /1542/96619?displayOrder=desc&displayType=none&displayColumn=cre ated&displayCount=1

Endersby, L. (2013). Book review: Learning is not a sprint. *Research and Practice in Assessment, 8,* 86–88.

Evergreen, S., & Metzner, C. (2013). Design principles for data visualization in evaluation. In T. Azzam & S. Evergreen (Eds.), *Data visualization, part 2. New Directions for Evaluation, 140* (pp. 5–20).

Evergreen, S.D.H. (2014). *Presenting data effectively: Communicating your findings for maximum impact.* Thousand Oaks, CA: Sage.

Ewell, P. T. (1988). Implementing assessment: Some organizational issues. In T. W. Banta (Ed.), *Implementing outcomes assessment: Promise and perils.* New Directions for Institutional Research, no. 59. San Francisco, CA: Jossey-Bass.

Ewell, P. T. (2001). The role of states and accreditors in shaping assessment practice. In T. W. Banta & Associates (Eds.), *Making a difference: Outcomes of a decade of assessment in higher education* (pp. 339–356). San Francisco, CA: Jossey-Bass.

Ewell, P. T. (2002). An emerging scholarship: A brief history of assessment. In T. W. Banta (Ed.), *Building a scholarship of assessment* (pp. 3–25). San Francisco, CA: Jossey-Bass.

Ewell, P. T. (2005a). Can assessment serve accountability? It depends on the question. J. C.Burke and Associates, *Achieving accountability in higher education.* San Francisco, CA: Jossey-Bass.

Ewell, P. T. (2005b). *Across the grain: Learning from reform initiatives in undergraduate education* (Discussion paper 3). York, UK: Higher Education Academy. Retrieved from http://jisctechdis.ac.uk/assets/documents/ resources/database/id548_complex_change_in_heis_paper3.doc

Ewell, P. T. (2008). *U.S. Accreditation and the future of quality assurance.* Washington, DC: Council for Higher Education Accreditation.

Ewell, P. T. (2009). Assessment, accountability, and improvement: Revisiting the tension (NILOA Occasional Paper No. 1). Urbana, IL: University of Illinois and Indiana University, National Institute for Learning Outcomes Assessment.

Ewell, P. T. (2011). Assessing student learning outcomes in college: The role of the states. In D. E. Heller (Ed.), *The states and public higher education policy* (2nd Ed.). Baltimore, MD: The Johns Hopkins University Press.

Ewell, P. T. (2012). *Making the grade: How boards can ensure academic quality, Second Edition.* Washington, DC: Associated Governing Boards.

Ewell, P. T. (2013a). *The Lumina Degree Qualifications Profile: Implications for assessment.* Urbana, IL: University of Illinois and Indiana University, National Institute for Learning Outcomes Assessment.

Ewell, P. T. (2013b). *Making the grade: How boards can ensure academic quality* (2nd Ed). Washington, DC: AGB Press.

Ewell, P. T. (2013c). *The changing ecology of higher education and its impact on accreditation.* Alameda, CA: Western Association of Schools and Colleges. Retrieved from https://wascsenior.app.box.com/s/36qe51avi9e99upn5vdg

Ewell, P. T (2014). The growing interest in academic quality. *Trusteeship, 1*(22), 8–13.

Ewell, P. T., & Boyer, C. M. (1988). Acting out state-mandated assessment: Evidence from five states. *Change, 20*(4), 40–47.

Ewell, P. T., Finney, J. E., & Lenth, C. (1990). Filling in the mosaic: The emerging pattern of state-based assessment. *AAHE Bulletin, 42,* 3–7.

Ewell, P. T., Ikenberry, S. O., & Kuh, G. D. (2010). Using student learning outcomes for accountability and improvement: The NILOA agenda. NCA Higher Learning Commission annual meeting, April 9–13, Chicago, IL.

Ewell, P. T., & Jones, D. P. (1985). *The costs of assessment.* Boulder, CO: National Center for Higher Education Management Systems.

Ewell, P. T, Paulson, K., & Kinzie, J. (2011). *Down and in: Assessment practices at the program level.* Urbana, IL: University of Illinois and Indiana University, National Institute for Learning Outcomes Assessment (NILOA).

Eynon, B., Gambino, L. M., & Török, J. (2014). What difference can ePortfolio make? A field report from the Connect to Learning Project. *International Journal of ePortfolio, 4*(1), 95–114.

Fain, P. (2013, November 4). In the dark on data. *Inside Higher Ed.* Retrieved from www.insidehighered.com/news/2013/11/04/metrics-college-performance-dont-reach-adult-students

Fain, P. (2014a, January 3). UC Davis's groundbreaking digital badge system for new sustainable agriculture program. *Inside Higher Ed.* Retrieved from http://www.insidehighered.com/news/2014/01/03/uc-daviss-groundbreaking-digital-badge-system-new-sustainable-agriculture-program

Fain, P. (2014b, February 19). Tough love for accreditation. *Inside Higher Ed.* Retrieved from http://www.insidehighered.com/news/2014/02/19/book-explores-how-make-accreditation-more-effective#sthash.zgEhl09H.dpbs

Fallow, S., & Steven, C. (2000). Building employability skills into the higher education curriculum: A university-wide initiative. *Education & Training, 40*(2), 75–83.

Fallucca, A., & Lewis, E. (2013). Promoting student affairs buy-in for assessment: Lessons learned. *Assessment Update, 25*(3), 4–14.

Ferren, A. (1993). Faculty resistance to assessment: A matter of priorities and perceptions. In *Conference discussion papers: the 8th annual assessment conference and the 1st continuous quality improvement conference, June 9–12, 1993, Palmer House, Chicago, Ill.* Washington, DC: American Association for Higher Education.

Finkelstein, M. J. (2010). The study of academic careers: Looking back, looking forward. In J. C. Smart (Ed.), *Higher education: Handbook of theory and research* (Vol. 21). Dordrecht, The Netherlands: Springer.

Fiske, E. B. (2013). *Fiske guide to colleges* (30th Ed.). Naperville, IL: Sourcebooks, Inc.

Friedlander, J., & Serban, A. M. (2004). Meeting the challenges of assessing student learning outcomes. *New Directions for Community Colleges, 126,* 101–109.

Fulcher, K., Bailey, M., & Zack, M. (2013a). *PLNU Degree Qualification Profile (DQP) pilot program.* Retrieved from http://www.learningoutcomeassessment.org/DQPInPracticePointLoma.html

Fulcher, K., Bailey, M., & Zack, M. (2013b). Point Loma Nazarene University Degree Qualifications Profile pilot program. *DQP In Practice.* Retrieved from http://illinois.edu/blog/view/1542/96616?displayOrder=desc&displayType=none&displayColumn=created&displayCount=1#blog-feature

Fulcher, K. H., Swain, M., & Orem, C.D. (2012). Expectations for assessment reports: A descriptive analysis. *Assessment Update, 24*(1), 1–2, 14–16.

Fung, A., Graham, M., Weil, D., & Fagotto, E. (2005, April 7). *From food to finance: What makes disclosure policies effective?* Cambridge, MA: Taubman Center Policy Briefs.

Gainen, J., & Locatelli, P. (1995). *Assessment for the new curriculum: A guide for professional accounting programs.* Sarasota, FL: American Accounting Association.

Gannon-Slater, N., Ikenberry, S., Jankowski, N., & Kuh, G. (2014). *Institutional assessment practices across accreditation region.* Urbana, IL: University of Illinois and Indiana University, National Institute for Learning Outcomes Assessment.

Gappa, J. M., Austin, A. E., & Trice, A. G. (2007). *Rethinking faculty work: Higher education's strategic imperative*. San Francisco, CA: Jossey-Bass.

Gaston, P. L. (2014). *Higher education accreditation: How it's changing, why it must*. Sterling, VA: Stylus.

Gentemann, K. M., & Fletcher, J. J. (1994). Refocusing the academic program review on student learning: The role of assessment. *New Directions for Institutional Research, 84*, 31–47.

George, M., & McLaughlin, D. (2008). Re-framing mainstream assessment. *Tribal College Journal, 19*(4), 18–22.

Gerstner, J. J., & Finney, S. J. (2013). Measuring the implementation fidelity of student affairs programs: A critical component of the outcomes assessment cycle. *Research and Practice in Assessment, 8*, 15–28.

Gilchrist, D., & Oakleaf, M. (2012, April). An essential partner: The librarian's role in student learning assessment (NILOA Occasional Paper No. 14). Urbana, IL: University of Illinois and Indiana University, National Institute for Learning Outcomes Assessment.

Gillen, A., Selingo, J., & Zatynski, M. (2013, May). *Degrees of value: Evaluating the return on the college investment*. Washington, DC: Education Sector. Retrieved from http://www.educationsector.org/publications/degrees-value-evaluating-return-college-investment

Gladwell, M. (2011, February 14). The order of things: What college rankings really tell us. *The New Yorker*. Retrieved from http://www.newyorker.com/reporting/2011/02/14/110214fa_fact_gladwell?currentPage=all

Glenn, D. (2010, January 24). Educators mull how to motivate professors to improve teaching. *Chronicle of Higher Education*.

Goals 2000: Educate America Act (1994). P.L. 103-227; 108 Stat. 125.

Gold, L., Rhoades, G., Smith, M., & Kuh, G. (2011, May). *What faculty unions say about student learning outcomes assessment* (NILOA Occasional Paper No. 9). Urbana, IL: University of Illinois and Indiana University, National Institute for Learning Outcomes Assessment.

Golden, S. (2013). How best to assess? *Inside Higher Education*, November 18, 2013. Retrieved from http://www.insidehighered.com/news/2013/11/18/debating-role-student-learning-federal-ratings-plan

Goldman, G. K., & Zakel, L. E. (2009). Clarification of assessment and evaluation. *Assessment Update, 21*(3), 8–9.

Graff, G. (2008). Assessment changes everything. *MLA Newsletter*. Retrieved from http://www.mla.org/blog&topic=121

Graff, G. (2010). Why assessment? *Pedagogy 10*(1), 153–165.

Green, M. F., & Bezbatchenko, A. W. (2014, January–February). An alternative model of philanthropy. *Change, 46*(1), 46–52.

Hagelskamp, C., Schleifer, D., & DiStasi, C. (2013). *Is college worth it for me? How adults without degrees think about going (back) to school.* New York, NY: Public Agenda.

Handley, K., den Outer, B., & Price, M. (2013). Learning to mark: Exemplars, dialogue and participation in assessment communities. *Higher Education Research & Development, 32*(6), 888–900.

Hanson, G. R. (1988). Critical issues in the assessment of value added in education. In T.W. Banta (Ed.), *Implementing outcomes assessment: Promise and perils. New Directions for Institutional Research*, no. 59. San Francisco, CA: Jossey-Bass.

Hatch, T. (2002). When improvement programs collide. *Phi Delta Kappan. 83*(8), 626–634.

Heiland, D., & Rosenthal, L. J. (2011). Introduction. In D. Heiland & L .J. Rosenthal (Eds.), *Literary study, measurement, and the sublime: Disciplinary assessment.* New York, NY: Teagle Foundation.

Hillman, N. (2014). College ratings: What lessons can we learn from other sectors. *NILOA guest viewpoints.* Retrieved from http://illinois.edu/blog/view/915/110544

Howard, M. A. (2013, May). Why the VSA is important to AASCU and our members. *VSA voice.* Washington, DC. Retrieved from http://vsavoice. blogspot.com/2013/05/why-vsa-is-important-to-aascu-and-our.html

Hrabowski III, F. A., Suess, J., & Fritz, J. (2011). Assessment and analytics in institutional transformation. *Educause Review, 46*(5), 15–28.

Huber, M. T. (2004). *Balancing acts: The scholarship of teaching and learning in academic careers.* Washington, DC: American Association for Higher Education and the Carnegie Foundation for the Advancement of Teaching.

Huber, M. T. (2009). Teaching travels: Reflections on the social life of classroom inquiry and innovation. *International Journal for the Scholarship of Teaching and Learning, 32*(2) [not sequentially paginated] Retrieved from http:// academics.georgiasouthern.edu/ijsotl/v3n2/invited_essays/_Huber/index.htm

Huber, M. T., & Hutchings, P. (2005). *Integrative learning: Mapping the terrain.* Washington, DC: Association of American Colleges and Universities.

Hunter, G., Abelmann, N., Cain, T. R., McDonough, T., & Prendergast, C. (2009). Interrogating the university: One archival entry at a time. *Change 40*(5): 40–45.

Hutchings, P. (2009). The new guys in assessment town. *Change, 41*(3), 26–33.

Hutchings, P. (2010). Opening doors to faculty involvement in assessment (NILOA Occasional Paper No. 4). Urbana, IL: University of Illinois and Indiana University, National Institute for Learning Outcomes Assessment.

Hutchings, P. (2011). From department to disciplinary assessment: Deepening faculty engagement. *Change, 43*(5), 36–43.

Hutchings, P. (2014a). *DQP case study: Kansas City Kansas Community College.* Urbana, IL: University of Illinois and Indiana University, National Institute for Learning Outcomes Assessment (NILOA).

Hutchings, P. (2014b). *DQP case study: Point Loma Nazarene University.* Urbana, IL: University of Illinois and Indiana University, National Institute for Learning Outcomes Assessment (NILOA).

Hutchings, P., & Clarke, S. E. (2004). The scholarship of teaching and learning: Contributing to reform in graduate education. In D. H. Wulff & A. E. Austin (Eds.), *Paths to the professoriate: Strategies for enriching the preparation of future faculty.* San Francisco, CA: Jossey-Bass.

Hutchings, P., Ewell, P. T., & Banta, T. W. (n.d.). *AAHE principles of good practice: Aging nicely.* Retrieved from http://www.learningoutcomeassessment. org/PrinciplesofAssessment.html#AAHE

Hutchings, P., Huber, M., & Ciccone, A. (2011). *The scholarship of teaching and learning reconsidered: Institutional integration and impact.* San Francisco, CA: Jossey-Bass.

Institute for Evidence-Based Change. (2012). *Tuning American higher education: The process.* Encinitas, CA: Author.

Jankowski, N. A. (2011a). *Capella University: An outcomes-based institution.* Urbana, IL: University of Illinois and Indiana University, National Institute for Learning Outcomes Assessment.

Jankowski, N. A. (2011b, July). *Juniata College: Faculty Led Assessment* (NILOA Examples of Good Assessment Practice). Urbana, IL: University of Illinois and Indiana University, National Institute for Learning Outcomes Assessment.

Jankowski, N. A. (2012a). *St. Olaf: Utilization-focused assessment.* Urbana, IL: University of Illinois and Indiana University, National Institute for Learning Outcomes Assessment (NILOA).

Jankowski, N. A. (2012b). *Mapping the topography of the evidence use terrain in assessment of U.S. higher education: A multiple case study approach* (Doctoral dissertation, University of Illinois, Champaign). Retrieved from https://www.ideals.illinois.edu/handle/2142/42316

Jankowski, N. A., Hutchings, P., Ewell, P., Kinzie, J., & Kuh, G. (2013). The Degree Qualifications Profile: What it is and why we need it now. *Change, 45*(6), 6–15.

Jankowski, N. A., Ikenberry, S. O., Kinzie, J., Kuh, G. D., Shenoy, G. F., & Baker, G. R. (2012). *Transparency & accountability: An evaluation of the VSA college portrait pilot.* Urbana, IL: University of Illinois and Indiana University, National Institute for Learning Outcomes Assessment (NILOA).

Jankowski, N. A, & Makela, J. P. (2010). *Exploring the landscape: What institutional websites reveal about student learning outcomes activities.* Urbana,

IL: University of Illinois and Indiana University, National Institute for Learning Outcomes Assessment. Retrieved from http://learningoutcomesassessment.org/documents/NILOAwebscanreport.pdf

Jankowski, N. A., & Provezis, S. J. (2011). *Making student learning evidence transparent: The state of the art.* Urbana, IL: University of Illinois and Indiana University, National Institute for Learning Outcomes Assessment.

Jankowski, N. A, & Provezis, S. (2014). Neoliberal ideologies, governmentality and the academy: An examination of accountability through assessment and transparency. *Educational Philosophy and Theory, 46*(5), 475–487.

Jencks, C., & Riesman, D. (1968). *The academic revolution.* Garden City, NY: Doubleday & Company, Inc.

Johnson, D. K., Ratcliff, J. L., & Gaff, J. G. (2004). A decade of change in general education. In *Changing General Education Curriculum* (special issue). New Directions for Higher Education, no. 125.

Johnstone, S. M., & Soares, L. (2014). Principles for developing competency-based education programs. *Change, 46*(2), 12–19.

Kegan, R., & Lahey, L. L. (2009). *Immunity to change: How to overcome it and unlock the potential in yourself and your organization.* Boston, MA: Harvard University Press.

Kezar, A., & Maxey, D. (2014). *The Delphi Project on the changing faculty and student success: Implications for assessment* (NILOA Occasional Paper No. 21). Urbana, IL: University of Illinois and Indiana University, National Institute for Learning Outcomes Assessment.

Kinzie, J. (2010). *Perspectives from campus leaders on the current state of student learning outcomes assessment: NILOA focus group summary 2009–2010.* Urbana, IL: University of Illinois and Indiana University, National Institute for Learning Outcomes Assessment (NILOA).

Kinzie, J. (2012). *Carnegie Mellon University: Fostering assessment for improvement and teaching excellence.* Urbana, IL: University of Illinois and Indiana University, National Institute for Learning Outcomes Assessment

Kinzie, J., Jankowski, N., & Provezis, S. (2014). Do good assessment practices measure up to the principles of assessment? *Assessment Update, 26*(3), 1–2, 14–16.

Krzykowski, L. (2012). Transparency in higher education as seen through accreditation (Doctoral dissertation, University of Albany, Albany, NY).

Krzykowski, L., & Kinser, K. (2014). Transparency in student learning assessment: Can accreditation make a difference? *Change, 46*(3), 67–73.

Kuh, G. D. (2003). A message from the director: More is not always better. *NSSE Annual Report.* Indiana University Bloomington: Center for Postsecondary Research, National Survey of Student Engagement.

Kuh, G. D. (2008). *High-impact practices: What they are, who has access to them, and why they Matter*. Washington, DC: Association of American Colleges and Universities.

Kuh, G. D. (2011). Foreword to Blaich, C. F., & Wise, K. S, *From gathering to using assessment results: Lessons from the Wabash National Study* (NILOA Occasional Paper No. 8). Urbana, IL: University of Illinois and Indiana University, National Institute for Learning Outcomes Assessment.

Kuh, G. D. (2013a). Culture bending to foster student success. In G. W.McLaughlin, R.Howard, J. S. McLaughlin, & W. Knight (Eds.), *Building bridges for student success: A sourcebook for colleges and universities* (pp. 3–17). Norman, OK: University of Oklahoma Consortium for Student Retention Data Exchange.

Kuh, G. D. (2013b, May). *What if the VSA morphed into the VST?* Washington, DC: AAC&U. Retrieved from http://blog.aacu.org/index.php/2013/05/15/what-if-the-vsa-morphed-into-the-vst/

Kuh, G. D., & Ikenberry, S. (2009). *More than you think, less than we need: Learning outcomes assessment in American higher education*. Champaign, IL: National Institute for Learning Outcomes Assessment.

Kuh, G. D., Jankowski, N., Ikenberry, S., & Kinzie, J. (2014). *Knowing what students know and can do: The current state of learning outcomes assessment at U.S. colleges and universities*. Champaign, IL: National Institute for Learning Outcomes Assessment.

Kuh, G. D., & Whitt, E. J. (1988). *The invisible tapestry: Culture in American colleges and universities*. ASHE-ERIC Higher Education Report, No. 1. Washington, DC: Association for the Study of Higher Education.

Kuh, G. D., & Whitt, E. J. (2000). Culture in American colleges and universities. In M. C. Brown III (Ed.), *Organization and governance in higher education* (5th Ed.). ASHE reader (pp. 160–169). Boston, MA: Pearson Custom Publishing.

Lattuca, L.R., Terenzini, P. T., & Volkwein, J. F. (2006). *Engineering change: A study of the impact of EC2000*. Baltimore, MD: ABET.

Lefever, L. (2013). *The art of explanation: Making your ideas, products, and services easier to understand*. Hoboken, NJ: John Wiley & Sons, Inc.

Leimer, C. (2012). Organizing for evidence-based decision making and improvement. *Change, 44*(4), 45–51.

Linkon, S. L. (2005). How can assessment work for us? *Academe, 91*(4), 28–32.

Linn, R. L. (2006, June). *Educational accountability systems*. CSE Technical Report 687, CRESST, Los Angeles, CA.

Lopez, C. L. (1999). *A decade of assessing student learning: What have we learned; what's next?* Chicago, IL: North Central Association of Colleges and Schools Commission on Institutions of Higher Education.

Lumina Foundation for Education. (2011). *The degree qualifications profile.* Indianapolis, IN: Author.

Lumina Foundation for Education. (2014a). *Call for a national conversation on creating a competency-based credentialing ecosystem.* Indianapolis, IN: Author.

Lumina Foundation for Education. (2014b). *The Degree Qualifications Profile 2.0.* Indianapolis, IN: Lumina Foundation for Education.

MacMahon, W. H. (2009). *Higher learning, greater good: The private and social benefits of higher education.* Baltimore, MD: The Johns Hopkins University Press.

Makela, J., & Rooney, G. (2012). *Learning outcomes assessment step-by-step: Enhancing evidence-based practice in career services.* Broken Arrow, OK: National Career Development Association.

Maki, P. L. (2004). *Assessing for learning.* Sterling, VA: Stylus.

Maki, P. L. (2010). *Assessing for learning: Building a sustainable commitment across the institution* (2nd Ed.). Sterling, VA: Stylus Publishing.

Marcus, D., Cobb. E., & Shoenberg, R. (1993). *Lessons learned from the FIPSE Project II (Fund for the Improvement of Postsecondary Education).* Washington, DC: U.S. Department of Education.

Martinez-Alemán, M. A. (2012). *Accountability, pragmatic aims, and the American university.* New York, NY: Routledge.

Mattingly, K. D., Rice, M. C., & Berge, Z. L. (2012). Learning analytics as a tool for closing the assessment loop in higher education. *Knowledge Management & E-Learning: An International Journal, 4*(3), 236–247.

McCormick, A. C. (2010). Here's looking at you: Transparency, institutional self-presentation, and the public interest. *Change 42*(6), 35–42.

McCormick, A. C., & McClenney, K. (2012). Will these trees ever bear fruit? A response to the Special Issue on Student Engagement. *Review of Higher Education, 35*(2), 307–333.

McFarland, S., Chandler, J., Patterson, E., Watson, C., & Williams, M. (2007). *Reading between the lives.* [DVD] Hayward, CA: Chabot College.

McGlynn, A. P. (2014). Report shares high-impact practices for student success. *Hispanic Outlook.* Retrieved from https://www.wdhstore.com/hispanic/data/pdf/march24-ccsse.pdf

Messick, S. (1989). Meaning and values in test validation: The science and ethics of assessment. *Educational Researcher, 18*(2), 5–11.

Miller, R., & Morgaine, W. (2009, Winter). The benefits of e-portfolios for students and faculty in their own words. *Peer Review, 11*(1), 8–12.

Muffo, J. A. (2001). Involving faculty in assessing the core curriculum. *Assessment Update, 13*(2), 4–5.

Muscatine, C. (1985). Faculty responsibility for the curriculum. *Academe, 71*(5), 16–21.

National Center for Education Statistics. (1992, June). *National Assessment of College Student Learning: Issues and concerns, a report on a study design workshop*. Washington, DC: Author.

National Center for Education Statistics. (2013). *Integrated postsecondary education data system*. Washington, DC: United States Department of Education.

National Commission on Excellence in Education. (1983). *A nation at risk: The imperative for educational reform*. Washington, DC: Author. Retrieved from http://www.ed.gov/pubs/NatAtRisk/risk.html

National Education Goals Panel. (2002). *About NEGP*. National Education Goals Panel. Retrieved from http://govinfo.library.unt.edu/negp/page1.htm

National Governors' Association. (1986). *Time for results: The governors' 1991 report on education*. Washington, DC: Author.

National Institute for Learning Outcomes Assessment. (NILOA). (2011). *Transparency Framework*. Urbana, IL: University of Illinois and Indiana University, National Institute for Learning Outcomes Assessment. Retrieved from http://www. learningoutcomeassessment.org/Transparency-Framework.htm

National Institute of Education. (1984). *Involvement in learning: Realizing the potential of American higher education*. Washington, DC: U.S. Government Printing Office.

National Survey of Student Engagement. (2012). *Moving from data to action: Lessons from the field–volume 2*. Bloomington, IN: Indiana University Center for Postsecondary Research.

Ndoye, A., & Parker, M. A. (2010). Creating and sustaining a culture of assessment. *Planning for Higher Education, 38*(2), 28–39.

New Leadership Alliance for Student Learning and Accountability. (2008). *New leadership for student learning and accountability: A statement of principles, commitments to action*. Washington, DC: American Association of Colleges and Universities and the Council for Higher Education Accreditation.

Nunley, C., Bers, T., & Manning, T. (2011, July). Learning outcomes assessment in community colleges (NILOA Occasional Paper No. 10). Urbana, IL: University of Illinois and Indiana University, National Institute for Learning Outcomes Assessment.

O'Meara, K. (2005). Effects of encouraging multiple forms of scholarship in policy and practice. In K. O'Meara and R. E. Rice (Eds.), *Faculty priorities reconsidered: Rewarding multiple forms of scholarship*. San Francisco, CA: Jossey-Bass.

Ochoa, E. M. (2012). *The state of assessment of learning outcomes*. Retrieved from http://illinois.edu/blog/view/915/73969?displayOrder=desc&displayType=none&displayColumn=created&displayCount=1#_ftn1

Palomba, C. A., & Banta, T. W. (1999). *Assessment essentials: Planning, implementing, and improving assessment in higher education.* San Francisco, CA: Jossey-Bass.

Paradis, T. W., & Hopewell, T. M. (2010). Recognizing progress in degree-program assessment: The seals of assessment achievement and excellence. *Assessment Update, 22*(4), 8–11.

Pascarella, E. T., Seifert, T. A., & Blaich, C. (2010). How effective are the NSSE benchmarks in predicting important educational outcomes? *Change, 42*(1), 16–22.

Pascarella, E. T., & Terenzini, P. T. (2005). *How college affects students, Vol. 2.* San Francisco, CA: Jossey-Bass.

Pathways to College Network. (2012). *The role of student learning outcomes for institutional accountability and transparency.* Washington, DC: Author.

Patton, M. (2008). *Utilization-focused evaluation* (4th Ed.). Thousand Oaks, CA: Sage.

Peck, D. (2013, December). They're watching you at work. *The Atlantic, 312*(5), 72–84.

Penn, J. D. (2011). *The case for assessing complex general education student learning outcomes.* New Directions for Institutional Research, no. 149.

Peter, K., & Forrest Cataldi, E. (2005). *The road less traveled? Students who enroll in multiple institutions* (NCES 2005–157). U.S. Department of Education, National Center for Education Statistics. Washington, DC: U.S. Government Printing Office.

Peterson, M. W., & Augustine, C. H. (2000). Organizational practices enhancing the influence of student assessment information in academic decisions. *Research in Higher Education, 41*(1), 21–52.

Peterson, M. W., & Einarson, M. K. (2001). What are colleges doing about student assessment? Does it make a difference? *Journal of Higher Education, 72*(6), 629–669.

Peterson, M. W., & Spencer, M. G. (1990). Understanding academic culture and climate. *New Directions for Institutional Research, 68*, 3–18.

Peterson, M. W., & Spencer, M. G. (2000). Understanding academic culture and climate. In M. C. BrownIII (Ed.), *Organization and governance in higher education* (5th Ed.). ASHE reader (pp. 170–181). Boston, MA: Pearson Custom Publishing.

Pink, D. H. (2014). *To sell is human: The surprising truth about moving others.* New York, NY: Riverhead Books/Penguin Group.

Porter, S. R. (2005). Survey research policies: An emerging issue for higher education. In P. D. Umbach (Ed.), *Survey research: Emerging issues.* New Directions for Institutional Research, no. 127 (pp. 5–15). San Francisco, CA: Jossey-Bass.

Powell, C. (2013). Accreditation, assessment, and compliance: Addressing the cyclical challenges of public confidence in American education. *Journal of Assessment and Institutional Effectiveness*, *3*(1), 54–74.

Powell, J. W. (2011). Outcomes assessment: Conceptual and other problems. *AAUP Journal of Academic Freedom*, *2*. Retrieved from http://www.aaup.org/sites/default/files/files/JAF/2011%20JAF/Powell.pdf

Princeton Review. (2013). *The best 387 colleges, 2014 edition*. New York, NY: Random House.

Principles for effective assessment of student achievement. (2013, July 19). Retrieved from http://www.wascsenior.org/files/principles_for_effective_assessment_of_student_achievement.pdf

Provezis, S. J. (2010, October). Regional accreditation and student learning outcomes: Mapping the territory (NILOA Occasional Paper No. 6). Urbana, IL: University of Illinois and Indiana University, National Institute for Learning Outcomes Assessment.

Provezis, S. J. (2011, July). *Augustana College: An assessment review committee's role in engaging faculty* (NILOA Examples of Good Assessment Practice). Urbana, IL: University of Illinois and Indiana University, National Institute for Learning Outcomes Assessment.

Provezis, S. J. (2012, June). *LaGuardia Community College: Weaving assessment into the institutional fabric* (NILOA Examples of Good Assessment Practice). Urbana, IL: University of Illinois and Indiana University, National Institute for Learning Outcomes Assessment.

Provezis, S. J., & Jankowski, N. A. (2012). Presenting learning outcomes assessment results to foster use. In C. Secolsky & D. B. Denison (Eds.), *Handbook on measurement, assessment, and evaluation in higher education* (pp. 602–612). New York, NY: Routledge.

Reindl, T. (2013, April 24). *Transparency in higher education* (Testimony). Washington, DC: National Governors Association. Retrieved from http://www.nga.org/cms/home/federal-relations/nga-testimony/edw-testimony-1/col2-content/main-content-list/april-24--2013-testimony—transpa.html

Reindl, T., & Reyna, R. (2011). *From information to action: Revamping higher education accountability system*. Washington, DC: National Governors Association Center for Best Practices.

Rhoads, T., & Finley, A. (2013). *Using the VALUE rubrics for improvement of learning and authentic assessment*. Washington, DC: Association of American Colleges and Universities.

Richman, W. A., & Ariovich, L. (2013). All-in-one: Combining grading, course, program, and general education outcomes assessment (NILOA Occasional Paper No. 19). Urbana, IL: University of Illinois and Indiana University, National Institute for Learning Outcomes Assessment.

Rising to the challenge: Meaningful assessment of student learning. (2010, January). A report from the Association of American Colleges and Universities, the American Association of State Colleges and Universities, & the Association of Public Land-grant Universities. Retrieved from http://www.aplu.org/document.doc?id=2555

Robinson, K. (2011). AAC&U Value rubrics at Calumet College of Saint Joseph. *AAC&U Case study.* Retrieved from https://www.aacu.org/VALUE/casestudies/calumet.pdf

Rogers, G., Holloway, A., & Priddy, L. (2014, April). Exploring degree qualifications: A descriptive analysis of the Quality Initiative Demonstration Project to test the Lumina Foundation's Degree Qualifications Profile. *Higher Learning Commission.* Retrieved from http://learningoutcomesassessment.org/documents/HLCFinalReport.pdf

Rosenthal, L. J. (2011). Assessment, literary studies, and disciplinary futures. In D . Heiland & L. J. Rosenthal (Eds.) with C. Ching, *Literary study, measurement, and the sublime* (pp. 183–198). New York, NY: Teagle Foundation.

Rutschow, E. Z., Richburg-Hayes, L., Brock, T., Orr, G., Cerna, O., Cullinana, D., & Martin, K. (2011, January). *Turning the tide: Five years of Achieving the Dream in community colleges.* New York, NY: MDRC.

Schmadeka, W. (2012). Case study of accreditation reaffirmation with emphasis on assessment-related ambiguities. *Journal of Case Studies in Accreditation and Assessment, 2,* 1–9.

Schmidtlein, F. A. (1999). Emerging perspectives on organizational behavior: Implications for institutional researchers. *New Directions for Institutional Research, 104,* 61–72.

Schmidtlein, F. A., & Berdahl, R. O. (2005). Autonomy and accountability: Who controls academe? In P. G. Altbach, R. O. Berdahl, & P. J. Gumport (Eds.), *American higher education in the twenty-first century: Social, political, and economic challenges* (2nd Ed., pp. 71–90). Baltimore, MD: The John Hopkins University Press.

Schneider, C. G. (2009, Winter). The proof is in the portfolio. *Liberal Education, 95*(1), 2–3.

Schuh, J. H., & Gansamer-Topf, A. M. (2010). The role of student affairs in student learning assessment (NILOA Occasional Paper No. 7). Urbana, IL: University of Illinois and Indiana University, National Institute for Learning Outcomes Assessment.

Schuster, J. H., & Finkelstein, M. J. (2006). *American faculty: The restructuring of academic work and careers.* Baltimore, MD: The Johns Hopkins University Press.

Seagraves, B., & Dean, L. A. (2010). Conditions supporting a culture of assessment in student affairs divisions at small colleges and universities. *Journal of Student Affairs Research and Practice, 47*(3), 307–324.

Serban, A. M. (2004). Assessment of student learning outcomes at the institutional level. *New Directions for Community Colleges, 126,* 17–27.

Seymour, D. (1995). *Once upon a campus: Lessons for improving quality and productivity in higher education.* American Council on Education Oryx Press Series on Higher Education. Westport, CT: Oryx Press.

Shah, P., Mayer, R. E., & Hegarty, M. (1999). Graphs as aids to knowledge construction: Signaling techniques for guiding the process of graph comprehension. *Journal of Educational Psychology, 91*(4), 690–702.

Shapiro, J. (2014, January 16). It ain't what I say. *Inside Higher Education.* Retrieved from http://www.insidehighered.com/views/2014/01/16/essay-way-administrators-and-faculty-understand-language#ixzz31ii5jPjz

Shulman, L. S. (2007). Counting and recounting: Assessment and the quest for accountability. *Change, 39*(1), 20–25.

Siefert, L. (2011). Use of AAC&U VALUE rubrics. *AAC&U Case study* Retrieved from https://www.aacu.org/VALUE/casestudies/documents/UniversityofNorthCarolinaWilmington.pdf

Signorini, A. (2013, December 9). *Involving undergraduates in assessment: Documenting student engagement in flipped classrooms* [Web blog post]. Retrieved from http://illinois.edu/blog/view/915/107512?displayType=month&displayMonth=201312.

Skinner, M., & Prager, E. (2013). Using the CAT for professional development at University of Wyoming. Presentation at the International Society for the Scholarship of Teaching and Learning, October, Raleigh, NC.

Southern Association of Colleges and Schools Commission on Colleges. (2014, January). *Making the case for the application of the Lumina Foundation's Degree Qualifications Profile.* Decatur, GA: Author. Retrieved from http://www.sacscoc.org/pdf/SACS-COCSTUDy.pdf

Stassen, M.L.A. (2012). Accountable for what? *Journal of Assessment and Institutional Effectiveness, 2*(2), 137–142.

Statement on government of colleges and universities. (1966). (Jointly formulated by the American Association of University Professors, the American Council on Education, and the Association of Governing Boards of Universities and Colleges). Retrieved from http://www.aaup.org/report/1966-statement-government-colleges-and-universities

Steen, L. A. (2005). *Supporting assessment in undergraduate mathematics.* Washington, DC: Mathematical Association of America.

Stein, B., & Haynes, A. (2011). Engaging faculty in the assessment and improvement of students' thinking using the critical thinking assessment test. *Change, 43*(2), 44–49.

Stensaker, B. (2003). Trance, transparency and transformation: The impact of external quality monitoring in higher education. *Quality in Higher Education, 9*(2), 151–159.

Student Right-to-Know Act (1990). 20 U.S.C § 1001.

Study Group on the Conditions of Excellence in American Higher Education. (1984, October). *Involvement in learning: Realizing the potential of American higher education.* Washington, DC: National Institute of Education.

Supiano, B. (2013, February 4). Straight answers on paying for college: Still too little, too late. *The Chronicle of Higher Education.* Retrieved from http://chronicle.com/article/For-Parents-Straight-Answers/136955/?cid=at&utm_source=at&utm_medium=en

Supiano, B. (2014, January 27). So much data, so little guidance. *The Chronicle of Higher Education.* Retrieved from http://chronicle.com/article/So-Much-Data-So-Little/144219/?cid=at&utm_source=at&um_medium=en

Suskie, L. A. (2004). *Assessing student learning: A common sense guide.* Bolton, MA: Anker.

Suskie, L. A. (2009). *Assessing student learning: A common sense guide* (2nd Ed.). San Francisco, CA: Jossey-Bass.

Swing, R. L., & Coogan, K. S. (2010). *Valuing assessment: Cost-benefit considerations* (NILOA Occasional paper No. 5). Urbana, IL: University of Illinois and Indiana University, National Institute for Learning Outcomes Assessment. Retrieved from http://learningoutcomesassessment.org/occasionalpaperfive.htm

Terenzini, P. T. (2000). Assessment with open eyes. In M. C. Brown III (Ed.), *Organization and governance in higher education* (5th Ed.). ASHE reader (pp. 339–351). Boston, MA: Pearson Custom Publishing.

The White House, Office of the Press Secretary. (2013). *Fact sheet on the President's plan to make college more affordable: A better bargain for the middle class* [Press release]. Retrieved from http://www.whitehouse.gov/the-press-office/2013/08/22/fact-sheet-president-s-plan-make-college-more-affordable-better-bargain-

Tocqueville, A. de. (1835). *Democracy in America.* Cambridge, MA: Sever & Francis.

Trow, M. (1988). American higher education: Past, present, and future. *Educational Researcher, 17*(3), 13–23.

Tufte, E. R. (1990). *Envisioning information.* Cheshire, CT: Graphics Press.

Tufte, E. R. (1997). *Visual explanations: Images and quantities, evidence and narrative.* Cheshire, CT: Graphics Press.

Tufte, E. R. (2001). *The visual display of quantitative information* (2nd Ed.). Cheshire, CT: Graphics Press.

U.S. Department of Education. (DOE). (1988). *Focus on educational effectiveness,* Federal Register 53:127, 602.17, p. 25098.

U.S. Department of Education. (DOE). (2006). *A test of leadership: Charting the future of American higher education.* Report of the Commission

Appointed by Secretary of Education Margaret Spellings. Washington, DC: U.S. Department of Education.

Upcraft, M. L., & Schuh, J. H. (1996). *Assessment in student affairs: A guide for practitioners*. San Francisco, CA: Jossey-Bass.

Volkwein, J. F. (2011). Gaining ground: The role of institutional research in assessing student outcomes and demonstrating institutional effectiveness (NILOA Occasional Paper No. 11). Urbana, IL: University of Illinois and Indiana University, National Institute for Learning Outcomes Assessment.

Walczak, M., Harper, V., McClure, B., & Hisey, A. (2010, February). Meaningful and manageable assessment at the department level. Presentation at the Collaboration for the Advancement of College Teaching and Learning, St. Paul, MN.

Walvoord, B. E. (2004). *Assessment clear and simple*. San Francisco, CA: Jossey-Bass.

Walvoord, B. E. (2010). *Assessment clear and simple* (2nd Ed.). San Francisco, CA: Jossey-Bass.

Weick, K. (1984). Small wins. *American Psychologist, 39*(1), 40–49.

Welch, J. (2013, October 14). *Student involvement in assessment: A 3-way win.* [Web blog post] Retrieved from http://illinois.edu/blog/view/915/98229

Wells, J., Silk, E., & Torres, D. (1999). Accountability, technology, and external access to information: Implications for IR. *New Directions for Institutional Research, 103*, 23–39.

Werder, C., & Otis, M. M. (Eds.) (2010). *Engaging student voices in the study of teaching and learning*. Sterling, VA: Stylus.

Werder, C., Ware, L., Thomas, C., & Skogsberg, E. (2010). Students in parlor talk on teaching and learning: Conversational scholarship. In C. Werder & M. M. Otis (Eds.), *Engaging student voices in the study of teaching and learning*. Sterling, VA: Stylus.

Werner, D. (2004). *Higher education accreditation: An overview.* Kyoto, Japan: LORC Presentation.

Western Association of Schools and Colleges. (WASC). (2002). *Evidence guide.* Alameda, CA: Author.

Western Association of Schools and Colleges. (WASC). (2013, March). *2013 Handbook of accreditation.* Alameda, CA: Author.

Western Association of Schools and Colleges (WASC). (2014). *Using evidence in the WASC accreditation process: A guide* (2nd Ed.). Alameda, CA: Author.

Wieman, C., Perkins, K., & Gilbert, S. (2010). Transforming science education at large research universities: A case study in progress. *Change, 42*(2), 7–14.

Wright, B. D. (1997). Evaluating learning in individual courses. In J. G. Gaff & J. L. Ratcliff (Eds.), *Handbook of the undergraduate curriculum:*

A comprehensive guide to purposes, structure, practices, and changes (pp. 571–590). San Francisco, CA: Jossey-Bass.

Wright, B. D. (2002). Accreditation and the scholarship of assessment. In T. W. Banta & Associates (Eds.), *Building a scholarship of assessment* (pp. 240–258). San Francisco, CA: Jossey-Bass.

Wright, B. D. (2013). Origins of the WASC assessment leadership academy. *Assessment Update, 25*(6), 1–2, 16.

Wyden, R., & Rubio, M. (2014, February 6). Reform starts with good data. *Inside Higher Ed*. Retrieved from http://www.insidehighered.com/views/2014/02/06/higher-ed-needs-better-data-spur-reform-essay

Yarbrough, D. B., Shulha, L. M., Hopson, R. K., & Caruthers, F. A. (2011). *The program evaluation standards: A guide for evaluators and evaluation users* (3rd Ed.). Thousand Oaks, CA: Sage.

Zenisky, A. L., & Laguilles, J. S. (2012). Reporting assessment results in higher education. In C. Secolsky & D. B. Denison (Eds.), *Handbook on measurement, assessment, and evaluation in higher education* (pp.593–601). New York, NY: Routledge.

Zis, S., Boeke, M., & Ewell, P. (2010). *State policies on the assessment of student learning outcomes: Results of a fifty-state inventory*. Boulder, CO: National Center for Higher Education Management Systems.

NILOA NATIONAL ADVISORY PANEL

NILOA National Advisory Panel

Joseph Alutto, Provost, The Ohio State University

Trudy W. Banta, Professor of Higher Education, Indiana University–Purdue University Indianapolis

Wallace Boston, President and CEO, American Public University System

Molly Corbett Broad, President, American Council on Education

Judith Eaton, President, Council for Higher Education Accreditation

Richard Ekman, President, Council of Independent Colleges

Mildred Garcia, President, California State University–Fullerton

Susan Johnston, Executive Vice President, Association of Governing Boards

Stephen Jordan, President, Metropolitan State University–Denver

Mary Kalantzis, Dean, College of Education, University of Illinois Urbana-Champaign

Paul Lingenfelter, President Emeritus State Higher Education Executive Officers Association

George Mehaffy, Vice President for Academic Leadership and Change, American Association of State Colleges and Universities

Kent Phillippe, Associate Vice President, Research and Student Success, American Association of Community Colleges

Randy Swing, Executive Director, Association for Institutional Research

Carol Schneider, President, Association of American Colleges and Universities

Michael Tanner, Chief Academic Officer and Vice President, Association of Public and Land-grant Universities

Belle Wheelan, President, Southern Association of Colleges and Schools

Ralph Wolff, Trustee, United States International University Kenya

Ex-Officio Members

Peter Ewell, Vice President, NCHEMS

Stan Ikenberry, President Emeritus and Regent Professor, University of Illinois

George Kuh, Director, NILOA, Adjunct Professor, University of Illinois Urbana-Champaign, Chancellor's Professor Emeritus, Indiana University

Past NILOA National Advisory Board Members (titles at time of service on board)

Douglas C. Bennett, President, Earlham College

Robert M. Berdahl, President, Association of American Universities

Joni Finney, Practice Professor, University of Pennsylvania, Vice President, National Center for Public Policy and Higher Education

Margaret Miller, Professor, University of Virginia, Editor, *Change Magazine*

Charlene Nunley, Doctoral Program Director, Professor Doctor of Management in Community College Policy and Administration, University of Maryland University College

David Shulenburger, Senior Fellow, Association of Public and Land-grant Universities

George Wright, President, Prairie View A&M University

NILOA STAFF, 2008 TO 2014

NILOA Senior Staff

Timothy Reese Cain, Senior Scholar, Associate Professor, Institute of Higher Education at the University of Georgia

Peter Ewell, Senior Scholar, Vice President, National Center for Higher Education Management Systems (NCHEMS)

Pat Hutchings, Senior Scholar, Senior Scholar, Carnegie Foundation for the Advancement of Teaching

Stan Ikenberry, Co-principal Investigator, Emeritus Regent Professor and President Emeritus, University of Illinois at Urbana-Champaign

Natasha A. Jankowski, Associate Director, Research Assistant Professor, Department of Education Policy, Organization, and Leadership, University of Illinois at Urbana-Champaign

Jillian Kinzie, Senior Scholar, Associate Director, Indiana University Center for Postsecondary Research & NSSE Institute

George Kuh, Co-principal Investigator and Project Director, Chancellor's Professor Emeritus of Higher Education, Indiana University

Paul Lingenfelter, Senior Scholar, President Emeritus, State Higher Education Executive Officers Association

NILOA Staff, 2008 to 2014

Staci Provezis, Project Manager

Kathryn Schultz, Project Manager

Carrie Allen, Research Analyst

Gianina Baker, Research Analyst

Sharanya Bathey, Graduate Research Assistant

T. Jameson Brewer, Research Analyst

Robert Dumas, Research Analyst

Nora Gannon-Slater, Research Analyst

Laura Giffin, Research Analyst

Jason Goldfarb, Research Analyst

Julia Panke Makela, Research Analyst

Nishanth Mandaara, Research Analyst

Balaji Manoharan, Research Analyst

Erick Montenegro, Research Analyst

Suhas Hoskote Muralidhar, Graduate Research Assistant

Paul Myers, Research Analyst

Jelena Pokimica, Research Analyst

Gloria Shenoy, Research Analyst

Terry Vaughan III, Research Analyst

INDEX

If you enjoyed this book, you may also like these:

Student Success in College
by George D. Kuh, Jillian Kinzie, John H.
Schuh, Elizabeth J. Whitt
and Associates

ISBN: 9780470599099

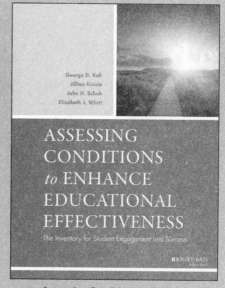

**Assessing Conditions to Enhance
Educational Effectiveness**
by George D. Kuh, Jillian Kinzie, John H. Schuh
and Elizabeth J. Whitt

ISBN: 9780787982201

Five Dimensions of Quality
by Linda Suskie

ISBN: 9781118761571

Assessment Essentials 2e
by Trudy W. Banta and Catherine A. Palomba

ISBN: 9781118903322

WILEY

Want to connect?

Like us on Facebook
http://www.facebook.com/JBHigherEd

Subscribe to our newsletter
www.josseybass.com/go/higheredemail

Follow us on Twitter
http://twitter.com/JBHigherEd

Go to our Website
www.josseybass.com/highereducation

WILEY